The American Disease

George C. Lodge

THE AMERICAN
DISEASE

Alfred A. Knopf   New York   1984

THIS IS A BORZOI BOOK
PUBLISHED BY ALFRED A. KNOPF, INC.

Copyright © 1984 by George C. Lodge

All rights reserved under International and Pan-American
Copyright Conventions. Published in the United States by
Alfred A. Knopf, Inc., New York, and simûltaneously in
Canada by Random House of Canada Limited, Toronto.
Distributed by Random House, Inc., New York.

LIBRARY OF CONGRESS CATALOGING IN PUBLICATION DATA
Lodge, George C.
The American disease.
Includes bibliographical references and index.
  1. Business and politics—United States.
  2. Industry and state—United States.
  3. Industrial relations—United States.
       I. Title.
JK467.L63   1984   322'.3'0973   83-48871
              ISBN 0-394-52903-0

Manufactured in the United States of America
First Edition

For E.S.L. and H.C.L.

Contents

Preface

The United States in the early 1980s confronted a set of structural difficulties that it was seeking to meet experimentally and pragmatically. Faced with recession and a loss of competitiveness, the country's institutions were changing their functions and relationships. The federal government was being forced as never before to set priorities; to limit the rights of its citizens, and to define their duties more stringently; to contemplate the role and dimensions of the country's great industries; and to recognize that the costs of unemployment necessitated, in addition to income maintenance, a program of job creation and training. Government was, in short, being required to think strategically about the nation as a whole, at a time when other nations' strategies were more competitive than ours.

Concurrently, great corporations were aware more than ever that their reason for being went beyond the satisfaction of their mythical owners, the shareholders, and that it was linked, vaguely but inexorably, to the interests of the several communities that they affected. Similarly, trade unions were realizing that the adversarial struggle to increase the wages and benefits of their membership was by itself no longer a practical mission in a world in which failure to keep costs competitive meant the erosion of the companies upon which those workers depended for employment. Furthermore, the rhetoric of their leadership notwithstanding, all three sets of institutions were realizing that their goals and policies were inseparably intertwined. None could succeed without the others.

There is nothing particularly new about these evolving trends. In 1959, for example, President Dwight D. Eisenhower devoted his Economic Report to Congress to the redefinition of "the respective rights and responsibilities of free government under a popular democracy." He spoke of the commitment of government to the growth of business; to expanding total production rather than redistributing the current product; to realizing the mutualities of interest that united the different elements of the American economy; to rethinking antitrust policy in order to promote efficiency; and to cooperating with business to assure the fulfillment of the nation's health and welfare. The distinctive feature of the 1980s was the degree to which crisis was forcing the change implicit in Eisenhower's vision.

The transition was difficult and confusing, because it represented a departure from traditional conceptions of institutional roles and relationships that were almost religious in nature. The tension between practice, born of necessity, and beliefs rooted in tradition caused a variety of psychological effects: a romantic yearning for a more glorious past, the denial of the reality that was forcing change, an escape into illusion, a loss of confidence, and an erosion of authority and responsibility. Together, these comprise the American disease.

This book attempts to describe the nature and symptoms of that disease, reveal its causes, and outline some remedies. But the first, most important step is the recognition of the disease itself. Once that is accomplished, remedies will appear in profusion; they will be many and varied. But until the disease is clearly recognized there can be no cure; it will continue to waste our resources, our institutions, and our people.

In light of recent political events, it may prove surprising to some readers that I perceive the transition from individualism to communitarianism—described in my last book, *The New American Ideology* (1975)—as continuing unabated. But the transition is not necessarily what the American people desire; it is what reality is imposing upon us. We must understand the tension that this uncomfortable circumstance generates; through the analysis of this tension, we can come to a greater understanding of our choices.

We shall examine the evolving relationships among large publicly held corporations, the federal government, and labor unions by focusing on a number of problems that shape those relationships, such as international competition, environmental pollution, electric generation, worker motivation, corporate governance, unemployment, and urban disintegration. To gain greater insight into these problems my research assistant, William R. Glass, and I interviewed many persons associated with business, government, and labor, whom I would like to thank for being so generous with their time and thoughts.

In and around government there were: Douglas D. Anderson, Deputy Counselor to the Secretary, Department of the Treasury, 1981–82; Joan Z. Bernstein, General Counsel, Environmental Protection Agency (EPA), 1977–79; Phyllis D. Bonanno, Director, Office of Private Sector Liaison, Office of the United States Trade Representative (USTR); Ambassador William E. Brock III, United States Trade Representative; Adolf Brueckmann, Senior Policy Analyst, Department of Commerce; Douglas M. Costle, Administrator, Environmental Protection Agency, 1977–81; William Diebold, Senior Research Fellow, Council on Foreign Relations; William Drayton, Environmental Protection Agency, 1977–80; Professor George Eads, member of the Council of Economic Advisors, 1979–81, School of Public Affairs, University of Maryland; Ambassador William D. Eberle, Special Representative for Trade Negotiations, 1971–75; Charles W. Ervin, Director of Operations, United States International Trade Commission; Geza Feketekuty, Assistant U.S. Trade Representative for Policy Development, Office of the USTR; John D. Greenwald, Assistant General Counsel, Office of the USTR, 1974–79, Department of Commerce, 1980–81; Matthew Holden, Jr., Commissioner, Federal Energy Commission, 1977–81; Richard John, Chief Scientist, Department of Transportation; Congresswoman Marcy Kaptur, former White House aide on Urban Affairs; Frederick T. Knickerbocker, Acting Director, Economic Policy Staff, Department of Commerce; Rebecca Lambert, Associate Deputy Secretary, Department of Com-

merce; Edward J. Logue, President, South Bronx Development
Organization, Inc.; Charles Mahoney, Secretary of Human Ser-
vices, Commonwealth of Massachusetts, 1979–81; Harald B.
Malmgren, Deputy Special Trade Representative, 1972–75; John
F. O'Leary, Deputy Energy Secretary, 1977–79, Administrator,
Federal Energy Administration, 1977; Joseph S. Papovich, Labor
Liaison, Office of the Private Sector Liaison, Office of the USTR;
Roger B. Porter, Deputy Assistant to the President; Richard R.
Rivers, General Counsel, USTR, 1977–79; Marjory E. Searing,
Director, Office of the International Sector Policy, Department
of Commerce; Thomas G. Sheehan, Assistant Director, Private
Sector Liaison, Office of the USTR; Harry Spence, Receiver/
Administrator, Boston Housing Authority; Ambassador Robert
Strauss, United States Trade Representative, 1977–79; Joseph
C. Swidler, former chairman of the Federal Power Commission
and N.Y. Public Service Commission, now Energy Consultant;
Jim J. Tozzi, Deputy Administrator, Office of Information and
Regulatory Affairs, Office of Management and Budget; Anne
Wexler, Deputy Undersecretary for Regional Affairs, Depart-
ment of Commerce, 1977–79, Assistant to the President for
Political Issues, 1979–81; and Mary Jane Wignot, Subcommittee
on Trade, Committee on Ways and Means, U.S. House of
Representatives.

Business leaders included: Jerr Boschee, Control Data;
Richard M. Brennan, Union Carbide; Charles L. Brown, AT&T;
Elizabeth A. Buckley, City Venture; Fletcher L. Byrom, Kop-
pers; Alan B. Cooper, ARMCO, 1953–82; Mark J. D'Arcangelo,
General Electric; Hugh P. Donaghue, Control Data; William J.
Durka, General Electric; Frank Fenton, American Iron and Steel
Institute; John H. Filer, Aetna Life and Casualty; Stephen H.
Fuller, General Motors; Brian I. Hollander, Aetna Life and
Casualty; Howard M. Love, National Steel; Charles F. Luce,
Consolidated Edison; Ruben F. Mettler, TRW, and chairman
of the Business Roundtable; Laura B. Morris, Digital Equipment;
Stanley Nehmer, Economic Consulting Service; William C.
Norris, Control Data; Paul M. Ostergard, General Electric;
Peter G. Peterson, Lehman Brothers Kuhn Loeb; Henry D.
Schacht, Cummins Engine; Irving S. Shapiro, E. I. duPont de
Nemours & Company; Oliver R. Smoot, Computer and Business
Equipment Manufacturers' Association; J. Bradford Stroup,

Data General; Alexander B. Trowbridge, National Association of Manufacturers; and Roger G. Wheeler, Control Data.

Labor leaders interviewed included: Edmund Ayoub, United Steel Workers of America; Irving Bluestone, United Auto Workers; Sam Camens, United Steel Workers of America; Thomas Donahue, AFL-CIO; John T. Joyce, International Union of Bricklayers and Allied Craftsmen; James W. Smith, United Steel Workers of America; Brian Turner, AFL-CIO; and Glenn E. Watts, Communications Workers of America.

In addition, there were: Jeremy Bacon, The Conference Board; Kevin Balfe, National Alliance of Business; Renee Berger, President's Task Force on Private Sector Initiatives, Committee for Economic Development; Professor David L. Birch, Program on Neighborhood and Regional Change, Urban Studies and Planning, MIT; Scott Fosler, Committee for Economic Development; Frieda Garcia, United South End Settlements, Inc.; Mary B. Green, KLH Child Development Center; Royce Hanson, Committee on National Urban Policy, National Research Council; Rebecca A. Lee, Local Initiatives Support Corporation; Leonard Lund, The Conference Board; Jack A. Meyer, American Enterprise Institute for Public Policy Research; Professor Gwen Morgan, Wheelock College; Robert E. Morgan III, Visiting Homemaker Service of Hudson County, Inc.; Robert P. Newsome, New York City Partnership; B. Warner Shippee, Center for Urban and Regional Affairs, University of Minnesota; Ted Small, New York City Private Industry Council; William Spring, Tri-Lateral Council on Quality Education, Federal Reserve Bank of Boston; Beverly Stadum, Center for Urban and Regional Affairs, University of Minnesota; Catherine Stratton, Boston Private Industry Council; Mitchell Sviridoff, Local Initiatives Support Corporation; Pat Wartts, City Venture; Millicent Woods, National Alliance of Business; and Robert L. Woodson, American Enterprise Institute.

I am also deeply grateful to my colleagues at Harvard, many of whom read and commented on all or parts of this book: Paul Achleitner and William Crum; Professors Alvin L. Alm, appointed Deputy Administrator of EPA in May 1983, Kenneth R. Andrews, Joseph Auerbach, Joseph L. Badaracco, Joseph L. Bower, John T. Dunlop, J. Ronald Fox, Thomas K. McCraw, D. Quinn Mills, Robert B. Reich, Malcolm S. Salter, Bruce R. Scott,

Richard H. K. Vietor, Philip A. Wellons, and David Yoffie. I owe special thanks to Professor Scott, whose thinking about the concept of national strategy has been central to my work. I am also most grateful to Dr. Miles F. Shore, professor at Harvard Medical School and director of the Massachusetts Mental Health Center, for his help in properly describing the "American disease."

John H. McArthur, Dean of the Harvard Business School, and E. Raymond Corey, director of the school's Division of Research, gave me essential support and assistance. My heartfelt thanks to them both and to the dedicated staff of the Research Division, especially Kathryn May and Judy Uhl. In addition, I am most grateful to Anne O'Connell and Joan O'Connor, who transcribed the tape recordings of my interviews, a painstaking and wearisome task of great importance.

Bill Glass's assistance was most valuable: in addition to helping with the interviews, he joined me in writing two *Harvard Business Review* articles, from which Chapters 7 and 10 were drawn. My thanks also go to Janet Porcaro, who has the uncanny ability to make sense of my scribbles, and never tired of typing drafts of this manuscript.

Jeffrey Cruickshank, editor of the Harvard Business School *Bulletin,* gave me the benefit of his extraordinary editing skills, and Peter Halasz diligently and accurately checked facts and endnotes. Ashbel Green has been, as always, a most valued friend, critic, and editor.

While none of these can be blamed for my errors, they must share credit for what is right and true in this book.

Finally, I thank my wife, Nancy, for her assistance and devotion, and my children and grandchildren for their patience and understanding in the face of the author's petulance.

Boston, Mass.   GEORGE C. LODGE
May 1983

The American Disease

1

The American Disease

The cold winter of 1982 brought home to Americans the realization that our economy, once the wonder of the world, was failing. The power and efficiency of the industrial system, which since World War II had been taken for granted, was eroding. The United States was aware, for the first time, of losing ground in the competitive race with other developed nations. We were particularly cognizant of our seeming inability to compete with Japan.

During the previous two decades, in virtually every line of industry she chose to enter, Japan had proved herself capable of making products as good as or better than their American equivalents, and of selling them at lower prices. In the early 1980s, the effects were plain to see in the production of color televisions, steel, automobiles, electronics, computers, semiconductors, and more. By 1981, Americans were spending $18 billion more on Japanese products than the Japanese were spending on American goods. And, increasingly, the nation's exports resembled those of a colony. Our rare success stories included agricultural products, tourism, timber, and coal—hardly representative of a vital and competitive economy. By 1982, the trade imbalance favored the Japanese by almost $25 billion.

Resentful, humiliated, and shocked, some Americans began to shout "foul!" *We* were playing fair, went the refrain; we were playing the game as it had always been played, but the Japanese (and Europeans) were changing the rules. Unfair advantages had been built into the structure of international trade. It was tariff barriers, suggested Lee Iacocca, that were preventing the Japanese from buying Chryslers.[1] The Japanese government, furthermore, thought coherently about its national goals and policies, and guided and assisted its strategic industries accordingly—an inappropriate function for government, many thought, particularly since Washington assumed no such responsibility.

Japanese workers were also at fault, failing to understand that the role of a respectable trade union was to fight for higher wages and benefits through an adversarial contract. Japanese corporations and banks were bound together in monstrously efficient machines, cooperating in ways which would clearly be illegal for their American counterparts. And the European steel makers, subsidized by their governments, were selling steel below U.S. prices in order to increase their share of the American market. Demands were heard for a counterpunch against this accumulating unfairness, which some began to perceive as a calculated evil.

But Americans have also begun to wonder whether the problem may not be rooted in the game itself, and in the assumptions upon which its rules were based. Facing a changed reality, they ask, by whose rules is the world going to play? If not by ours, then a critical question arises immediately: How long will it take us to learn the new rules, and organize our economy to play by them? Other fundamental questions ensue, focusing on the roles and relationships of government, corporations, and trade unions. The answers to these questions—so recently posed—have only just begun to be sought.

Japan is not the enemy; its success is but the mirror of our own failure. In that sense, Japan is peculiarly valuable to us as the best measure of what we have not done, the standard against which we must compare our future efforts. But our focus must be on the American reality, and not the reflected image that Japan represents. The roles and relationships of America's great institutions are indeed changing, but the change is slow and costly, attended by mounting crisis. The purpose of this book is to consider how that change can be made more efficient, less painful, less bloody. In short, how do we effect a maximum of change with a minimum of crisis? In the answers to this question lies the remedy for the disease which afflicts us.

The symptoms of the American disease were clear in the performance of the economy in 1982. They were even more dramatically revealed by an examination of the cumulative impact of the 1970s: economic growth was slow, lagging consistently behind that of Japan and most of Western Europe, and interrupted by periods of decline in the mid-1970s and early 1980s; the real incomes of the American people fell further and further behind inflation; and both public and private borrowing increased, even as the cost of borrowing reached all-time highs. In the first quarter of 1982, corporate profits took one of their worst plunges on record, with earnings down 17% from a year earlier.[2] Investment in new plants and equipment was sluggish.

In fact, every indicator, social as well as economic, revealed sickness. Nearly 12 million Americans were looking for work in 1983, and several million more had given up the search in despair. By another measure, more than 10 million people were counted as being part of an underclass increasingly unreachable by the legitimate institutions of our country. Populated largely by the disaffected—by welfare mothers, dropouts, addicts, hustlers, and ex-offenders—the underclass was young, mostly female, mostly black or Hispanic, and mostly hopeless. The bridges which had once tied their disintegrating communities to the mainstream of American society had been destroyed.

The productivity levels of American industry were stagnant and labor costs were rising; as a consequence, foreign industry, mostly Japanese, was acquiring ever larger shares of both the U.S. and world markets. During the 1970s the United States lost more than 2 million jobs to foreign competition, about half of them in the hard-pressed Northeast and Midwest. Foreign auto manufacturers, again mostly Japanese, had seized nearly 30% of the U.S. market and American companies in 1980 and '81 had suffered losses of more than $5.5 billion. By 1981, twenty-five auto plants had closed and another hundred factories related to the industry had shut down. These trends struck at the very heart of the American economy: the automobile industry had traditionally accounted for 8% of the gross national product and had employed some 4 million Americans. Of these, close to half a million were out of work in 1982.[3]

Although America's principal economic competition was coming from Japan, and although the automobile industry was suffering most obviously, there was trouble on other fronts as well. The manufacture of jetliners, for example, had been a virtual U.S. monopoly for years. But at the turn of the decade, a consortium of European governments and companies called Airbus Industries began to threaten that monopoly. By 1981, Airbus had captured a fourth of the world market for big jets; during the first five months of 1982, Airbus won almost half of the new orders for large aircraft, even gaining a toehold in the U.S. market.[4] In what was becoming a familiar refrain, U.S. manufacturers complained that the Europeans were cheating, relying on government subsidies and loans.

The steel industry was in a comparable state of disarray, the victim of cheaper imported steel, in part the result of the cooperative relationships established among the government, business, and labor sectors of our foreign competitors. Imports had accounted for about 20% of the U.S. market, and the American share of world steel production had declined from 28% in 1958 to less than 17% by the end of the 1970s.[5] The manufacture of machine tools—essential for the development and use of new technology—had suffered an even more ominous deterioration. In 1972 the United States enjoyed a $146-million trade surplus in machine tools, $16.6 million of which was with Japan. Only six years later the surplus had turned into a $155-million deficit, including an incredible $182-million deficit with Japan.[6] In fact, U.S. manufacturing exports were declining across the board, and not only in relation to Japan. Throughout the 1970s, Britain, France, Germany, and Italy also outperformed the United States in the rate of growth of manufactured exports, as did the "new Japans" of East Asia: Taiwan, South Korea, Singapore, and Hong Kong. Overall, by 1983 the American trade deficit was approaching $60 billion.

Part of the problem, it was clear, was uncompetitive labor costs. The American trade-union movement, born in the nineteenth century and nurtured in the early years of the twentieth, came of age after World War II. Founded in an adversarial relationship with management—a posture which was reinforced with the negotiation of collective contracts—unions demanded and won an ever-increasing share of the fruits of production for American workers. Wage raises, linked to the cost of living, grew dramatically in the 1960s and '70s, to the point where they contributed to the decline of entire industries. The automobile industry was a clear case in point. The average wages of automobile workers in the United States in 1980 were about twice those in Japan. This difference, combined with the greater efficiency of Japanese workers (about 20% more productive than their American counterparts), gave their autos a cost advantage of between $1200 and $1500 when landed on our shores.[7] To make matters worse, American consumers perceived Japanese products to be of superior quality.

But the competitive problems of American industry could by no means be blamed exclusively on labor. William J. Abernathy and Robert H. Hayes saw "a broad managerial failure" in the United States, "a failure of both vision and leadership that over time has eroded both the inclination and the capacity of U.S. companies to innovate."[8] They charged American managers with a variety of shortcomings: a short-term focus on quarterly dividends, a fixation on short-term cost reduction rather than long-term innovation and risk-taking, a neglect of quality and production processes, and unimaginative work-force management.

Another visible symptom of the American disease was the discouraging record of incoherent, fragmented, and shortsighted government policies. Government had failed consistently to consider the long-run and cumulative impact of what it was doing. America's energy policy during the mid-1970s, for example, was designed to insulate consumers from the real increase in the price of oil. Americans were thus encouraged to purchase gas guzzlers, and automobile companies were encouraged to continue their production. (Manufacturers, of course, were otherwise enticed: profit margins were higher on larger cars.) With the sharp rise in the price of oil and gasoline in 1979, however, small cars became dramatically more desirable, even to American consumers. Foreign producers were there with the right product, while the U.S. industry was caught with uncompetitive cars.

One might well wonder why leaders in American industry and

government in the early 1970s did not discuss the implications of the clear trend of rising gasoline prices, and develop a considered response to it—a response which could perhaps have been accompanied by a less disruptive application of environmental and safety regulations. One might well ask how labor, industry, and government could entirely fail to see how the game was developing. (Chrysler's dismal plunge began, after all, in the early 1970s.) In part, that failure was inherent in the relationships among the principal players, and in the rules of the game itself. Ours was an economy based on the rules of adversarialism. During the 1970s, for example, big business was "bad," the target of powerful interest groups who saw it as an ugly, profiteering, and polluting force. National polls revealed a marked "antigrowth" bias in the American people.[9] A concurrent assumption, of course, was that big business was as indestructible as it was objectionable, and that the cow would still give milk even as it was being battered with unpredictable and frenzied blows.

Even American industries at the frontiers of technology, the potential giants of the future, were in trouble. In the field of semiconductors, for example—those miraculous silicon chips that have emerged as the key component in new computers, telecommunications devices, machine tools, and dozens of other products—America once held a seemingly insurmountable edge. But by 1982, U.S. and Japanese manufacturers were competing head to head for a world market estimated to be worth more than $80 billion by 1990. Robert B. Reich, formerly the director of planning for the Federal Trade Commission and later a lecturer at Harvard's Kennedy School of Government, predicted in November 1981 that the U.S. would lose the battle.

"United States manufacturers, in partnership with the U.S. government, took an early lead in the Chip Wars," Reich wrote. "Research in radar and sophisticated communications equipment during World War II led to the invention of the transistor in the late 1940s, and of the integrated circuit a decade later. By 1967, the U.S. government was the largest single purchaser of semiconductors, accounting for almost one-third of the market—thereby giving new chip makers the volume they needed to bring costs down. . . . In 1962 an integrated circuit cost $50; by 1968 its cost had dropped to $2.33, making it commercially attractive for use in many civilian products."[10]

In the early 1970s, the Japanese government gave its chip makers tax privileges and direct subsidies of about $400 million a year, and imposed a 10% tariff on imported chips. But it was not until 1975 that the Japanese began to make substantial headway. "In a sluggish economy that was trying to adjust to the oil-price rise," Reich continued, "commercial purchasers of semiconductors in the U.S. reduced their demand sharply." The Defense Department also retrenched. "U.S. chip makers cut their capital equipment purchases by half and laid off thousands of skilled workers. By contrast, the Japanese chip makers—with their tax privileges, loans, subsidies, and tariffs in place—could afford to expand their production and improve their technology in anticipation of the next economic upturn."

In 1978 the demand for chips took off. "Just to keep its own customers supplied, Intel (one of the major U.S. producers) was forced to buy chips from Hitachi at the rate of 200,000 a month. IBM had to purchase 10 million Japanese chips for its small computers. By the end of 1978 the Japanese chip makers had captured 40% of the world market for 16K RAMs (Random Access Memory), the most advanced memory devices in production."

Reich saw history repeating itself in the winter of 1982, as high interest rates and sluggish demand forced the U.S. industry to cut back, while the Japanese, less mindful of short-term profits, proceeded to gobble up increasing shares of the world markets. They had already beaten the U.S. to market with the sophisticated 64K RAM chip, and seemed to have a clear lead with the 256K chip of the future.

"American chip makers' only real hope at this point," said Reich, "is the U.S. Department of Defense." Increased military expenditures will spur demand for chips, but it will also bias innovation and production away from commercial uses and toward military uses. Reich concluded that Japan will win the "Chip Wars" largely because of a failure of U.S. industrial policy. It is a particularly dismal example: because the government/business relationship was poorly designed and incoherently administered, a once-dominant American industry faced defeat in the international marketplace.

It has been almost a hundred years since Andrew Carnegie wrote *Triumphant Democracy,* which began:

The old nations of the earth creep on at a snail's pace; the Republic thunders past with the rush of an express. The United States, in the growth of a single century, has already reached the foremost rank among nations, and is destined soon to outdistance all others in the race. In population, in wealth, in annual savings, and in public credit; in freedom from debt, in agriculture, and in manufactures, America already leads the civilized world.

What has happened to Carnegie's America? As my colleague Bruce Scott has pointed out, the old wealth of the United States —land, labor, capital, raw materials, and markets—is no longer enough to ensure a competitive advantage. The winners in today's world—those who "thunder past with the rush of an express"—possess little in terms of land or raw materials. Their capital has come from savings; their markets are the world. What they do possess is an extraordinary capacity to bind together government, business, and labor in the formulation and implementation of explicit national strategies. "In industrial terms," writes Scott, "the star performers of the last 30 years are a group of countries whose critical resources are not land or minerals but rather people and savings—and the policies and institutions to mobilize and periodically redirect both." [11]

Stephen Fuller, who returned to the faculty of the Harvard Business School in 1982 after serving as vice-president of personnel at General Motors, put it another way:

> There are two areas where Japanese industry has a competitive advantage. They have no superiority in manufacturing or engineering technology, but they have a non-adversarial relationship with their government and they give full strategic importance to the management of people. Japanese management makes sure that employees at every level understand the company's strategy, goals and objectives. In this country, no major company can develop and implement its strategic goals without considering the adversarial nature of government and union relations. We'll restore our competitive strength as we learn to make those relationships more cooperative. [12]

At the end of World War II, Japan was a shattered nation, with 85 million impoverished people crowded onto a small, infertile island chain, devoid of resources, dejected and depressed. Appalled at the prevailing conditions, and seeking to stabilize the vanquished enemy, General Douglas MacArthur and his occupation forces undertook to set the country on the road to prosperity. "The world has never seen . . . so abnormal an economic system," said MacArthur, referring to the remnants of the prewar system, which featured extensive collaboration between large private entities—the *zaibatsu*—and the government.[13] By introducing typically American antitrust laws, MacArthur sought to sever what he perceived as the overly close relations between government and business. He brought an unaccustomed militancy to Japan's traditional company unions by inviting the United Automobile Workers and other U.S. unions to teach his wards how to wage a proper strike. In short, he sought to instruct them in the "rules" as understood by Americans.

Given the circumstances, the Japanese were accommodating and respectful, and sought to implement the general's innovations; but these were plainly not their ways. Eventually, the American pressure for economic reform eased: MacArthur was distracted by the Korean War, and the United States began to focus more on building Japan's strength as an ally than on purifying its economic system. Japan seized the opportunity to revert to more traditional precepts. Government undertook to guide and assist industry so that Japan could earn the foreign exchange she desperately needed for her survival. Antitrust laws were set aside in favor of the efficiencies of consolidation, under the watchful eye of the Ministry of International Trade and Industry (MITI). Trade unions and management, after a rash of conflicts, concluded that a relationship based on mutual antagonism would not benefit either side. Far more constructive than the adversarial contract was a working consensus, through which the mutuality of interests of both labor and management could be made manifest. It was a decision that would have far-reaching consequences: by 1980, 16% of the board members of Japanese companies would be former trade-union leaders.[14] (William Abernathy reports that young managers at Toyota serve two or three years in the union, during which time they are expected to be elected to a position of leadership.)

In the years following World War II, Westerners looking at Japan tended to be pessimistic about her chances. Even such a friendly and astute observer as Edwin O. Reischauer wrote in 1950:

First of all, there is the problem of whether or not Japan, regardless of the political and economic system she eventually chooses, can maintain any satisfactory standard of living in the future. She cannot grow enough food to feed all her people. She cannot produce the greater part of the fibers from which she must spin her clothes for her millions. She has very little oil or iron and is lacking in adequate quantities of most of the other minerals and raw materials needed to maintain a modern industrial economy. Nylon and other synthetic fibers have destroyed most of the demand for silk, the one major export item she produced entirely within her boundaries. All she has to offer on the world market is her own energy—manpower and the energy of coal and water. With these she can transform imported raw materials into goods for re-export. The slim margin of profit from this re-export trade must be sufficient to pay for all the imports Japan must have to support her own people. To do this, Japan's export trade must be huge. But where is she to find her markets in a divided world and in a Far East disrupted by revolutions and bitterly determined not to trade with her? Japan's situation is basically similar to England's but infinitely worse. She is far less richly endowed with the vital resources of coal and iron than are the British Isles. She is less highly industrialized. She has no overseas empire to aid her but instead an international legacy of distrust and hate. And she has almost twice the population of Great Britain to support on her more meager resources.[15]

What Westerners could not understand, and still have not completely understood, is that Japan conceived of herself as a coherent community whose survival depended upon an effective national strategy.[16] Her people looked outwards, not inwards, and realized that the dangerous and competitive world described by Reischauer necessitated an agenda of national priorities, and policies to accomplish that agenda. The war had reemphasized a vital lesson: all sectors of Japanese society had come to realize that they were dependent on each other. Consensus was a necessity; an educational system that contributed to consensus-building was as essential a part of an effective economic strategy as the organization and management of workers, technology, processes of production, or investment for trade expansion. Japan was a nation that had learned to think systematically about herself, and had developed the institutions which enabled the lessons of systematic thought to be implemented effectively.

By 1970, Japan's economic output had surpassed that of every

country in the world except the United States and the U.S.S.R.
The reasons for this "economic miracle" are not mysterious,
only subtle. Their perception requires a holistic approach. They
lie in the structure of the relationships among the different sectors of society, a structure which enabled Japan's leaders to think
coherently about the requirements for success in the real world.
It was not a matter of imposed uniformity. It was, as Peter
Drucker put it, "the result of something far more interesting,
habits of political behavior that use the diversity in Japanese
national life to produce effective economic action." [17] Among
these habits was a consciousness of dependence on the outside
world for energy and raw materials, which necessitated an understanding of the impact of any policy or action on the competitive strength of Japan in the world. Japan, as Drucker
emphasized, does not have a monolithic social structure; it includes as many powerful interest groups as any country, which
lobby "brazenly" for their own interests, "in ways which would
make a Tammany boss blush." But each group is "expected to
fit its self-interest into a framework of national needs, national
goals, national aspirations and national values." [18] The acid test
is the national interest.

To fuel its industrial machine with low-cost capital, the Japanese government has created a system that provides the highest
savings rate in the world. In 1981, more than $42 billion was
deposited into the Postal Savings system and converted into long-
term borrowings at low or no interest rates for companies which,
in the opinion of the Ministry of International Trade and Industry
and other government agencies, were critical to Japan's continued success in world market competition. In addition, in 1981
some $1.8 billion of the government budget was allocated to pro-
mote science and technology, including computer technology. [19]

Evidence of the efficacy of this approach abounds. For example, private investment in plant and equipment as a share of gross
national product during the 1970s averaged 17% in Japan, as
opposed to 10% in the United States. Consumer prices at the end
of the decade were increasing by about 13% a year in the United
States, but only by about 4% annually in Japan. Interest rates by
the end of the decade were about 12% (Federal Reserve discount
rate) in the United States, and 6.2% in Japan. Productivity—
output per hour of work—was declining in the U.S., while it was

growing at about 4% in Japan. U.S. plant and equipment in 1978 was approximately seventeen years old; in Japan it was ten.[20] "Japan is a nation like a juggernaut with all of the pieces in place going in one direction," said J. Thomas West, director of engineering at Data General Corporation. "It has a tendency to succeed at anything it decides to do."[21]

This outstanding economic performance, it must be emphasized, has been the result of a strategy. Government policies have promoted investment in new plants producing goods for export. They have supported education in the skills required to operate new plants and equipment—simply put, they have trained engineers, not lawyers or financiers—and they have provided retraining for those needing relocation within the economy. Management, for its part, has looked for long-term market share in highly profitable industries, rather than a short-term return to shareholders. Managers have realized that new technology requires new methods of organizing workers; new education demands new procedures to ensure high levels of motivation and commitment. Workers have understood that their standard of living is inseparable from Japan's competitive posture.

In short, across the spectrum of her society, Japan has seen the world as it is, not as she would wish it. She has defined her position and her vital interests in that world. And she has defined her institutional functions and relationships in such a way as to fulfill those vital interests. Her comparative advantage lies in her ability to be both realistic and holistic—that is, conscious of herself as a combination of elements, which, when properly assembled, constitute a whole which is manifestly different from and more powerful than the sum of its parts.

Many have attributed this ability to the peculiarities of the national culture. To be sure, culture is important; but we had better understand clearly what we mean by the term. Is it reasonable to argue that Japan's culture makes it, inevitably, the superior of the United States? I cannot accept that premise. Japan's success is more properly attributed to a concept related to, but different from, culture. That concept is ideology—the set of ideas that defines and justifies the roles and relationships of a community's institutions. If I am correct, then Americans do indeed have a choice, and therefore a responsibility. Whereas culture tends to be inherent and congenital—that which is predetermined for a society—a change in ideology can be undertaken and accomplished. What the Japanese possess that we have yet to achieve is an appreciation of the world context in which their nation exists, and an awareness of the necessities which that reality imposes.

The American disease is importantly a psychological ailment. Observers of the American scene in 1981 reported that "three out of four Americans, shocked by the reverses the country has undergone since 1973, have concluded that 'We are fast coming to a turning point in our history. The land of plenty is becoming the land of want.' "[22] Survey data in 1980 showed that 55% of the population was convinced that "next year will be worse than this year."[23] The past looked rosier than the future. There was the inarticulate but wistful hope that Ronald Reagan would take us back to a lost state of grace.

But despite Reagan's appealing rhetoric—about tax cuts and budget cuts, about unsnarling government regulations, about returning power to the people and getting government off their backs—there was an ominous disquiet in the winter of 1982. Perhaps the very simplicity of the President's vision emphasized the true complexity of the situation: there seemed to be too much institutional rot around to be so easily disposed of. Many of the nation's school systems, for example, were in a shambles. They were accomplishing little; and of what they did manage to convey, not much seemed especially relevant to the needs of society. (Japanese children outscored U.S. children in mathematics at every grade level.[24]) The physical infrastructure was in an appalling state of deterioration—sewers leaked, roads and bridges needed repair, and mass transportation systems were obsolescent. Richard Schneller, the majority leader of the Connecticut state senate, estimated that it would require $1.5 billion just to fix the roads and bridges of Connecticut. "Business depends on healthy infrastructure," he said. "They should be working in partnership with the government to improve the situation, but they are not. Old antagonisms get in the way. Somehow business does not think the community's business is theirs."[25]

Other resources even further removed from the pressures of the marketplace were in serious trouble. The nation's electric utilities, for example, faced unprecedented costs due to rising oil prices. Their revenues were restrained by both rate limitations and environmental regulation. In 1982, many were near bankruptcy, and were essentially paralyzed. Although there seemed to be enough generating capacity in place to keep the lights on through the 1980s, there was a real possibility of extensive regional power failures in the following decade.With ten- to twelve-year lead times needed for new plants, these failures could be inevitable.

Such internal difficulties only exacerbated our growing doubts about the nation's ability to maintain a posture of world leadership. Many, indeed, were concluding that the effort was not worth the price. Having fallen to tenth among nations in per capita gross national product—behind almost every country in northern Europe except the United Kingdom—Americans were loath to increase military expenditures. Lester Thurow, viewing the deteriorating American economy, wrote: "If adventurism is what the Soviet Union wants, it will have even more opportunities (in the 1990s) given the likely disarray in Western alliances. In short, the major American foreign policy problems lie at home. Unless these domestic problems are cured, there is no panacea to be found abroad in projecting military power or displaying diplomatic skill."[26]

Perhaps the most disquieting and unfamiliar aspect of the reality facing America was the growing perception of interdependence. Americans had begun to sense that they would never again experience the sense of self-sufficiency and indestructibility they had enjoyed during the thirty years following World War II. In a profound sense, we, too, had become dependent on the other nations comprising our fragile world. Roughly half of the oil which fueled our industries had to be imported from one of the most unstable quarters of the world. And while the economy was being battered by competitive systems in Japan and Europe —systems we found not only difficult to understand but in many ways distasteful to emulate—the pervasiveness of trade in the economy, and thus the necessity of a competitive posture, was more and more evident.

As a proportion of gross national product, trade increased substantially in all industrialized countries during the 1970s. It rose by 44% in Japan, 36% in West Germany, and 80% in France. But in the United States, it grew an incredible 140%.[27] More than 20% of the nation's industrial output in 1982 was exported. One out of every six jobs in U.S. factories produced for export. The products of two out of every five acres of U.S. farmland was sold abroad. Almost one-third of the profits of American corporations came from their exports to, or investments in, foreign countries. The share of trade in the gross national product doubled during the 1970s. The cost of oil imports alone rose from $3 billion in 1970 to more than $80 billion in 1982. Many of the largest U.S. companies depended on the rest of the world for more than half their sales and profits. America's dependence on imports manifested itself in many ways: when the value of the dollar fell in 1977–78, for example, the increased cost of imports added at least two points to the rate of inflation.[28]

Much of this rise in interdependence was an outgrowth of the rapid escalation in oil prices which began in 1973. By 1980, the oil-exporting countries enjoyed a combined trade surplus of $110 billion, up from $60 billion in 1974. It was a breathtaking transfer of money and power. For the United States, the most powerful nation in the world, the shock was as profound psychologically as it was economically and politically. In a twinkling, the world —and our role in it—had been transformed.

But the oil shock has to be understood also as a unifying, integrating force. The oil producers had to do something with their sudden infusion of revenues. What they did was to increase greatly their purchases of goods and services from the industrialized world, fueling a competition to satisfy their new demands: for armaments, industrial equipment, consumer goods, financial services, and social and educational programs. Much of their money was deposited in Western banks, and subsequently loaned to developing countries. For these countries to be able to afford the interest payments on these huge loans—Mexico, for example, had obligations of more than $80 billion in 1982—they had to export their products to the consuming nations. Here the ties began to bind: in order for Brazil and Mexico to pay their debts to American banks, they had to increase their exports of steel, autos, and agricultural products to American markets.

Another route traveled by the oil producers was investment in the capital markets, through the purchase of real estate, commercial properties, industries, or debt. With such purchases, of course, came political and economic influence. While Americans, when they considered these trends, tended to focus on their sense of being "in hock," "over a barrel," the overriding effect was one of increased interdependence.

In short, the United States was becoming as dependent on the rest of the world as Japan had been for a century. But there was a difference: we didn't realize it. President Reagan's 1982 State of the Union address contained multiple references to the virtues of states' rights, but it made no reference to the fact or the consequences of interdependence. Perhaps most interesting was the glow of good feeling that the address generated, even in as jaundiced an observer of the American scene as Roger Mudd of NBC, who responded to the President's words with what appeared to be a heartfelt admiration. The reason can be inferred: the President was taking us back to a happier day, to a more secure time, to long-cherished virtues.

But, speeches and nostalgia to the contrary, by the early 1980s there was evidence that Americans were absorbing the profound implications of global interdependence. The effects of the American disease were coming clear: America had been living beyond its means. We had grown inefficient and careless. We had to consume less and invest more.

Belatedly aware of the problem, Americans began their search for solutions. Appropriately, the remedies proposed were directed primarily at the roles and relationships of government, corporations, and labor. They focused on the proper role of government and how it could be carried out effectively; on the purpose of the great corporation and the most desirable relationship between its activities and those of government; on the authority and practice of management, and the relationship of managers to those whom they manage. These concepts, of course, had been discussed previously; the difference was that in earlier discussions, they had invariably been considered separately. This isolated approach to economic problems was in itself among the causes of the disease, and it was now perceived, if only dimly, that they could not be managed or even grasped unless their interrelationships were clear.

Some proposed a return to protectionism, to the erection of

trade barriers around the failing institutions of America to insulate them from competition. This remedy, which had been acceptable in the past, was in 1982 generally perceived as self-defeating because of the unalterable dependence of the nation on the world. Opponents of protectionism also challenged the logic of insulating the unproductive or uncompetitive sectors of our economy. Others promoted "local content" legislation, requiring foreign producers who sell in the U.S. to manufacture here also. "The long range goal has to be to get the Japanese to locate and produce here," said Douglas A. Fraser, the then president of the United Automobile Workers.[29] This was perceived as a means of retaining jobs in the United States while importing foreign capital and management techniques. But the approach also had its risks, carrying with it the threat of retaliation from other countries, whose cooperation already benefited many industries. Could we afford to jeopardize existing relationships in the attempt to create new ones?

These budding changes in the American approach to management and competition were paralleled by developments in American trade unionism. "It's time our adversary system was changed," said Donald F. Ephlin, UAW vice-president at the ailing Ford Motor Company. "It's a system that is causing us to run in second place."[30] Indeed, in many sectors besides automobile manufacturing—in construction, trucking, communications, rubber and steel production, and the airline industry, for example—the old adversarial conception of the role of the trade union weakened as the interests of workers became more clearly identified with those of the enterprise as a whole.

But what new concept would take the place of the old? Unions representing some 4.5 million workers faced demands for wage restraint and other concessions in 1982. What they would and could seek in return was unclear. With organized labor now comprising little more than 20% of the work force, and with its political influence and bargaining power at a correspondingly low ebb, the American labor movement felt itself vulnerable to increasingly sophisticated attacks by managers eager for "a union-free environment." But it seemed unlikely that the new concept of American labor would be no concept at all; the unions would not give up something for nothing, and they would certainly not die gently. The new grounds for negotiation appeared most likely to lie in that fuzzy area formerly protected by the terms "management prerogatives" and "corporate governance": access to corporate financial records, a voice in pricing and investment policies, participation in the management of the workplace, and an influence on the distribution of profits.

Keichi Takeoka was appointed in 1974 to manage Motorola's Quasar television plant in Franklin Park, Illinois, which had been bought by Matsushita Electric, one of Japan's largest producers of consumer electronics. "What we found when we took over," said Takeoka, "was a manufacturing operation with a quality level of 150 defects for every 100 finished sets manufactured and a high rate of claims under warranty. Faced with such thorny problems, we tried using many productivity and quality control techniques employed in Japan. These techniques proved to be the right solution, since our preshipment defect rate is now three or four per hundred, and our warranty claims rate has decreased by 80%."

This achievement is particularly noteworthy because most of the plant's workers and managers were carried over from Motorola days. Takeoka's solution was neither exotic nor mysterious: he changed the relationship between workers and managers to inspire a commitment to both quality and efficiency. The existing hierarchical approach was abandoned, and workers were encouraged to become involved in areas formerly reserved for management. "When workers feel they directly participate in management," summarized Takeoka, "they are motivated to perform and to actively improve the entire system from production to management."[31] (Motorola, incidentally, later suggested that it would have moved in the same direction had it decided to stay in the business.[32])

The example is not exceptional. Sanyo, one of Matsushita's major Japanese competitors, acquired Warwick's color television assembly plant in Arkansas in 1979, and in about two months reduced the product-defect rate from about 30% to less than 5%. In 1981, Sony's San Diego facility achieved productivity and quality levels equal to those of comparable plants in Japan. But the problems inherent in changing concepts of the workplace should not be minimized: Akio Morita, chairman of Sony, has noted the difficulty that he encountered in trying to persuade

American engineers and managers at the San Diego plant to get involved on the production floor, to "mingle with foremen and workers to learn how things were really being made."[33]

In the summer of 1982, Nissan began building a $500-million light-truck plant in Smyrna, Tennessee. The company announced plans to send 425 key workers to Japan for training, and the UAW announced its intention to organize the plant. Marvin Runyon, Nissan's American manager, felt the latter activity was unnecessary: "I have no distaste for unions," said the former Ford vice-president, "but the reasons for a union thirty-five years ago do not exist in this company."[34]

However uncomfortably, the lessons were beginning to take root. As Anthony Athos and Richard Pascale conclude in their 1981 book, *The Art of Japanese Management,* "There is a growing consensus—both at home and abroad—that to a significant extent the management practices which had seemed to serve America so well, and were admired around the world, were failing us. Reginald H. Jones, chairman of General Electric, recently commented, 'The indictment in many cases is justified. It should be taken very seriously.' "[35] (Athos and Pascale also noted that the American companies generally considered to be outstanding performers—such as IBM, Boeing, Procter and Gamble, Delta Airlines, 3M, and Hewlett Packard—were in many ways similar to companies like Matsushita.[36])

The Japanese, of course, were mindful of the hostility with which their successes were being met in the United States, and in the early 1980s were becoming increasingly generous with advice and assistance. The Nikko Research Center of Tokyo, for example, sent a team of experts to America in 1980 to help out. "Both nations," the team observed, "will continue their competition in the future. It is necessary for Japan to help American industry in such sectors where Japan holds an advantage. The way to prevent the spreading protectionism and [to keep] the free trade principle from becoming a mere skeleton is that the nation standing at advantage assists and helps the nation in distress."[37]

Noting that since 1950 Japanese productivity had grown at twice the American rate, the Nikko team cited a familiar list of reasons: lack of investment in new plant and equipment, inefficient use of capital, stagnation of technological development, "management policy aiming at short-term return on investment, and various problems contained in the conventional style of man-

agement in the U.S., especially labor-management relations."
Also condemned were the failure of government to control inflation, "excessively expanded and fattened governmental structures," and incoherent government regulations. Perhaps most
serious, from the researchers' perspective, were the "many un-
favorable factors rooted deeply into the very system of American
society, such as declining work ethic resulting from change in
personal values, and excessive social welfare plus increase in
crime, deterioration of social discipline and order, degraded quality of education and the like." It was an ironic reversal, in a scant
thirty years: now the Japanese were saying to us, as General
MacArthur had said to them decades earlier, "You have a most
abnormal system."

On the positive side, the visitors found "mounting enthusiasm
for the Japanese style of management . . ., the so-called 'respect
for humanity' and 'collective value system' seeking the harmony
of personal benefit and the collective profit." More than two
hundred companies, they said, had adopted "Japanese style
quality circle activities," but they predicted that "a great deal of
brain working [sic] may be necessary" because of "cultural differences."

The report also included a sobering note: "In order to avoid
the most deplorable possibility of a frontal clash between two
partner nations, there may be no other alternative for Japan than
to cooperate with U.S. industry for its revitalization."

"A real management revolution," the report concluded,
"might be required."

Not all remedies had to be imported. While the Japanese were
prodding us to become more effective competitors, the late Congressman Richard Bolling of Missouri and John Bowles, an investment banker with Kidder, Peabody and Company, were
seeking to rally the nation around the development of a new
national consensus, a coalition of strength and purpose to deal
with our competitive challenge.[38]

In their book *America's Competitive Edge,* Bolling and Bowles
emphasized the achievements made possible when government,
business, and labor had organized themselves for concerted actions in the past: the Marshall Plan for the reconstruction of
Europe after World War II; the Hoover Commission, which ef-

fectively made the President the manager of the executive branch; and the Employment Act of 1946, which established the Council of Economic Advisors, and assigned to government the implicit obligation of assuring jobs to all those willing to work.

It is unfortunate that *America's Competitive Edge* did not receive the attention it deserved. The nation, distracted by the advent of Ronald Reagan and his very different conclusions, did not fully benefit from Bolling and Bowles's research, the lessons of which are worth recalling. The decline of American strength they attributed to weakness in the "economic triangle of trade, energy, and productivity."[39] This weakness was compounded during the Johnson-Nixon decade by a proliferation of incoherent government activities at the federal level, and by short-term economic policies which seriously neglected the nation's capital base. Excessive and conflicting regulation, an aimless and often ineffective collection of social and welfare programs, and short-sighted fiscal and monetary policies were the inevitable result.

The authors' remedies included "the re-creation of a governmental system that works," and a revision of the Employment Act which would place emphasis on "productive jobs and not just jobs themselves."[40] Implicit in the Bolling-Bowles recommendations was the endowment of government with the responsibility and the power to define coherent national priorities, to work with business, labor, and other interest groups to establish a consensus for those priorities, and to create imaginative public policies for the efficient implementation of that consensus by American corporations, in cooperation with government and labor.

Philip Caldwell, the chairman of Ford, echoed these beliefs when he said, in 1981: "We need a new, sensible national industrial policy to provide an effective framework for action." To Caldwell, it appeared to be a matter of survival: "Much as we might hope for greater independence in our affairs, . . . today U.S. companies are really competing with the country of Japan rather than with another private company."[41] "What we have never been able to master in this country," he lamented, "is the articulation of goals in the industrial sector."

Debates about the establishment of a "national industrial policy" will surely mark the decade of the 1980s and beyond. Proponents of such a policy argue that the United States will not recover economic health and competitiveness without it. Says

Robert Reich: "Today competitive leadership requires the ability to adapt to a changing world economy, and government can help reduce the cost of adaptation in two ways: 1. By smoothing the movement of capital and labor out of declining industries; and, 2. By ensuring the availability of both capital and labor to promising sectors of the economy—that is, by accelerating the adjustment that capital and labor would otherwise achieve more slowly on their own." [42]

Other proponents of industrial policy have noted that, to a great extent, our need is to make coherent and explicit that which government already attempts to do, and that which it must do in addition. Government policies already have enormous impact on industry, through military procurement, through research and development contracts, through environmental regulation, through tax and trade policies, and through outright subsidies. This school of thought raises the issue of governmental self-awareness: will the government continue to design and implement these policies oblivious of their very real effects on industry, or will it lift the veil of ignorance, as it were, and ponder what it is doing? [43]

If the United States has had an explicit industrial policy in this century, it has been antitrust. Our semi-religious faith is that if the marketplace were kept open and unobstructed, the resulting competition among numerous—and preferably small—proprietors to satisfy consumer desires would assure the definition and fulfillment of the national interest. This was both more and less than an economic policy; this was a statement of political and social beliefs. As Judge Learned Hand wrote in explaining the 1945 decision to break up Alcoa, "great industrial concentrations are inherently undesirable regardless of their economic consequences."

But the antitrust posture—like so much of traditional U.S. policy—has assumed that America is an essentially closed economy. This posture has become increasingly untenable. Just as our outmoded policy failed to cope with the enormous flows of Eurodollars in the early 1970s, so our antitrust stance has proven slow to adjust to the realities of world competition. As an industrial policy, antitrust has discouraged consolidation, cooperation, and combination, regardless of how necessary these responses might be in order for American firms to compete with the rest of the world. Examples abound: the Federal Trade Commission was still considering taking antitrust action against the four U.S. automobile companies in the 1970s, until their troubles with imports rendered the commission's contemplated actions politically and economically absurd.

The Reagan administration adopted a radically different approach to antitrust matters. In response to the dramatic rash of large corporate mergers and acquisitions in 1981, Attorney General William French Smith declared that "bigness doesn't necessarily mean badness." He had allies in unexpected quarters. Douglas Fraser of the UAW, for example, agreed: "I'm for mergers when you can strengthen companies," he explained, adding that in the auto industry, the problem of monopolistic practices had become "a completely moot question because you have the fierce competition with the Japanese."[44] Support also came from more predictable sources. Clifton C. Garvin, Jr., chairman of Exxon, said, "If you believe in our economic system, you are not opposed to mergers or acquisitions. The history of our economic growth has been based on these kinds of things."[45]

A series of actions by the Justice Department presented dramatic evidence of the government's attitude toward antitrust as industrial policy. Ford and GM were allowed to cooperate in the development and testing of antipollution devices.[46] The department's long-standing suit against IBM was dropped, and its equally significant case against AT&T was settled, both because of concern in the Commerce Department about Japanese competition, and national-security worries of the Defense Department. In each case, Assistant Attorney General William F. Baxter was concerned about the effects of industrial structure on consumer prices, being mindful of the efficiency and economy which had been derived from combination and consolidation.[47]

Thus many were saying that the national interest, the needs of the American community in 1982, required consolidation. But there was concern about the definition of that interest and those needs. House Judiciary Committee Chairman Peter Rodino expressed the obvious point that some mergers were better than others, and that criteria were needed for determining the nation's interest in such situations. Did it reside in consumer prices? Or in enhanced competitiveness in the world economy? Or in more jobs in a given location or industry? "If the cash in corporate treasuries isn't invested in long-term growth," said Rodino, "but is spent instead to acquire the assets of other firms, a major potential source of investment has been dissipated. . . . Cash in the hands of stockholders usually doesn't find its way readily into productive investment." In a more traditional vein, he also expressed concern about the future of small business if "all our economic assets are concentrated in the hands of a few large corporations."[48]

So while there was a new conception of industrial policy emerging in the 1980s, there was also a new concern about its purposes, and about whether it would be guided by some clear definition of community need. Was a more explicit industrial policy required? If so, how would it be determined? Existing models —for example, Japan's deliberative councils, which bring together government officials, business managers, union leaders, and others for consensus-building and joint planning—would profoundly disturb traditional antitrusters in America. In short, the new order was undecided on the subject, and the subject was critical.

Peter G. Peterson, former Secretary of Commerce and later chairman of Lehman Brothers Kuhn Loeb, believed that for all of its appeal, an industrial policy might constitute a remedy that could worsen the disease. "You have to ask where the scheme ends up politically," he said in an interview. "What worries me is that we would inevitably support the losers, as the British did with British-Leyland and we did with Chrysler. I also believe that protectionism would be almost the certain result of industrial policy in this country. It's unfortunate, but it's the way the system works."[49]

According to Peterson, Americans have chosen to consume, rather than invest. The government has been a principal offender. "Accumulated budget deficits have pushed the national debt to more than $1 trillion, involving annual interest charges of nearly $100 billion. In addition, we have quietly incurred 'off-the-books' liabilities of more than $2,000 billion. Half of that will be needed to meet future shortfalls between scheduled benefits and scheduled payroll taxes in the Social Security system. Other government pension commitments will take up the other half."[50]

Peterson saw these government claims on the capital market as inexorably denying to the private sector the resources it needed in order to compete effectively in the world. The so-called "safety net" programs, which in 1982 were spared President Reagan's budget knife, shared one characteristic: "Poverty or financial need is not a test for receiving the benefits."[51] By 1985, said Peterson, these programs would cost some $400 billion a year, "probably 10 times greater than all the cuts made in the fiscal 1982 budget." And these cuts would, he feared, hurt the poor. "Unless we now launch a counter-revolution against middle- and upper-class entitlements, budget control and economic recovery will elude us." Government, said Peterson, should determine who is poor and who isn't, and make sure that its assistance goes only to those who need it. In this way sufficient funds would be available for investment by business, and the current relationship between business and government could continue largely unchanged.

Convinced of the necessity for drastic belt-tightening, Peterson was also concerned about the divisive questions of fairness which would inevitably result from such an effort. While the economic pie was growing, unequal shares were acceptable, because everyone continued to receive a little more. But when the pie begins to shrink, unequal shares bring absolute pain for those who are too weak to make their influence felt. Austerity, Peterson concluded, must be fairly shared.

Other business and labor leaders were doubtful about the government's ability to create desired economic effects. American presidents from Franklin Roosevelt to Ronald Reagan had used fiscal policy to combat both inflation and unemployment, while simultaneously encouraging investment; during the past decade the tools had obviously not worked; they were blunt and clumsy. The Reagan tax cuts—which were supposed to encourage investment—were apparently focused as much or more on increased consumption, and on consumption by the rich, at that. There seemed to be no way to raise investment levels sufficiently (from 10% of GNP to 30%, if U.S. workers were going to acquire new equipment as quickly as their Japanese competitors) without reducing consumption. But, as Peterson asked, who was going to do the sacrificing—the rich or the poor? The strong or the weak? (Recent experience was not promising. Office of Management and Budget director David Stockman, in his celebrated confessions in *The Atlantic,* bemoaned the ability of powerful interests in Congress to evade his budget-cutting knife. "The hogs were really feeding," he complained.[52])

And if it was indeed new investment that was required, and if funds were scarce, then would not some industries need to be identified as more important than others? For thirty years, the Japanese had been skillful at ensuring that high-technology, export-oriented companies received the credit they required, even though resources were generally scarce. Was that kind of targeting appropriate for the United States? Typically, we had maintained that it was not appropriate; we did not know enough, we said, to pick winners. But was that an adequate response? Were we truly unable, for example, to distinguish between semiconductors and fast-food chains?

Monetary policy had proved an equally ineffective tool. Throughout the decade, the Federal Reserve Board had experienced increasing difficulty both in measuring money and controlling it. As soon as the Fed learned how to control one kind of money, another, more ingenious variety appeared—credit cards, Eurodollars, and so on. By 1982 there was a general irritation with the Fed: President Reagan, the AFL-CIO, members of Congress, and business representatives were all expressing their complaints. Even the Fed's supporters had their doubts: if we want the Fed to do its job, they asked, does it not need more teeth? Some even went so far as to suggest that the Fed's vaunted independence—to this point sacrosanct—should give way to a posture of closer coordination with the rest of government, as in other advanced countries.*

In short, all of the mechanisms of government policymaking

---

* Treasury Secretary Donald Regan conceded in January 1982 that managing the money supply was "a mammoth job," adding, "It doesn't help when the tools [the Fed] has to use are imprecise ones." There was some indication that he was coping adequately with the independence of the Fed, assuring his audience that the administration planned "to work with the Fed to keep its money supply growth on target."[53]

were separate and fragmented, while the problems they attempted to address were inseparably related. High interest rates restrained investment and therefore the economy. They also created a massive demand for dollars on the world market, which led to an overvalued dollar and an undervalued yen. This, in turn, made U.S. exports more expensive, while foreign (and especially Japanese) imports to this country grew cheaper. As the trade deficit grew, the economy stagnated and unemployment rose. Welfare costs climbed, and government incurred greater deficits to pay for them; inflation persisted as public money fed consumption, rather than production. The rising government deficits necessitated increased government borrowing, which kept interest rates high, thereby completing the vicious circle.

To reiterate, all elements of the circle were related, but the fragmentation of American government precluded such a coherent analysis. No policy divorced from the holistic reality could conceivably work.

There was by this point a fairly broad consensus that not only were the government's social and welfare programs (amounting to something like $300 billion in 1981) more than we could afford, but they were actually hurting many of those whom they were designed to help. Many agreed that the programs—conceived with the best of intentions—were eroding work incentives, promoting the disintegration of families, and nourishing a criminal subculture. Sixty-five million Americans, some 30% of the population, were receiving some variety of tax-supported income transfer payment from the government. Even with these massive expenditures, many of our urban communities were disintegrating, and the underclass within them was becoming increasingly alienated from the mainstream of American life. But was it sufficient merely to cut government expenditures for the poor? Faced with the prospect of starvation, would the underclass jump into the legitimate economy? Or would they move instead into the criminal economy? Seeing the second outcome as being as likely as the first, many observers felt that a coherent replacement for the poverty program was a necessity.

Felix Rohatyn, chairman of New York's Municipal Assistance Corporation and general partner in the investment banking firm of Lazard Frères, argued that the revitalization of the United States required the same kind of business-labor-government cooperation that saved New York City from financial ruin in the late 1970s. Labor had accepted a temporary wage freeze and substantial reductions in the workforce; banks had provided long-term low-interest loans; the state had stepped in with additional aid, credit assistance, and budgetary controls, and the federal government had guaranteed a small portion of the city's loans. The public assumed the burden of higher taxes and transport fares, and tuition fees at City University. "Stringent expenditure control coupled with rapid, inflation-driven growth in revenues turned a $1.7 billion deficit in 1975 into a $500 million surplus in 1981." [54]

Like Peter Peterson, Rohatyn saw the necessity of reducing government spending drastically. "Fairness requires that additional budget cuts include programs benefiting the middle class (social security, cost of living allowances, federal pensions, Medicare), as well as those benefiting the poor (federally-funded training programs for the unemployed, Medicaid, welfare)." But even with these cuts, he foresaw serious problems resulting from slow growth and inflation, as well as from regional disparities, "as oil, defense and sunshine favor half the United States, while the other half drifts more and more off into the shadows."

"No democracy, not even ours," he said, "can survive half suburb and half slum."

Rohatyn argued that "the linchpin"—effecting and securing the cooperation between business, government, and labor which was essential to the nation's recovery—was a contemporary version of the Reconstruction Finance Corporation (RFC) of the 1930s. It would provide capital to ruined northern cities, as well as to older industries temporarily unable to face foreign competition. "The free market is inadequate to the task," he said. Addressing Peterson's concern, and drawing on his own experience in New York, he added: "Far from simply bailing out failing companies or politicians unwilling to face reality, the RFC would offer its capital only to those entities willing to make the sacrifices required to make them viable: corporations whose unions are willing to make wage and productivity concessions and rely more on profit sharing; managements which will make equivalent sacrifices and limit price increases; stockholders who will forgo dividends in order to maximize investments. . . . The damage caused by excessive government regulation and interference in the 1970s will not be cured by government abdication in the 1980s."

New York City arrived at its solution only when it reached the brink of bankruptcy. (Many have argued that it actually plunged over the brink.) The question naturally arises: How much crisis will be required before the nation moves to a similarly cooperative course of action? What will it take to force us to inspect the assumptions which underlie the existing relationships between government and business and management and labor, to consider their utility, and to make changes? What is it that precludes certain remedies, and permits others? What is it that guides our perception of our environment, providing a relatively clear view of parts of it while leaving much of it in shadow? Self-interest, one might answer: those in the seats of power can't be expected to delight in change. But what if those in power fully recognize the worms that are eating at their chairs—what then prevents them from responding realistically? The answer is ideology. "Unfortunately," says Rohatyn, "[America] faces this future with an ideology . . . more suitable to the past than to the present."

The truth is even more complicated, however. As we have seen in this overview, America's institutions—government, industry, and labor—are changing radically, especially in terms of their relationships with one another. If these institutions and their behavior have been in harmony with traditional ideology, they must now be moving away from it. While their managers sing the old hymns to justify their behavior, they are of necessity moving further and further from the convictions represented in those hymns. They are not practicing what they preach. And indeed they cannot and should not do so. If change is essential, what then? If we cannot and should not practice what we preach, should we learn to preach what we practice, and thus act with a full consciousness of what we are doing?

2

The Concept of Ideology
and Transformation in
the United States

The diagnosis and treatment of the American disease can be aided greatly through the use of the concept of ideology, as a framework for understanding both the implications of what we are currently doing and what we must undertake to do. The word "ideology" first emerged in the early 1800s, when a group of French philosophers used it to refer to the body of ideas that have a formative effect upon a community.[1] Since then, the word has been bandied about a good deal, and occasionally misappropriated, but its usefulness as a concept persists.

What is ideology? I have already suggested one metaphor: the "hymns" we sing to justify and make legitimate what we are doing (or, perhaps, what we would like to do). Simply put, ideology is the collection of ideas through which a society translates its values into action. We may posit that values persist from epoch to epoch, and are often shared by very diverse cultures; ideology, however, must evolve in order to retain its usefulness. Justice, for example, is a value that every community has cherished, in one manifestation or another. In this sense, the concept of justice is noncontroversial. Obviously, though, different communities at different times have achieved "justice" in very different ways. Each approach represents an ideology: a bridge of ideas for carrying justice and other values into the real world. This bridge gives a general value specific meaning, and makes it serve in such time- and space-bound contexts as government, corporations, and labor organizations.

Values are what a society cherishes most deeply. Ideology— serving values as intimately as it does—is almost inescapably controversial. Its inspection evokes a controversy that we generally seek to avoid. Who, after all, enjoys subjecting his society's standards to a rigorous examination? But the practical result is that an outmoded ideology tends to linger on, uninspected, while institutions depart from it in many pragmatic ways. Eventually, we can no longer practice what we preach, and we are not yet able to preach what we practice.

Ideology, as I have defined it, serves as the bridge between values and their contexts in the real world. Because those contexts change over time, ideology is not rigid; it is not dogma. Sooner or later it changes to accommodate reality. In that process, the new reality is made legitimate in light of enduring values.

Ideology is crucial to managers, because it justifies their role and behavior. It is the wellspring of their authority. (The concept of "property rights," for example, has long served as an ideological basis for managerial authority.) The problem is that managers must live dangerously: for a time they may be able to act consistently with the prevailing ideology, but as circumstances in the real world change, managers must respond to take advantage of (or merely cope with) the change. In so doing, they run the risk of departing from the traditional ideology, and thus being found illegitimate by its adherents. Their authority erodes; they must either return to the old ideology, or articulate a new ideology that justifies what they are doing (see Figure I).

On the other hand, of course, managers may find themselves reluctant to adapt to change in the real world because of their attraction to the old ideology. The irony is that this course is no less risky. Society may applaud their orthodoxy, but if their subscription to an outmoded ideology makes them progressively irrelevant, inefficient, and ineffective, they will lose their authority with equal finality, but for a different reason: their businesses will fail.

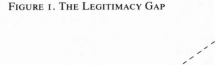

Figure I. The Legitimacy Gap

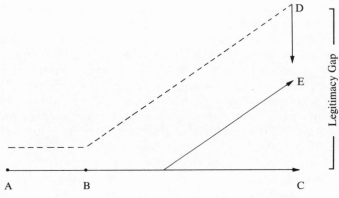

The solid line ABC in Figure I represents a traditional ideology proceeding through time. The dotted line represents institutional practice—that is, what government, business, and labor are actually doing and how they are related to one another. During time period AB, institutional practice conforms to the prevailing ideology, and after that, departs: changes in the real world compel the institutions to behave differently than they did. By time C, institutional practice is very different from what the ideology presumed: the old hymns are being sung, but they are not being practiced. There is a gap, DC, which may be called a "legitimacy gap." There is an ideological schizophrenia: the new practice brings forth a new ideology to justify itself, but loyalty to the old ways discourages its articulation. As the legitimacy gap widens, two conflicting pressures converge on managers: one seeks to force errant institutions back into conformity with the ABC ideology; the other argues for a more forceful and articulate expression of the new ideology, which is the only means of legitimizing what is actually occurring (ABE).

During the last decades of the twentieth century, changes in the "real world" of the United States have stimulated many institutional changes. Predictably, institutional responses have taken two forms:

1. Some institutions have responded quickly, moving pragmatically to a new set of justifications for their actions.

2. Others have found the transition difficult to manage, being constrained by traditional ideological assumptions and by the perceptions and decision-making patterns that flow from them.

Both responses have generated uncertainty, waste, and crisis. Institutions in the first category—whose managers may lack a clear understanding of what they are doing ideologically—often fail to perceive the full set of possible consequences of their actions, and thus exacerbate the natural suspicion and opposition of traditionalists. Those in the second category confront mounting crisis—bankruptcy, loss of influence, inefficiency, and intellectual deterioration—as they fail to adapt effectively to changes in their environment. With both types of failure, the community as a whole suffers.

In summary, ideological analysis can provide a way of understanding institutional change, inspecting assumptions about it, and managing it more effectively. It can be equally useful to the director of the Office of Management and Budget, the chairman of General Motors, the president of the United Automobile Workers, or the president of Amherst. In times of rapid societal change, a tool must be brought forth to grapple with that change. Ideological analysis is that tool.

We need to refine further our definitions of *values, ideology,* and *the real world,* and of how they are related to one another. Values, as I have defined them, are the timeless, universal notions that every community has cherished. They include, for example, survival of the community, justice, economy, self-fulfillment, and self-respect. It would be difficult to identify a national leader, in any age or culture, who would not come out four-square in favor of such notions. The controversy arises, of course, when these values are interpreted, and are made explicit in organizations and decision-making procedures which are intended to implement the values. This is the task of ideology, as we have said: to serve as the bridge that connects values to the world. Inasmuch as the world constantly changes, ideology changes too, albeit more haltingly. Many communities expend huge amounts of time, money, and blood trying to keep their ideology rigid, but unless their world is static, such efforts must eventually fail.

One might say that a community is successful—that is, effective in setting and implementing its goals—to the extent that it manages ideological change so as to keep institutional pace with change in the real world. Applying this thesis to today's world, it is reasonable to say that Japan is relatively more successful than the U.S.S.R. and the United States, because its ideology achieves a better fit with reality. Stated another way, Japan's comparative advantage—the topic of so much of the controversy outlined in the preceding chapter—is ideological.

Every community worthy of the name has an ideology. Sometimes there are several ideologies, which may exist either in harmony or in conflict with each other. Today, it is generally the developed nations that enjoy a relatively clear ideological framework; those that are less developed tend to be ideologically confused. This is not to say that ideologies that were in place in developing countries for millennia were not clear or compelling to their adherents. Unfortunately, however, one of the most pervasive effects of colonialism was the destruction or dispersion of indigenous ideologies, and the replacement of them with a superficial overlay that lacks indigenous roots.[2]

The phrase "the real world" means the collection of events, actions, circumstances, scientific insights, and institutional phenomena occurring at a particular time within and around a particular community. The real world is what might be called the community's existential reality. Ideology, then, is connected to the real world in several ways. The components of the real world at a given time will tend to reflect the prevailing ideology at that time. For example, the behavior of government in the real world will tend to conform to the community's idea of what the role of government should be. But as change occurs in the real world—as in the emergence of the large publicly held corporation around the turn of the century, or the Great Depression of the 1930s—the role of government changes, resulting in an inconsistency between the new practice and the prevailing ideology, which in turn produces strains. If the inconsistency grows, there will be increasing amounts of confusion until a new ideology emerges to justify the new ways.

What are some of the more important characteristics of the real world which may come to bear on ideology? First, there is geography, including demography. Resources are scarce or plentiful; populations are sparse or dense. There is also economic performance: a given economy may be growing or contracting; labor may be plentiful or scarce, prices high or low. The community may be competitive in the world economy or not—i.e., a "winner" or a "loser." Changes in these realms—in resources and economic performance—will force changes in institutional practice, which in turn may necessitate changes (implicit, if not explicit) in the underlying ideology.

Reality is defined not only by its physical and economic characteristics, but also by accepted notions about the nature of matter, of spirit, and of feeling. Whereas this was once the realm of poets and priests, in the last three hundred years scientists have taken over the field. In the Middle Ages the generally accepted view of the world was that of a hierarchically ordered organic society, under God's tutelage and sanctioned by Church doctrine. In modern times, though, people have tended to regard reality as a collection of elements, ordered according to "natural" laws that can be deduced by scientific experimentation. As long as the bulk of the evidence produced by that experimentation supported that concept of reality, we were in good shape.

Currently, however, we are not in good shape: the trouble is that continuing scientific discovery has refuted what we took to be irrefutable laws of nature. For Sir Isaac Newton, reality derived from an understanding of the particles of nature, and of the laws of motion and mechanics that governed those particles. But Einstein found that an accurate perception of reality depended on an understanding of the relationship among those particles in time and space. Today, our scientists—the ecologists, microbiologists, geneticists, and the rest—are supplying us with visions of a profoundly different reality, and their separate visions are not necessarily compatible. Even the concept of distinct scientific disciplines is in question: while some scientists continue to peer down the dark tunnels of specialization, others have reached the jarring realization that reality may well require a conception of wholes, not merely of pieces. These new perspectives are necessitating technological and institutional change with profound ideological implications.

At any given time, the real world is dominated by a particular set of institutions. Inevitably—although not predictably—new ones appear on the horizon that challenge the old, and force them to adapt or perish. In the 1970s the Organization of Petroleum Exporting Countries (OPEC) became one such institution, and the government/business partnership of Japan emerged as another. These two have precipitated change in the structure and behavior of every institution in their path: in industries, such as financial services and the producers of oil, autos, steel, and semiconductors; in governments, of both rich and poor nations; in trade unions, especially those dependent on the more severely impacted industries; and in the more specialized departments of our universities, forced for the first time to think holistically. Institutional adjustment to these challenges will continue to strain our traditional ideological assumptions, and will of necessity evoke different ones.

Traditional assumptions are an important feature of the current reality, rooted deep in the collective heart of the community. Some of these ideological touchstones are useful; others are less so. The characters portrayed by John Wayne are an interesting example, at once superficial and profound. Surely there is something glorious about Wayne's stock character, the lone gunman, who swaggers down the streets of Dodge City rooting out—and shooting up—sinners. Steeped as we are in our individualistic ideology, we respond instinctively to Wayne's example; we internalize it. But the same performance would take on a different cast in Times Square; a John Wayne would be likely to hit innocent bystanders in the course of the purification. Americans are fully aware of this incongruity, and yet we find it extremely difficult to control the use of guns. Foreigners examine our reality and find it difficult to comprehend: they see a deadly romance with weapons; they do not fully understand the power of traditional myths in contemporary America. These myths effectively retard institutional change, even as other patterns are demanding it.

Approaching the same phenomenon from another vantage point, let us examine briefly the effect of the real world on the Japanese ideology. A collection of small, infertile islands, with limited natural resources and a population of 120 million people, Japan is almost totally dependent on an often hostile world for its survival. As would be expected, Japan's ideology—again, the framework of ideas that are used to make values explicit and to justify institutions—is very different from that of nineteenth-century America, in which a sparse population was attempting to tame a wilderness of almost unlimited scope and resources. Without much exaggeration, we can trace many contemporary attitudes in Japan to limits imposed by the real world. Japanese attitudes about the role of government, the role of business, and the relationship between the two; the role of trade unions; and the means of self-fulfillment and self-respect for the individual in the family, the village, the firm, and the nation are very much rooted in that reality.

To argue, therefore, that the Japanese "cheat" in their competition with the West, that they violate the accepted rules of the game, is specious. It is far more productive to examine the rules in their context, and to extrapolate from that examination. How do the competitors' approaches to the game differ? If the world is likely to choose one approach over another—and it will; it will adopt the more successful strategy—then whose rules are likely to be picked? Ultimately, these questions require an inspection of ideology, because that is where the rules are rooted.

During the last eighty years, and particularly in the 1960s and 1970s, the real world in America has forced upon institutions a variety of changes that demand an ideological transformation. Understandably, leaders have been reluctant to make this ongoing transformation explicit, because the traditional ideology has great appeal. And although the election of President Reagan caused some to conclude that America was reverting to its traditional ideology, this does not in fact appear to be the case. Our current posture, then, has both advantages and disadvantages. On the plus side, we are recognizing—if only implicitly—the need for change. On the other hand, we are still dragging our feet. (To revive an earlier metaphor, we see the need for some new hymns, but we are only grudgingly learning the new words.) The consequences are unfortunate: further delay in recognizing the ideological implications of what we are doing merely makes the task of transition more difficult, the related costs higher, and the final outcome less certain.

What constitutes an ideology? For our purposes, an ideology can be conveniently divided into five components:

1. The relationship between the human being and the community—that is, between the individual and the group.

2. The institutional guarantees and manifestations of that relationship, such as property rights.

3. The means of controlling the production of goods and services.

4. The role of the state.

5. The predominant perceptions of reality and nature, which determine, for example, the role of science and the functions of education.

There are today two dominant ideologies in the world: individualism and communitarianism. There are many variations of each (see Figure 2). The traditional ideology of the United States is an individualistic one. It consists of five great ideas that first came to this country in the eighteenth century, having been postulated in seventeenth-century England by John Locke, among others.[3] These ideas, as noted, found fertile ground in the vast, underpopulated wilderness of America, and served the country well for the first century of its existence. It is important to understand how appropriate and useful these principles have been to America: although they have been buffeted and eroded throughout our history by communitarian practices—particularly in times of crisis—they continue to be remarkably resilient. They are, says Samuel Huntington, "at the very core of [our] national identity. Americans cannot abandon them without ceasing to be Americans in the most meaningful sense of the word—without, in short, becoming un-American."[4]

A review of the five great Lockean ideas provides a starting point for understanding the transformation we are now experiencing. Let us look at twentieth-century America through the eyes of John Locke.

1. INDIVIDUALISM. The community, as Locke would see it, is no more than the sum of the individuals within it. The values of self-fulfillment and self-respect are realized through an essentially lonely struggle. The fit survive; if you do not survive, it is because you are somehow unfit.[5]

FIGURE 2. IDEOLOGY: A BRIDGE BETWEEN VALUES AND THE REAL WORLD

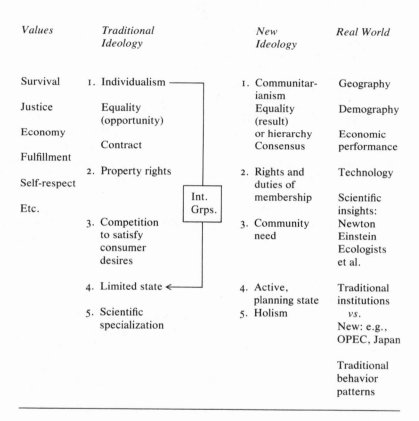

Values	*Traditional Ideology*	*New Ideology*	*Real World*
Survival	1. Individualism	1. Communitarianism	Geography
Justice	Equality (opportunity)	Equality (result) or hierarchy	Demography
Economy	Contract	Consensus	Economic performance
Fulfillment			
Self-respect	2. Property rights	2. Rights and duties of membership	Technology
Etc.	Int. Grps.		Scientific insights:
	3. Competition to satisfy consumer desires	3. Community need	Newton Einstein Ecologists et al.
	4. Limited state	4. Active, planning state	Traditional institutions
	5. Scientific specialization	5. Holism	*vs.* New: e.g., OPEC, Japan
			Traditional behavior patterns

Some corollary principles:

a. Individuals are equal in the sense of deserving equal opportunity.

b. Although inherently separate, individuals are tied together by the notion of contract: as buyers and sellers, employers and employees, and—in earlier times—husbands and wives. The contract, in its pure state, is individualistic; however, the contract became collectivized (and therefore corrupted) with the rise of the trade-union movement.

Pure individualism, of course, has been augmented in the real world of American politics by interest-group pluralism. Individuals who have found themselves unable to reach the levers of power have banded together, and the direction of the community has been determined largely by the pressure of conflicting interest groups: sheepherders, ranchers, the railroads, environmentalists, black-power advocates, feminists, and so on.

2. PROPERTY RIGHTS. Property consists of one's body and one's estate, and property rights are the guarantor of individualism. Through this notion, the individual is protected against the predatory inclinations of the sovereign, and from it the corporation derives its right to exist, and its authority to act. By extension, the authority of managers is rooted in the property rights of the corporation's owners—that is, its shareholders.

3. MARKETPLACE COMPETITION. The control of the uses of property is best left to proprietors (preferably of small firms) competing in an open marketplace to satisfy individual customer desires. Adam Smith's "invisible hand" assures that the good community results. (This idea has been explicit in traditional United States antitrust law and practice.)

4. THE LIMITED STATE. Government is a necessary evil. Its fundamental role is to protect property and enforce contracts. Smaller is better: government should be kept divided, checked, and balanced. It should not plan or act coherently, even if the result of not doing so is a fragmented instrument responsive only to crises and interest groups. "Because of the inherently antigovernment character of the American Creed," says Samuel Huntington, "government that is strong is illegitimate, government that is legitimate is weak."[6]

5. SCIENTIFIC SPECIALIZATION. Knowledge, the justification for education and science, is obtained through specialized analysis. If experts understand the parts, the whole will take care of itself.

Implicit in individualism is the assumption that man has the desire to acquire power—that is, to control external events, property, nature, the economy, politics, or whatever. In combination with the concept of the limited state, this drive serves to guarantee progress through competition. In one sense, this is a corruption of Darwin's theory that the inexorable processes of evolution are constantly working to improve on nature. (Darwin himself might have been made uncomfortable by this extension of his theory.) Scientific specialization has been understood to be a part of this progress.

How can we assess the impact of these five concepts on our history and our contemporary culture? Taking the last idea first, we may fairly say that specialization has produced notable achievements over the past century, including penicillin, computers, and atomic bombs. It is not so simple to label such developments as examples of "progress," however. If "progress" implies change for the general good, we must stop short of that implication. Ballistic missiles are magnificent machines, for example, but they are not necessarily more "progressive" than bows and arrows. We can also perceive other difficulties: to cite a contemporary example, individualistic competition does little to assure healthy water supplies.

If we take a longer view and consider the past five thousand years of human history, one is struck by the extent to which the individualistic ideology is a fundamental aberration. Historically, the norm has been communitarian, not atomistic. Individualism constitutes a revolutionary (and in many ways noble) experiment, which achieved its most extreme manifestation in nineteenth-century America. Bringing our review up to the present, it appears that during this century, pure individualism has been deteriorating in the face of various real-world challenges—wars, depressions, new economic and political systems, the concentration and growth of both population and corporations, ecological degeneration, and perceptions of scarcity.

Today our difficulties are twofold:

1. The old ideas serve less and less well to define values in the real world, and

2. Many of our most important institutions—notably the large, publicly held corporations, trade unions, and the federal government—have departed radically from the old ideology, or are in the process of doing so, in order to achieve such goals as efficiency, economies of scale, productivity, and global competitiveness.

Although many small enterprises remain comfortably and acceptably consistent with the five basic Lockean concepts, and probably can remain so, large institutions in both the so-called private and public sectors cannot so easily practice what they preach. Yet Locke's concepts are what is meant by "the free enterprise system," and that system is regarded as the basis of institutional legitimacy. Because Americans cling to the old ideology, much of institutional America lacks legitimacy, and thus authority.[7] So illegitimacy—and dubious authority—abounds.

Reginald Jones, former chairman of General Electric, addressed the problem when he spoke to a group of Harvard students in 1982. "The legitimacy of democratic capitalism," he said, "derives from its pragmatic success; it has produced the greatest good for the greatest number. Its greatest failing is that it has no theology."[8] Jacques Maritain expressed the same thought poetically, telling Americans: "You are advancing in the night bearing torches toward which mankind would be glad to turn, but you leave them enveloped in the fog of a merely experiential approach and mere practical conceptualization with no universal idea to communicate. For lack of an adequate ideology, your lights cannot be seen."[9]

Communitarianism is the emerging rival to individualism in contemporary America. Although this ideological structure might appear to be new in our eyes, it is by no means new to the world, or even to our culture.

If we were to substitute the notion of *hierarchy* for equality of result, what we would have would closely resemble the medieval and neomedieval ideologies of Europe. These ideologies, or variations descended from them, came to the United States with successive waves of European immigrants. Altered to accommodate an ample dose of egalitarianism, they then manifested themselves in such institutions as the New England town meeting and the farmers'-cooperative movements of Wisconsin and Minnesota. But individualism, it should be noted, remained the dominant ideology.

Once given the five basic Lockean concepts, it is a simple task to outline their counterparts in communitarianism (see Figure 2):

1. COMMUNITARIANISM. The community, says the communitarian, is more than the sum of the individuals in it; the community

is organic, not atomistic. It has special and urgent needs as a community. The survival and the self-respect of the individuals in it depend on the recognition of those needs.

Individual fulfillment derives from a sense of identity, participation, and usefulness in a community. In the complexity of today's societies, says the communitarian, few can live the life that Locke envisioned.

Again, we can distinguish a number of corollary principles:

a. Equality of result or hierarchy. There has also been a shift away from the old notion of equality, according to the communitarian vision. Formerly, equality meant equality of opportunity, in terms of which all members of the society had a fair position at the starting line, and all could go as far and as fast as their talents would take them. Around 1970, however, this approach began to be altered radically. Representatives of the federal government responsible for enforcing equal-opportunity legislation began to argue that the starting line itself was suspect.

AT&T, for example, was accused of systemwide discrimination, given the fact that all telephone operators were female, all company vice-presidents were male, and most minority-group representatives were crowded at the bottom of the pay scale. The company, shocked by the implications of the government's charge, responded in effect that women preferred to be telephone operators, men preferred to be vice-presidents, and minority groups were happy to be employed at all. The government, in turn, said that it was not particularly interested in theories about what individuals might or might not prefer; rather, it wanted to see AT&T as a whole respond to inequalities in the surrounding community, in order to produce what amounted to equality of representation at all levels.

This business/government interaction was extremely significant for its ideological and practical implications, and we should digress for a moment to consider it at length. Initially, many company managers reacted in a Lockean fashion. They saw in the government's policy a troubling shift to an equality of result, which seemed a serious threat to efficiency. How could the company avoid the elevation of mediocrity, and the imposition of lead belts on the speedy?

Problems of fairness also arose: there was a tendency to suppose that the Supreme Court would "set things right" when the complaints of white males about reverse discrimination came to its attention. There was, therefore, the expectation that the nation would return to the old idea of equality of opportunity. More realistic observers, though, reached the opposite conclusion: given the activism sure to arise in new quarters—whether as a result of perceived sexual or racial discrimination, or from other wellsprings—a return to the old standards was not likely.

This opinion prevailed among AT&T's managers, and it led them to an effective embrace of the new approach. Under continuing pressure from the government, AT&T set targets—or quotas—and effectively redesigned itself as a community. In the end, AT&T accomplished the task with considerable skill, recruiting, training, motivating, and promoting appropriate employees to make a difficult situation more efficient and humane.

The specific ideological implications are clear: the government's action amounted to the imposition of an ideological consensus on AT&T from the outside. Not only was it a threat to old notions of equality; it was also a threat to the contract that had existed between management and the union, which previously had been the device used to resolve inequities in seniority and promotion policies. When the union protested this intrusion, however, those protests were overridden by the government.

In more general terms, as managers of government and business contemplate the implementation of the idea of equality of result, a variety of issues come to mind. How does one manage the propensity toward mediocrity in society as a whole—the "lead belts" problem? How does one handle the appeals of countless groups for representation? Most fundamentally, one must ask: Can the idea really last? Is it viable?

In all other communitarian societies, whether in medieval Europe or modern Japan, this slot in the ideological framework is occupied by the notion of hierarchy. In other words, the individual's fulfillment and self-respect result from the recognition of one's place in the social structure. That position could be fixed in a variety of ways: by God, by the King, or—as in modern Japan—meritocratically, by a sequence of rigorous examinations, with the elite being the *summa cum laude*'s from the University of Tokyo.

The vestiges of medieval communitarianism in the United Kingdom are still plainly evident in the recurrent theme of class consciousness. To a great extent, the working class perceives itself as pitted in an inexorable struggle against the ruling class. The fact that the "ruling class" has for the most part dissolved into the government, an anonymous stock market, and the banks has had little impact on the ancient ideological strain between hierarchy and equality.

In the 1980s, only a few years after its inception, the "affirmative action" represented by the AT&T case is under attack in the United States for several reasons. The idea of "reverse discrimination" offends those—particularly white males—who feel it penalizes them. It is regarded by some as demeaning to those it was designed to help. In the school systems, some say, it has produced what might be called the "nobody-fails" syndrome, eroding educational standards. If one grants that these objections have merit, one must consider the range of possible ideological responses:

1. We can persist in seeking equality of result, and try to make that approach work. Realistically, big institutions like AT&T would have a hard time in the short run doing anything else, because of their current commitments, existing law, and the expectations of their employees. If we shifted course, managers of such institutions might well miss the forceful hand of government, at least temporarily.

2. We can return to a vigorous support of equality of opportunity. This would require, above all, equality of education for blacks and whites. But would this goal be achieved through integration—as the Supreme Court mandated almost thirty years ago —or some other way?

3. We can attempt to shift to a concept of hierarchy, such as meritocracy, within which one's place would be determined by knowledge and skills, without regard for the concept of "equality." If we choose hierarchy, of course, the question becomes: Who is at the top, who at the bottom, and how will these designations be made acceptable?

b. Consensus. If the example of AT&T represents an external consensus being imposed by government on a contractual relationship, there are many examples of similar disruptions—which are actually transitions—originating from within. Especially given the economic contractions of the early 1980s, companies and unions have sought ways in which to restrain wages, close plants, increase productivity, and improve employee motivation, all the while seeking some semblance of "fairness." In Europe, the new arrangements are called "industrial democracy," "co-determination," "workers' councils," and the like. They tend to replace the adversarial contractual relationship between managers and the managed with a consensual one, which proceeds both from the top down and from the bottom up. In Japan, of course, manager-managed relationships have always been consensual—at first feudal in nature, and gradually adapting to meet changing needs and expectations. In the United States, such transitions are being described in a number of ways: organization development, job enrichment, workers' participation in management, and quality of work life (QWL) programs. Whatever the form, the result is the same, and it is for our culture a radical one: the right to manage is coming increasingly from the managed, and not from the owners.

In Europe and the United States, such transitions are impeded by the residue of traditional ideology. Trade unions are naturally loath to surrender the power and legitimacy they have enjoyed under the terms of the adversarial, bargained contract. Managers, for their part, are nervous about moving away from their traditional bases of authority, implicit in property rights and the contract. But if improved productivity depends on a transition from these concepts of authority to a new one, the issue is clear: How much crisis must we endure in the process of recognition and acceptance? Can we—and will we—accomplish the process soon enough?

Finally, it is worth remembering that the idea of contract was invented to protect the individual against the excesses of the medieval group. It would be dangerous to abandon the protection afforded by the contract before a consensual approach takes its place and its implications are clearly perceived and managed. There are signs, for example, that the transition from contract to consensus is contributing to, if not causing, the weakening of trade unions in the United States. Union membership has been declining, to the point where today it encompasses only about 20% of the work force. The influence of unions has been eroding; they are less confident of their role and mission. Artful managers are increasingly seeking means of "union avoidance," employing the techniques of consensualism without necessarily assuming its full obligations. We should, therefore, ask ourselves: Is a strong trade-union movement important for America and its corporations? If so, then we must help redefine the union's mission. Pragmatic innovation without ideological renovation is not sufficient.

2. RIGHTS AND DUTIES OF MEMBERSHIP. Since Locke's ideas were first brought to this continent by European settlers, the concept of property rights has been paramount in our society. In recent years, however, a set of rights has been superseding the idea of property in both political and social realms. These include survival, income, pensions, health maintenance, and other entitlements which have come to be associated with membership in the American community, or in some component of that community, such as a corporation.[10] (These new rights constitute the "safety net" which President Reagan, early in his tenure, promised to maintain.) The rights do not derive from any individualistic action or need, nor do they emanate from a contract. Rather, they are communitarian rights that Americans and others now hold to be consistent with a "good" community. This is indeed a revolutionary departure from the old conception, under which only the fit survived.

Inevitably, the escalating rights of members in society have strained our ability to pay the bill. All levels of government have been forced to "limit" rights through various budgetary caps, and some entitlements have been deferred, reduced, or abandoned. This process has prompted a debate—at times rancorous —which has in turn generated some new, shared perceptions. For example, many have come to realize that if the community is to assure rights, it must also require duties. But who decides a citizen's duty? In Japan, from time immemorial, the community has imposed a sense of duty. But in America, our legacy of individualism has made us inclined to leave the question of duty to the individual—to the dictates of upbringing, religion, and conscience.

The inexorable advances of communitarianism, however, are beginning to force government to define the duty of those who do not seem to be doing it for themselves. In one manifestation, this has been called "workfare." If everyone has a right to a job, as the Humphrey-Hawkins Act suggested in 1977, does not everyone who is able-bodied have a duty to work? If so, how does a nation implement this idea? Having granted that the idle have a right to survive, there are only three practical ways of dealing with them: government can support them, government can subsidize them through public employment, or government can coerce or subsidize business to employ them. In practice, Europe and the United States have tended to favor the first two options, while Japan has preferred the third. The U.S., however, appears to be moving toward the third option; if this proves to be true, we must soon consider the inherent implications for the role of government, and its relationship to business.

The continuing debate naturally tends to focus on those whom society must subsidize. But if the duties of the poor and the weak are to be made more explicit, does it not follow that those of the rich and powerful must also be clear? This is largely unexplored territory; even today, we hear echoes of *noblesse oblige* in the calls for increased charitable donations by the rich to make up for cuts in public spending. Such an archaic approach has its clear limitations. As noted in the last chapter, while the Reagan budget cuts were making their way through Congress in the summer of 1981, Office of Management and Budget (OMB) director David Stockman found himself shocked at the failure of government to require sacrifice from well-organized and powerful economic interest groups. Significantly, his response was ideological and unconsciously communitarian: he felt that the moral premise of austerity had been eroded.[11]

Perhaps the single most important ideological shift in our society has been the erosion of the concept of "private property" as a legitimizing force. It is quite obvious, for example, that our large public corporations are not "private property" at all. The shareholders of General Motors do not and cannot control, direct, or in any real sense be responsible for "their" company. Furthermore, the vast majority of them have not the slightest desire for such a responsibility. They are investors, pure and simple; if they don't earn an adequate return on their investment, they will put their money elsewhere.

Attempts to foster "shareholder democracy"—often viewed with suspicion by managers—are in fact ideologically conservative strategies, designed to force shareholders to behave like owners, and thus to legitimize corporations as property. But such actions, simultaneously naïve and heroic, are fraught with practical difficulties, not the least of which is their tendency to be misinterpreted. It is a singular irony that General Motors chairman James Roche branded such agitation as the radical machinations of "an adversary culture . . . antagonistic to our American ideas of private property and individual responsibility." In truth, of course, General Motors was the radical; Ralph Nader *et al.* were trying to bring the corporation back into line with a conservative ideology.

If General Motors and hundreds of similar corporations are not property, then what are they? Currently, they are no more than collections of people, machinery, and resources. They drift in a philosophical limbo, vulnerable to the charge of illegitimacy, and to the charge that they are not subject to community control. It is an awkward and dangerous position.

Consider, for example, how the management of these nonproprietary institutions are selected. Our mythology tells us that stockholders select the board of directors, which in turn selects the management. This is not generally true, however; more often, management selects the board, and the board blesses management. Managers thus achieve that rank through a hierarchical process of questionable legitimacy. Under such circumstances, it is not surprising that "management's rights" are fragile, and its authority waning. Alfred Sloan, hardly a communitarian, warned us of this problem in 1927:

> There is a point beyond which diffusion of stock ownership must enfeeble the corporation by depriving it of virile interest in management upon the part of some one man or group of men to whom its success is a matter of personal and vital interest. And, conversely, at the same point the public interest becomes involved when the public can no longer locate some tangible personality within the ownership which it may hold responsible for the corporation's conduct.[12]

To date, we have not foundered on this ideological shoal because the unquestioned effectiveness of the corporate form has made such a discussion moot. In the past, when economic growth and progress were synonymous, we tacitly concurred with the premise that managers should be as free as possible from stock-holder interference, all in the name of efficiency. But today, much less is certain, including the definition of efficiency, the criteria for (and the limitations of) growth, and the general con-text of the corporation. So the myth of corporate property—once a strength—is fast becoming a corporate Achilles' heel.

The large corporation is a reality and a necessity, and there is no doubt that some means will be found to legitimize it and make it responsive to community needs. Even now, several trends are discernible:

1. More coherent and balanced regulation by the state is evolving.

2. Worker-management schemes are being put in place by some companies.

3. Partnerships with government are increasing, especially in troubled sectors such as the steel, automobile, and utilities industries.

The rights and duties of ailing giants like Chrysler pose partic-ularly interesting ideological questions. Most obvious among them: Does such a corporation have a "right to survive"? Under the terms of the traditional ideology, the answer is no; such com-panies should die when they no longer serve the interests of their owners or of consumers. But because the politics of the real world make such corporate deaths unacceptable, they are snatched from oblivion at the last possible moment. Propped up in the name of an ill-defined community need, publicly "humili-ated" in the eyes of the individualists among us, they are made to continue their uneasy existence.

What are the alternatives? A more efficient, humane, and com-petitive approach is suggested by Japan's communitarian system. The sick corporation is diagnosed when its disease first manifests itself—about 1974, most would say, in Chrysler's case. Industry, government, and labor officials confer; a consensus is reached about the best remedy. The Japanese response to the Chrysler crisis might have been an industry consolidation through merger, with retraining and relocation for displaced workers. (Indeed, there is periodic discussion in Japan of just such consolidation.) An early diagnosis gives all parties time to adjust to the remedy, thereby minimizing disruption and cost. These last considera-tions alone will probably prove enough to force an ideological overhaul in America; perhaps the only question is when and how this overhaul will take place.

3. COMMUNITY NEED. The needs of the community—for clean air and water, safety, energy, jobs, competitive exports, and the like—are becoming increasingly distinct from, and more important than, the desires of the consumer. As a consequence, the ways we determine community need demand greater attention. This becomes more urgent with the recognition of economic limits: when it is impossible for the community to meet all its needs at once, priorities must be carefully established.

Sometimes the concept of "community need" manifests itself in unexpected quarters. In 1971, when the Justice Department was attempting to force ITT to divest itself of Hartford Fire Insurance, ITT took an unusual approach. Its lawyers argued, in effect, that the public interest required ITT to be powerful at home so that it could withstand the blows of Allende in Chile, Castro in Cuba, and the Japanese in general. Before you apply the antitrust law to us, the lawyers concluded, perhaps the Secretary of the Treasury, the Secretary of Commerce, and the Council of Economic Advisors should jointly determine—in the light of America's balance-of-payments problems and domestic economic difficulties—what the national interest is.[13]

Although the company's tactic was eminently pragmatic, the full ideological implications of this stance should not be ignored. Simply put, ITT was claiming to be a partner with the American government—and more specifically, with the Cabinet—in the definition and fulfillment of the nation's needs. In fact, the claim was partly true. (Cynics might express some doubts about which was the senior partner, but a partnership it was, and is today.) But this concept is radically different from our traditional ideas, and particularly those underlying the antitrust laws—namely, that the public interest emerges naturally from free and vigorous competition among numerous companies attempting to satisfy consumer desires.

In the face of real competitive threats from Japanese and European business organizations (which, as we have seen, originate in ideological settings quite different from our own), there will be additional compelling pressure to set aside the old ideology— which essentially addressed a domestic competition—to enable

American businesses to prosper in worldwide competition.[14] Managers will probably welcome such a step, but they will almost certainly be less willing to accept the concomitant principle: if we allow restraints on the full sway of competition in the domestic market, then other forces will have to be empowered to define and protect the public interest. These "other forces" will of necessity consist of more effective control by the political order, in one form or another.

4. ACTIVE, PLANNING STATE. The role of the state is changing radically. For better or worse, it is fast becoming the arbiter of community needs. Inevitably, it will take on unprecedented tasks of coordination, priority-setting, and planning in the largest sense. It will need to become far more efficient and authoritative, capable of making the difficult and subtle choices that we now face—for example, between environmental purity and energy supply, between economic stability and growth, and between the rights of membership and a competitive posture in the world marketplace.

Ironically, President Reagan's radical 1981 economic program —which aimed to cut taxes, increase defense spending, balance the federal budget, increase productivity, cut inflation, and promote full employment—may signify the beginnings of an explicit recognition that the U.S. economy requires government planning, if not a planned economy. Analyzing the difficulties that the Reagan plan soon encountered, OMB director David Stockman arrived (albeit haltingly) at the definition of a planned economy:

> The reason we did it wrong—not wrong, but less than the optimum—was that we said, Hey, we have to get a program out fast. . . . We didn't add up all the numbers. We didn't make all the thorough, comprehensive calculations about where we really needed to come out and how much to put on the plate the first time, and so forth. In other words, we ended up with a list that I'd been carrying of things to be done, rather than starting the other way and asking, What is the overall fiscal policy required to reach the target?[15]

Of course, our governmental leaders have from time to time found it necessary to plan.[16] But invariably they have masked their departures from the limited state in the music of the old hymns, attempting to make their interventions appear pragmatic, and without ideological implications. The charade may be reassuring, but it is costly; it only postpones the moment when we will recognize the planning functions of the state for what they are, and must be.

Does this mean more government, and therefore higher costs? Actually, the opposite is true. If the role of government were more precisely and consciously defined, the government itself could be smaller. To a great extent, our burdensome plethora of bureaucracies is the result of a lack of focus and comprehension, the costly and ironic by-product of the notion of the "limited state." With a more conscious approach, furthermore, we could better identify those issues which can be addressed on the local or regional levels, and those which require a broader approach.

Presidents Nixon, Ford, Carter, and Reagan each realized this in turn. Each tried to make the executive branch of government more coherent. (His rhetoric notwithstanding, Reagan has moved most radically, giving unprecedented centralized power to the Office of Management and Budget.) All have attempted to close the separation between the executive branch and the Congress, an obvious prerequisite to the consensus upon which any form of planning depends.

Great corporations have also begun to recognize two unavoidable facts: that we require definitions of community need (what's safe, what's clean, etc.), and that the government, sooner or later, will supply those definitions. We are already witnessing increased cooperation between big business and big government toward this end. But the forms of cooperation need careful scrutiny. Industry often has the information and analytical skills— the competence—that government requires in order to make an intelligent definition of community need, but it lacks the authority to define. Government has the authority, but is short on competence. Cooperation is in order, but the procedures for combining private competence with public authority must be legitimate, as well as efficient. The ideological implications of any particular procedure must be carefully considered and managed. We can anticipate increased ideological anxiety—and indeed, cries of "fascism" from the Lockeans—as more and more decisions are made cooperatively by big business and big government.

5. HOLISM—INTERDEPENDENCE. Finally, and perhaps most fundamentally, the old idea of scientific specialization has given way to a new consciousness of the interrelatedness of all things. New phrases have entered our vocabulary—spaceship earth, the limits of growth, the fragility of the biosphere—which dramatize the ecological and philosophical truth that everything is related to everything else. (Anne Burford's error was that she set out to resist this irresistible transition.)

During the 1970s, regulatory response to this new realization had two characteristics: incoherence, and an ecological bias rather than a holistic balance. In the 1980s, government regulation appears to be moving toward more coherence and holism; there is a recognition that jobs, tax revenue, and the trade balance are as much a part of the environment as air, water, and safety.

Even so, there are still serious intellectual and political problems to consider as we make the necessary tradeoffs. Do we scan the environment in a specialized way, as has been the scientific tradition, or do we seek to grasp wholes, looking for the inherent systemic relations? If we choose the latter course, we will be departing radically from our rational tradition, which not only has informed scientific endeavor but has legitimized our educational establishment. We will, therefore, need quite new scientific, technological, and educational procedures. These, in turn, will undoubtedly cause changes in the political institutions that allocate resources for research and education.

Until rational approaches to holistic thought can be created, we will be confronted with nonrational beliefs, mysticism, and a new religiosity. This is not to suggest the superiority of the rational over the nonrational, but rather to point out that ideological analysis leads to a discernment of inevitabilities. Nor is it to suggest that specialists will not be necessary; rather, they will need to be managed by those with a holistic consciousness.[17]

In one sense, ideological analysis allows us to prepare for the worst, to provide safeguards against the ignorance and abuses that historically have accompanied ideological transition. If it is communitarianism toward which the West is tending, ideological analysis serves to warn us of the dangers of collectivism, of the threats to liberty and the rights of the individual for which many have bled and died. Communitarianism need not be totalitarian, but it can be. It need not lead to antihuman and bureaucratic centralization, but it can. It does not require an increased nationalism, but that is a possibility unless our leaders give careful thought to what the appropriate community is for various institutions, products, and processes.

Changes emanating from ideological transition are, by definition, radical—they go to the roots of things—and they are therefore difficult to introduce into large bureaucracies. Resistant hierarchies rest on the old ideas. Change invariably entails crisis, but not necessarily catastrophe. Ideological inspection can help managers understand the nature of crisis early and precisely, so they can use that crisis effectively as an instrument for organizational change, avoiding catastrophic waste and violence. Ideological analysis helps to prevent misinterpretation of trends and events, a mistake which is all too likely when those trends and events seem to reinforce the perspective of the observer.

In the United States, some observers have concluded that the nation is witnessing a resurgence of individualism. This conclusion is a snare and a delusion, existing more in hope than fact. In the general communitarian tide, evidences of heightened individualism are akin to the last roses of summer. Let us examine some specifics.

Proposals for deregulation abound in such areas as transport and energy. But does deregulation represent a movement back toward the limited state? On the contrary, it more than likely indicates a step toward a coherent governmental approach to transportation, energy, and other such necessities. To be sure, the consequences of such thought and planning may sometimes be a greater use of the market mechanism. However, the reason for this use is a calculated one, not the exercise of an ideological commitment to the marketplace.

Many liberal welfare programs that reflect only rights of membership are in low repute. This fact does not necessarily reflect a resurrection of property rights and the survival of the fittest. More than likely, it will serve to clarify the duties of membership: i.e., if you are able-bodied, you must work; if you cannot find a job, government will provide one, and perhaps even coerce you into taking it.

Many persons, especially the young, yearn to "do their own thing." This is the perfectly predictable result of educating children according to the precepts of individualism and then confronting them with the pressures of communitarianism. Such yearnings either wither under the pressures of reality, or lead to disastrous forms of escapism. The desires themselves have no power to return us to individualism.

Daniel Yankelovich, the social surveyor, has described the problem well in his book *New Rules*. Over two decades he has attempted to discern what he calls the "psychoculture"—"the webs of meanings Americans hold in common,"[18] a concept close to my definition of ideology. What is occurring in America today, he observes, is "nothing less than the search for a new American philosophy . . . the leading edge of a genuine cultural revolution."[19]

On the one hand, Yankelovich found a variation of the traditional notion of individualism, one which was heavily laced with Calvinism: self-denial, hard work, and sacrifice so that our children's lives might be better than our own. Not only was this conception endorsed as morally right; it had also been shown to be pragmatic in economic terms.

On the other hand, said Yankelovich, this "web of meanings" was being systematically eroded by institutional change in the real world, and by the coming of the idea of rights of membership. Big government, far-flung multinationals, and big unions tended to remove even the hardest-working individual from any significant control over his life, and equalized his return with that of the less productive. If one had a right to income and other benefits regardless of work, some said, why work at all? In the 1970s, furthermore, inflation discouraged hard work and savings. Finally, the entrance of large numbers of women into the labor force eroded the traditional male sense of an obligation to support his family.

As the self-denial ethic became economically unwise—indeed, it gained the stamp of the "sucker"—it lost a good deal of its moral appeal. Many young people, feeling the pressures of onrushing communitarianism, lashed out in individualistic protest, insisting on the full promise of the Enlightenment. They nurtured a "duty-to-self" ethic, that remarkable norm of the 1970s, under which one was obliged to do what one wanted to do. This was individualism with a vengeance, a militant rejection of self-denial by both men and women, and one which was blessed by psychologists, psychiatrists, and all their various mimics.

In the 1950s and '60s, individualism expressed itself as follows: "If I work hard, observe the rules, and learn to keep my personal desires largely suppressed, I may find myself well rewarded— with moral self-esteem for my self-denial, with the acceptance of others for my respectability, and with worldly goods from an affluent economy." [20]

But in the 1970s, this was turned upside down: "I have a duty to myself, and satisfying rather than denying myself becomes the ascendant norm." [21] The consequences of this conception for the family and for the community were, of course, appalling. It constituted self-indulgence, pure and simple. People had come to think of themselves as a bundle of needs which had to be filled "as if they were sections of an ice-cube tray." [22]

Ideologically, the duty-to-self notion was a costly and romantic reversion to a waning Lockeanism, at a time when many were apprehensive about the changes around them. The old had gone, but there was nothing new to take its place. Institutional pragmatism had destroyed individualism, but our leaders—political, religious, and academic—had ignored the need to clarify the new ideology that reflected the change. The result: chaos.

The duty-to-self ethic is dying in the 1980s, undercut by its own premise that the self can survive in an autonomous, solitary, contained, and egocentric condition. That discredited concept is being replaced by an ethic of commitment, a longing for connectedness and creative expression. The worker wants to take pride in his work and have a sense of control over his environment. The manager is finding it more feasible and efficient to derive his right to manage from the managed, through teamwork, rather than from a hierarchy rooted in the old notion of property rights. Cooperation with government at all levels, for the good of the community, is replacing the old antagonisms which characterized the Lockean ideas. In other words, after a decade of waste and disappointment, we are assessing the fit between our reality and two competing ideologies. We are, with understandable reluctance, embracing crisis to avoid catastrophe.

3

The Unwanted Transition:
Its Meanings for Managers

The transition from individualism to communitarianism is proceeding vigorously in the 1980s. In general, evidence to the contrary can be attributed to confusion resulting from the transition, as in the case of many young "individualists"—or, as in the case of deregulation, may represent a simple misinterpretation. But not all such evidence can be dismissed so easily. There is the example of the 1980 elections: a significant majority of Americans seemed to be voting for a return to the "good old days," of which Ronald Reagan appeared to be the near-perfect embodiment.

But let us look more closely. What most voters wanted in the 1980 election, according to the Harris poll, was a program "to curb inflation, cut government spending, find a way to transform our economic capability into a modern, technologically superior vehicle for growth, turn around productivity and improve America's standing in the world."[1] The real world was presenting very real demands, as we have noted: a growing international interdependence in terms of both imports and exports of goods and services; increased competition from efficient communitarian systems like Japan; the shrinkage of the U.S. economic pie; the fact of scarcity; the necessity of defining duties as well as limiting rights; the requirement of choosing among national priorities; the retrenchment and concentration of industry in the face of inflation and high interest rates; the growing blight of unemployment and urban disintegration; and the emergence of new technologies upon whose successful development and marketing our standard of living for years to come will depend.

What were Americans voting for? On the one hand, they were seeking a reassuring leader, who would forcefully invoke the old ideology. On the other hand, they desired solutions to the long litany of problems facing them.

Why did Americans choose Ronald Reagan? On balance, it seems that they chose to be ideologically reassured, rather than challenged. The fact is that the transition we are experiencing is ideologically unwanted; it runs counter to our sense of national purpose and identity. Such a divergence has ample precedent in our history. Samuel P. Huntington has identified several periods when America has strayed from the individualistic ideology to a form of communitarianism, in order to meet the exigencies of the real world. The end of each such experience is marked by what Huntington calls "a creedal passion period"[2]: angry and indignant at the recognition of what has transpired ideologically, the nation demands a return to the former ideology, and attempts to haul its wayward institutions back into the fold of legitimacy (as in Figure 1, Chapter 2). Creedal passion periods are reactionary, and produce no new political theory. Ironically, though, they are distinguished by the revelation of new political facts that run counter to the central tenets of the old ideology.[3] In effect, by seeking reassurance in the election of Ronald Reagan, Americans have lent more visibility to the revelations of communitarianism.

It is also useful to remember that for Americans, ideological revelations have an aura of sin about them. This is because for most of us, individualism is not an ideology at all, but a revealed truth, as it was for Locke. Indeed, Americans have only grudgingly accepted even the concept of ideology as being relevant to their national experience. For many, it is a "foreign" notion, and one which was the bane of the lands from which their ancestors fled. Under such circumstances, then, departures from individualism are doubly objectionable. They are heretical both because they raise the issue of orthodoxy, and more fundamentally, because they raise the issue of ideology at all.

What are the characteristics and consequences of this inevitable transition, which is at best unwanted and at worst sinful?

First, as it proceeds, there is a predictable effort by the creedally passionate to defy and to thwart it, to linger with the old ideology for emotional or religious reasons. Since the 1930s, in response to a wide variety of challenges springing from events in the real world—such as the Great Depression, World War II, the Cold War, the rise of OPEC, and intensified international competition—American institutional behavior has been changing. Government, big business, and big labor have been acting at variance with Lockean traditions. This gap between practice and preachment grew wide during the 1970s; by 1980 it had become a yawning chasm. We had only two choices: first, to identify the new practice that seemed to be working best, and then construct an ideology to justify it; or second, to cry "sin!" and seek a return to the old ideology. This was the epitome of a creedal passion period; predictably, longing for the security of the old principles, many cried "sin!" Nevertheless, the transition continued, and continues today. The biggest problem facing us in this process is our continuing ignorance of it. Because we do not admit the existence and the power of ideology, we neither understand nor manage it.

Thus the second consequence of the transition's being unwanted: it tends to be surreptitious, inexplicit, careless, and wasteful. We have resolutely ignored the ideological implications of our actions during the past fifty years, and have therefore been the victims of a good deal of inadvertence. We tolerate, for example, a large, expensive, and interventionary government, which is unable to think or act coherently. This stance was feasible during the decades that we were ahead in the world economic race, but now it is not. If we remain ideologically confused, we can only fall further behind.

The third consequence of the transition's being unwanted is that we have steadfastly pretended that it was not occurring. As a result, while the social norms and relationships which rested on the old ideology have deteriorated, no new ones have been substituted. Old bases of authority—in families as well as the multinational corporations—have rotted away, and nothing has come forward to take their place. The resulting disorder is eerily famil-

iar to the historian: four and five centuries ago, as medieval communitarianism gave way to individualism in Europe, there was a
similar blight of upheaval, confusion, and corruption. (In this
light, it is clear why Barbara Tuchman titled her history of the
fourteenth century *A Distant Mirror.*)

The blurred definition of social arrangements in America in the
1980s has given rise to the two diametrically opposed "passions"
that one might expect: a renewed rush to individualism, traditionally defined, and a search for new forms of community and commitment. In what may be taken as a typically American response
to this dilemma, Ronald Reagan artfully invoked both passions
during an election-eve broadcast in 1980, when he exalted both
John Wayne and John Winthrop; the former a prototypical indi-
vidualist whose cinematic six-gun tamed the West, the latter a
Puritan communitarian in search of a "city on a hill." Never
fussy about ideological contradictions, as long as they are not
made explicit, Americans cheered him on, hoping to regain their
lost self-confidence. But President Reagan's subsequent policies
have incorporated the same ambivalence, and the result has been
far from reassuring. Real-world problems have only intensified,
and what is needed in response is not ambivalence, but further,
sharper departures from individualism.

These three characteristics of our unwanted transition—the
creedal passion to stay with the old, the inefficient and illegitimate transition to the new, and our confusion about the bases of
authority—begin to define the disease that afflicts America. It is
a disease about which little is known, and for which there is as
yet no remedy. It is in the realm of collective psychology, which
has only begun to be recognized as a field of study. Given these
obstacles, perhaps the most productive approach is to examine
current knowledge of the individual psyche, and to extrapolate
from that base to the larger community.[4]

In these terms, the American disease is a pathological condition, deriving from a severe developmental crisis in the evolution
of American society. It is a psychotic condition, characterized
by the denial of reality and the inability to develop solutions to
the problems being forced upon the community by a new and
unfamiliar environment. In its extreme manifestations, the American disease has the symptoms of schizophrenia, a condition for
which there is essentially no cure; but in fact, the disease more

closely resembles the ailment of a troubled adolescent whose grief at growing up causes him to deny reality, or to cope with it through wishful thinking or a regression into immature, counter-productive behavior.

The treatment of the American disease will necessarily include a rebuilding of the foundations of our society. We will need to rediscover those communitarian elements which emerged period-ically during our history, to build upon them, and combine them with compatible aspects of individualism. From this effort will emerge a new basis for the community and its institutions.

A crucial first step in the treatment of a psychiatric malady is to recognize its manifestations and consequences in one's rou-tines. In this chapter and those which follow, we will examine the processes of the American disease. We will identify depar-tures from traditional ideology, and interpret their successes and failures; we will analyze the awakening of creedal passions which such departures cause; and we will explore further the costs of lingering with the old, and the consequences of transition to the new. We will begin this investigation with a specific and practical focus: the perspective of the corporate manager, who is so often at the cutting edge of the ideological transition.

The consequences of ideological ambivalence for the managers of large, publicly held corporations can be conveniently analyzed by looking at two general categories of relationships. The first, between government and business, concerns the means of con-trolling the impact of the corporation on the communities which it affects. The second has to do with the governance of the corporation internally, and the relationship between managers and those whom they manage. It will be clear that these two sets of relationships are increasingly intertwined and interdepen-dent.

This growing interconnection can be clearly seen with the help of two simple models. The first involves community need. Every community has an implicit or explicit set of needs or goals. On the national level, these may include economic growth, a high standard of living, world leadership, environmental purity, full employment, stable prices, competitiveness in the world econ-omy, and so on. In reviewing such a list, it is apparent from recent experience in the United States that needs are frequently contradictory, or must compete for limited resources. Obviously, a community cannot achieve them all at once. The investment allocated for national defense impinges upon our standard of living. Economic growth collides with environmental purity. Measures to control prices increase unemployment. The establishment of priorities, therefore, becomes a necessity.

Some communitarian nations, such as Japan, tend to be very good at defining their goals and working out priorities, in part because this is recognized as being the role of government. The community, furthermore, is equipped with consensus-making mechanisms which ensure that the definition and implementation of its needs are generally acceptable. Other communitarian societies, such as the Soviet Union, achieve what might be called an "enforced consensus" through coercion from the top. Lockean communities such as our own have a more difficult time defining needs and goals: the role of government is limited, consensus-making mechanisms are less well developed, decision-making is decentralized, and coercion is generally held to be unacceptable. But even across this wide spectrum of societies, there is at least one shared characteristic: all communities are assisted in the definition of their needs by crisis, especially that which comes from outside. To effect change, however, some communities require a great degree of crisis; others less. Some can use a limited crisis to alter their institutions; others waste that opportunity.

There are four ways in which the activities of corporations can be made harmonious with community need. (See Figure 3.) The first is through competition in the marketplace—the Lockean approach. This approach has the unique advantage of both defining community need and aligning the corporation with it. It depends entirely on the price mechanism to coordinate economic decisions, allocate resources, and provide incentives. It is inherent in antitrust law and practice in the United States: numerous privately owned firms are meant to compete to satisfy individual consumer desires, and "the invisible hand" ensures that the good community will unfold.

The second avenue is government regulation. It presupposes that there are some needs that government, and not the marketplace, must meet. While granting its manifest virtues, an objec-

tive observer must soon conclude that competition to satisfy consumer desires will not necessarily meet all the needs of the community. Meatpackers, perhaps because of that same compe-

FIGURE 3. COMMUNITY NEED: DEFINING IT AND
PROCEDURES FOR ALIGNING BUSINESS WITH IT

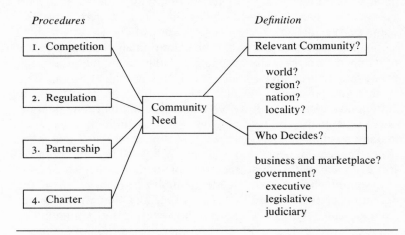

tition, adulterated their hot dogs, presumably to the detriment
of consumers. The result was the Pure Food and Drug Act,
along with a slew of other regulations intended to augment market
forces. In our society, government regulation has become pervasive, with each new area of regulation representing a new
definition of community need by government in response to specific crises.

But the structural incoherence and fragmentation of our government, prescribed by our ideology, has meant that regulatory
intervention by the government must be largely unplanned and
uncoordinated. The totality of regulation's effects has been, until
very recently, essentially unmeasured. Furthermore, its general
inefficiency and occasional misapplication have led to an adversarial and litigious relationship between government and business; as a result, the competence of the latter—its skills,

resources, and information—has often been unavailable to those in government.

A third procedure, therefore, has had to evolve. This may be called cooperation, or partnership: government decides the community need, generally with the assistance of business, and business joins in the effort to meet it. But with the exception of times of great crisis, the partnership route is fundamentally suspect in our society. Unless it is carefully constructed, it tends to be considered illegitimate. This problem of illegitimacy can be exacerbated in a number of ways: if the community need has not been clearly defined; if it is obviously not being met; or if it does not rest on a clear consensus of the community—the sort that results from "good" wars, like World War II, or the race to the moon.

A fourth way of harmonizing business and the community need is through the device of the corporate charter, granted by the community, and setting forth the terms of the corporation's existence. This procedure tends to make explicit the terms of a government/business partnership, and also limits the activities of the corporation to the achievement of a particular need. It was the preferred approach during our nation's first three decades, when corporations were chartered by legislatures to perform specific functions—erecting a bridge, digging a canal, or building a highway, and so on. It still is used for such undertakings as the Tennessee Valley Authority and COMSAT.

It is important to note that regulation, partnership, and charter are ideologically quite different from competition. They are communitarian; they presume that the community, through government, has defined its needs, and has resolved any conflicts among them. Under competition, as Lockeans would employ it, community needs are simply the sum of consumer desires. This is not to suggest that the device of marketplace competition cannot be used in a communitarian fashion; on the contrary, it may, and the spate of recent deregulation in the transportation industry is a good example of such a process. When Congress decided that air fares should and could be lower, for example, it met that community need by removing air transport from the realm of regulation and allowing it to enter that of competition. But the success of this process—at once individualistic and communitarian—depends on a wise definition of a need in the first place, and on the subsequent selection of the most effective procedure to implement it.

Energy is another example of a community need whose definition and fulfillment might well require an extensive use of the price mechanism. If this is to be made politically acceptable, however, a communitarian approach will be required. Recent history is illuminating: as the price of energy rose during the 1970s, the politically salient need was that of the consumer, so prices were regulated. The result was that other needs were sacrificed: the nation was slow to conserve and to develop more efficient ways of using energy, U.S. dependence on the Middle East grew, and alternative forms and supplies of energy closer to home were discouraged. Finally, when the price of oil could no longer be controlled, the inevitable adjustment came with a greater shock than if prices had been allowed to rise more gradually.

An alternative (and more effective) approach would have been based on a calculation of the full range of community needs. The price mechanism would have come into play much sooner, while the government aided the poorest consumers and simultaneously made a concerted effort to improve the energy efficiency of homes and businesses.[5] But this approach was not taken because our governmental decision-making systems were not designed for the long-range, coherent planning that must precede such a policy. Instead, those systems were fragmented, and overly responsive to short-term interest-group pressures.

An important—and increasingly controversial—aspect of this discussion is the definition of the relevant community. Out of that definition emerges the definition of the appropriate jurisdiction. "Community needs" for oil, food, and money, for example, now extend beyond national boundaries, and require transnational forms of government for their adequate definition. During the 1970s, therefore, institutions such as the International Monetary Fund, the General Agreement on Tariffs and Trade, and the International Energy Agency became increasingly important as elements of world government, and as organs capable of meeting the "community need" writ large.

The same debate has taken place on all levels of government. The "New Federalism" proposed that the relevant community for many needs is the state. Municipal governments often find themselves competing with the separate neighborhoods in their jurisdiction as the legitimate definer of community needs.

If, as the evidence suggests, the marketplace alone is inadequate or unacceptable as a definer of community needs, then the task must fall to government, with or without the help of business, labor, and other groups. But to which level and which branch of government? Some extreme cases are easily assigned: it is as inappropriate for Alabama to define our military needs as it is for Washington to control stray dogs. But all cases are not so obvious, as we shall see when we examine the crisis of the automobile industry and its relationship to community need. Even after successfully assigning a responsibility to a level of government, we must still choose among the branches of our governments—the executive, legislative, and judiciary. When we settle on the last alternative, we often find that our Lockean heritage—which causes many questions of definition to be resolved through adversarial pulling and hauling in the courts—is particularly time-consuming and expensive. The alternative of legislative action is at least as inexact and unpredictable, and its failings, when combined with those of the judicial approach, often force us into a definition of need by executive agency.

By the 1970s, the idea of the limited state had spawned in America a government whose authority and power was so fragmented that any kind of coherent definition of community need was difficult, if not impossible. Lamenting his inability to persuade Congress to embrace comprehensive solutions in the health and welfare fields, former Secretary of Health, Education, and Welfare Joseph A. Califano said, "Washington has become a city of political molecules, with fragmentation of power, and often authority and responsibility, among increasingly narrow 'what's-in-it-for-me' interest groups, and their responsive counterparts in the executive and legislative branches. . . .

"There are today nearly 300 congressional committees, subcommittees and select committees, each meticulously attended by narrow interest groups that have weight with committee and subcommittee members (whose political campaigns depend upon private financing) far beyond their power in the electorate as a whole. And it is now a truism that over the past decade the power of subcommittees in Congress has increased, as have the size and influence of congressional staff." [6]

We should not abandon hope, though, that our government can organize itself to begin to define and serve the community need. As in the economic sphere, there is evidence that the inexorable is being recognized and incorporated. On the legislative side, several significant strides away from fragmentation have been taken during the past decade. The Congressional Budget Act of 1974, for example, established an orderly, binding process for setting spending limits; it created congressional committees to oversee the whole budget process; and it established the Congressional Budget Office to work with the Office of Management and Budget in the executive branch to provide comprehensive analyses of the impact of budgetary changes. At the same time, the OMB was strengthened, and given increased control over several departments of the executive branch. In the international sphere, the Trade Acts of 1974 and 1979 established useful procedures for insulating Congress from interest-group pressures, and for linking the legislative and executive branches of government with business and labor. (We shall look at this apparatus in more detail in Chapter 10.)

In summary, before our hypothetical managers can begin to formulate corporate strategy, they must understand and be prepared to use this model of community-need definition. Unless managers are perceptive, their companies' relationships with the community will be needlessly messy, expensive, and inefficient. The manager must understand precisely which procedures align his corporation's actions with community need at any given time, and whether other options are open to him. He must know what the relevant community is for the particular needs that he affects (and that affect him), and he must know which institution can supply a clear definition of those needs.

The first critical relationship with ideological implications, as we have noticed, is between the corporation and its community. The second is between the manager and the managed. This relationship delineates the possible sources of authority for the managers of corporations—that is, the locus from which they derive rights and prerogatives, the base from which they impose discipline upon their organizations, and the justification for their decision-making. There are again four possibilities. (See Figure 4.)

FIGURE 4. SOURCES OF MANAGEMENT AUTHORITY

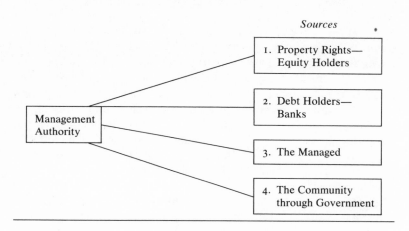

Sources

1. Property Rights— Equity Holders

2. Debt Holders— Banks

3. The Managed

4. The Community through Government

First, managers may obtain authority from the owners, who— according to the Lockean ideology—have God-given rights deriving from their property. Under this scheme, relations with the managed are contractual, and the manager hires what he requires in the labor market and fires the superfluous. Relations with government are minimal; the role of government is essentially limited to the protection of property rights and the enforcement of contracts. Such a scheme naturally suggests that the principal obligation of management is to maximize the return to shareholders over a given period of time. Equally predictable is an adversarial relationship with both labor and government, since both represent potential costs which management must minimize. Property rights have been the dominant source of authority in the United States; they are relatively unimportant in Japan, where managers' authority derives from other sources, described below.

A second source of authority is the debt holders or the banks. These are growing in importance, as the proportion of debt to equity in American companies increases. In Japan, where debt-to-equity ratios have generally been four to one, the banks are very important in the governance of the corporation; however, the relationship between the banks and the government has been close, so that the aims and purposes of the financial institutions have tended to be aligned with the community need as defined by government.

The third possible source of authority is the managed. Management can secure the right to manage through a variety of procedures in which some or all of the members of the corporation actively acknowledge that right. This represents a participative or consensual managerial procedure, through which all corporate members gain a sense of identity and control. (Delta Airlines, for example, has proven itself mindful of this source of managerial authority; in 1973, when the company faced lower profits due to higher oil prices, it reduced dividends, not employees.[7] By 1982, perhaps not coincidentally, Delta was one of the nation's most profitable carriers.)

The fourth possibility is the community, as represented by different levels and branches of government. Japanese management has always derived a considerable degree of authority from its alliance with the national government to promote the national interest. The management of America's great oil companies gained considerable authority from a somewhat similar (albeit covert) alliance between the 1920s and the 1960s. On the largest scale, the managers of multinational companies—which affect the community needs of many nations—may derive authority from many governments.

The authority of managers who draw on each of these four sources tends to rise and fall with the performance of the firm, as measured by its efficiency and competitiveness in serving its customers. Shareholders, banks, workers, or governments can prop up noncompetitive firms for a while, but their willingness and ability to bear such costs is understandably limited.

The lessons of the community need model in Figure 3 pertain equally to the managerial authority model in Figure 4: it is crucial for managers to know precisely where they and their corporations stand. Where are they deriving their right to manage today, and where is it likely to come from tomorrow? Authority may originate from all four sources, in which case other questions arise: How much emanates from which quarter? How is it changing? What are the consequences of the change? Is the process harmonious, or is it characterized by conflict, with the managers paralyzed in the middle?

In Japan and other countries, the relationships among these four sources are more carefully coordinated than in the United States, giving Japanese firms a key competitive advantage over many of their U.S. counterparts.

In the 1960s, for example, Japanese steel makers, their banks, and the government jointly decided that the national interest would best be served by creating the most modern steel factories in the world, and pricing their product below that of U.S. competitors in order to gain market share. Japanese labor was soon satisfied that its long-term interests were served by such a strategy, and a powerful consensus emerged. With a unanimity of opinion behind them, the authority of managers was clear, and they set about achieving the agreed-upon results with confidence. The situation of managers in the U.S. steel industry presents a sharp contrast. Long hampered by uncertainty about what is expected of them—shareholder dividends, high wages, jobs, clean air, or competitiveness—these managers have been unable to achieve any of these ends effectively.

These two models are, of course, inextricably interrelated. If, for example, marketplace competition is used to determine community need, a company's owners are an effective source of authority. On the other hand, if the corporation is aligned with community need through regulation, partnership, or charter, managerial authority will tend to come from government (and from workers, to the extent that workers are affected by government policy). The corner grocery store rests comfortably in the first category, while large, publicly held corporations tend to be in the second. Both are called "business," but their ideological bases are quite different.

Not only are these models interrelated; they are also universal and all-inclusive. That is, there appear to be no other models to choose from: all contemporary societies can be located on this spectrum. The Soviet Union uses an extreme—and inefficient—form of the charter route (Procedure 4 in Figure 3), with managerial authority coming from the state (Source 4 in Figure 4). Japan presents an efficient blend of the four procedures, with a careful arrangement of sources. The United States, as noted, displays a profound ambivalence, for which it is paying an increasingly high price in terms of efficiency and competitiveness.

Let us use our two models to analyze several examples of institutional change, and consider the effects of those changes on managers. The first shift is the increasing concentration of American business through mergers and acquisitions, and the second is the deterioration of the American automobile industry in the early 1980s.

Alfred Chandler has described the consolidation and concentration of business in America, a process which made possible the efficient volumes of production and distribution required by the real world of the United States. Few of the two hundred largest corporations in America are privately owned.[8] The vast majority of the publicly held companies in that group are controlled by their managers, rather than by their shareholders. Those managers, in turn, select their own boards of directors. This creates a self-perpetuating hierarchy, as we have seen, consisting of well-trained and experienced professionals, for the most part competent in the techniques of modern management.

Their weakness lies in their conception of their purpose and that of their firms. The traditional ideology holds that their role is primarily to serve the interests of the owners—i.e., the shareholders. Who decides what that interest is? When shareholders truly owned companies, they were present, or were clearly represented on boards of directors. A manager could ask whether their interests were long-term or short-term, whether they desired quick money or future market share. But today's shareholders are an anonymous body, essentially unable and unwilling to govern the corporations they "own." So the manager finds himself unable to reach, or be reached by, the shareholders, and is driven to "play to the mercurial tics and prejudices of a small cadre of stock price influencers' shifting ideas of value, rather than to value itself," to use consultant John Schnapp's language.[9]

This is not how the great corporations of the United States—or any other country—were created. Firms like Caterpillar, John Deere, Procter and Gamble, Eastman Kodak, and IBM were the creations of inventive managers, who singlemindedly dedicated themselves to designing and improving their products, expanding their delivery and support systems, manufacturing more efficiently, and adapting to changing world conditions. They could do so in part because they possessed unchallenged authority, which few contemporary managers enjoy. Our current situation has other problems as well. Ironically, the financial manipulations that it encourages have not proven very rewarding to the shareholders. More seriously, it is demonstrably unhealthy for the economy of the country as a whole.

Dubious authority feeds upon and reinforces itself, especially when combined with financial pressures. The 1970s and 1980s, for example, saw a dramatic increase in corporate size and concentration through mergers and acquisitions. The movement, according to Malcolm S. Salter and Wolf Weinhold, was a response to changes in the real world: low growth, low profitability, high inflation, rising energy costs, and financial, economic, and geopolitical instability.[10] It was easier—both financially and ideologically—for managers to expand their corporations by acquiring other companies than by investing and building new plants and equipment.

In many cases, expansion was beneficial to the stockholders, particularly since most of this "growth" was financed by borrowing from the banks. But while shareholders may have benefited financially, they lost even more control over what they theoretically owned. Growth by merger was a form of retrenchment and rationalization at a time of economic stagnation and instability. In effect, the tactic pooled corporate assets for the minimization of risk; but in so doing, it further undermined the idea of property rights as a source of managerial authority, by increasing the distance between ownership and control.

Others argue that the concentration of industry has entailed a more active and malevolent abuse of the shareholders. It is, says this camp, the means and the end of managerial greed: for higher salaries, more power, and greater prestige.[11] This notion of management—as self-serving and completely disconnected from shareholder or any other kind of control—is supported by Carol Loomis's 1982 study of executive compensation. She found that the compensation of leading executives had no relation to corporate performance—that is, to the return on their stockholders' equity. In fact, the guiding principle appeared to be: take what you can get, but be sure to disguise it from the press and the stockholders.[12]

In any case, the concentration of American business under the control of professional managers without accountability to own-

ership—whether in response to economic and political change or
due to baser motives—is clear and understandable. But is it desirable? Is it justifiable or legitimate? Does it serve the national
interest? Is the traditional criterion for answering these questions
—return on shareholder equity—sufficient? Is a manager doing a
good job if dividends and the stock price rise regularly?

No, argue Robert Hayes and William Abernathy. According to
these researchers, the managerial mentality and financial-control
systems inherent in the large and diversified creations of corporate mergers have fostered a short-term outlook, one which di-
verts management away from the research and technological
experimentation so necessary for economic competition in the
world.[13] It is entirely understandable: a short-term focus on financial returns is a very straightforward basis for management promotion and compensation. It is measurable, and suited to the
neat mathematical analyses that are in such favor at our business
schools. It is understandable, but probably unacceptable, producing as it does executives who are unmindful of long-term
results, who remain aloof from the stickier problems of the production line and the marketplace, and who refrain from engaging
in the process of innovation.

By the 1980s, the cost of invoking the old procedures in contemporary conditions was alarming. Retrenchment and consolidation for short-term gain appeared increasingly to be putting
America out of business, and Americans out of jobs. The old idea
of property rights, far from inspiring the traditional entrepreneurial zeal, was causing capital to be concentrated in institutions
that were notoriously risk-averse, including many that were looking to government for protection against foreign competition.

The nation's large integrated steel companies in 1982 suffered
huge losses, which resulted from their outmoded facilities, high
labor costs, foreign competition, domestic recession, and overcapacity. Many steel companies scrambled to diversify out of
steel into more profitable industries, while others sought government help and protection. The situation was so dire that even
traditionalists began to ask, What kind of a steel industry, if any,
does the United States need, and who will make that decision?
Will we leave it to a distant and ephemeral body of shareholders,
imprecisely represented in an institutionalized stock market, or
must other elements of the community, including government
and workers, be involved?

The profundity of the ideological problem confronting the large, publicly held corporations of America is underlined by comments of Donald T. Regan, Secretary of the Treasury and former chairman of Merrill Lynch. "I stand before you a capitalist, and proud to be one," he told the students at Bucknell University in March of 1982. "I believe capitalism to be an honorable way of life, and one that encourages man's better nature.

"Don't get me wrong," he went on to say. "I have no intention of defending big business or corporate America. Those impersonal institutions no longer belong to individuals—much of their stock is held by groups—so they feel less strongly the constraints of individual values, needs, and morality. Belonging to no one in particular and responsible only to the bottom line, too many have become more like government bureaucracies than cradles of risk-taking and entrepreneurial spirit." [14]

In other words, the Treasury Secretary proudly subscribed to the traditional ideology, from which, he felt, the major corporations of America had departed with unfortunate consequences. (A related irony, of course, was that these companies were in many cases responding to the pressures of Wall Street, of which Mr. Regan was once an accomplished leader.) What are the available alternatives? Should—and could—big business revert to the days when shareholders were individuals who actually controlled what they owned? I suspect that Mr. Regan would doubt the feasibility of such a reversion, if not the desirability. So then what? The Secretary wants our great corporations to regain the risk-taking spirit they have abandoned. I submit that such a spirit requires clarity of purpose, confidence of mission, and certainty of authority, attributes which spring from a secure ideology consistent with the real world.

Again, we must look to the model of Japan. Japanese communitarianism has produced exceptional corporate formations, notable in part for the entrepreneurial verve that Secretary Regan finds wanting in America. Japan's international giants have emerged from extremely tough competitive battles in their home marketplace. They are the survivors of a struggle to serve their own interests, within the context of serving Japan. They enter the world economy aided by government policies, and determined to gain market share for long-term growth regardless of short-term returns to shareholders. Japanese computer companies in Brazil and Australia, therefore, offer substantial discounts to governments and central banks in order to persuade them to replace IBM computers with their own, which offer somewhat more processing power and can use IBM's software. Once governments are hooked on Japanese products, surmise the Japanese, the local private sector will demand them, too. Fujitsu announced plans to move from number five in the worldwide computer market in 1981 to number two—just behind IBM. The Japanese plan to capture 30 percent of the U.S. computer market by 1990.[15]

IBM, on the other hand, finds it hard to disconnect from the traditional idea of shareholder return, and is doubly constrained by the old antitrust concept of competition (or at least the memory of it). Among the more fascinating papers uncovered during IBM's long bout with the Justice Department was a memorandum sent to fourteen managers of IBM's Data Processing Group by its legal counsel, H. Bartow Farr, Jr., in October of 1966. The memo contained advice on avoiding antitrust action; it is rich in irony, given the realities of Japanese competition in 1982. In general, it counseled against using militant language about "going after" the competition, and, in particular, warned, "Never imply that we would be willing to sacrifice profit for market share."[16]

The need for managers to think about the long-term interests of their corporations is clear, and yet the responses of American business leaders who are questioned about the problem are confused. As six *Business Week* editors reported, regarding a survey they made in 1982:

> It is a rare [chief executive officer] who has not publicly expounded the need to focus on the future, usually in a speech castigating government or labor unions for short-term policies. Yet the compensation system in their companies, the financial requirements for investing in new projects, the criteria for management-by-objective goals and performance appraisals all point to an extremely short-term orientation.[17]

"In a number of our biggest companies, you have men who have risen for years through the ranks, and they have a very short stewardship as chief executive officers," says Julian Scheer, a senior vice-president of LTV Corporation. "They try to deal with long-range problems in the short term. They want to demonstrate to their directors, their stockholders, and the financial community that this year's rate of growth is as projected, and they'll meet this year's targets this year. What gets lost is the strategy that will take the company over twenty-five years or thirty years." [18]

"No matter how much I say about building the company longer-term," lamented Edson W. Spenser, chairman of Honeywell, "short-term performance is the issue that seems to take on most importance." [19]

It is a discouraging refrain. What is happening, of course, is that the ghost of property rights—and it is today scarcely more than a ghost—is exacting a high price. Most thoughtful managers know or suspect that the right to manage no longer derives substantially from shareholders, and that the return to the owners is not the primary aim of business. "All of us should understand," said Fletcher L. Byrom while he was chairman of Koppers, "that the principal function of the business corporation in our society is to produce goods and services in a manner which will provide an expanding base of production, thereby making it possible for society to support improvements in its quality of life. Profit, by providing rent for the savings invested in the capital structure of the enterprise and the funds needed for new plant and equipment to expand production capabilities, is the mechanism which maintains the economic viability of the enterprise and allows it to continue to make a positive contribution to the well-being of society. Profit-making is not the primary corporate purpose." [20]

We have discussed the advantages and risks of corporate concentration in America. We have begun an examination of the sources of managerial authority, both realized and potential. And we have glimpsed the consequences when these elements are combined in America today: a society in ideological confusion. Let us apply this framework to a painful example—the American automobile industry—and see what lessons are to be learned, keeping in mind the concepts of community need and the sources of management authority.

Before considering how our models relate to the choices facing the managers of U.S. automobile companies, we should recount the dismal prospects that confronted them by 1982. The industry (including its suppliers, but not its dealers) had very recently employed about 2 million people, roughly half of whom were located in fifteen counties of three states: Michigan, Ohio, and Indiana. By the spring of the year, the industry had laid off about half a million workers. Congressmen and union leaders representing those 2 million proclaimed loudly that the automobile industry had to be saved—it was important to the industrial base of the United States, and, by extension, to the national defense. But others were reluctant to prop up the ailing industry. They concluded that it deserved to die.

American auto workers' wages and benefits in 1981 were some 70% above the average manufacturing wage. They amounted to $8 more per hour than the Japanese auto workers' package. Japan, by landing cars in the United States at an average cost of between $1000 and $1500 a unit, had already captured 22% of the U.S. market, up from 12% in 1978. Japan was making a car with about twelve hours of labor, compared to General Motors' thirty-two hours. Not surprisingly, the Japanese auto industry was operating at virtually full capacity, while the four American producers were down to 70%.

The Japanese were in no sense "dumping"—that is, selling their cars for less than they cost to make or below the domestic price. (In fact, their cost advantages were such that they could have afforded to cut prices, if necessary.) Even the halting steps that America had taken to stem the tide had had negative consequences: trade restraints imposed on the low-priced Japanese imports had forced Japanese manufacturers to concentrate on more luxurious models. This, of course, was where Detroit's highest profit margins were.

Sales of the U.S. auto industry were down in both 1980 and 1981, and losses totaled $5.5 billion in the two years. In 1978–1979 the industry planned a massive $60-billion investment in new plant and equipment to make small cars with front wheel drives and smaller engines. Half of that investment had been completed by 1982; there was no working capital left to do more. Still heavily burdened with obsolete factories, the industry had a debt in 1982 of some $14 billion. The banks were not eager to lend more.[21]

Perhaps the most ominous development had occurred two years earlier, in 1980, when Chrysler had been forced to seek a multimillion-dollar loan guarantee from the federal government.

The request was granted; the reason, according to a government official who had participated in the drafting of the legislation, was that "nobody knew what to do with the 40,000 people in East Detroit that would be laid off if Chrysler went bankrupt."

Responsibility for the automobile industry in Washington had been assigned to Robert G. Dederick, Undersecretary for Economic Affairs of the Department of Commerce. The list of community needs demanding attention from Undersecretary Dederick was sobering. It included:

• *Employment*. It appeared as if the nation might suffer the permanent loss of half-a-million or more jobs, mostly in the Midwest.

• *Our balance of payments*. The United States was incurring increasing deficits in its trade account, importing some $60 billion more in goods than it was exporting.

• *The structure of the economy*. Was it indeed important for the United States to retain within its borders a strong manufacturing base? If so, were the automobile manufacturers and their suppliers an essential component of that base?

• *The health of the banking system*. What would defaults on some or all of $14 billion in loans mean to U.S. banks? Surveying the governmental landscape in the spring of 1982, Dederick would have discovered the following major government policies affecting the industry:

• *Trade*. Government negotiators had persuaded the Japanese to restrict their auto exports, an effort which almost no one felt would address Detroit's problems. Other officials were "monitoring" the Japanese—or, more simply put, watching them.

• *Tax subsidies*. Under the leasing provisions of the 1981 Reagan tax bill, the Ford Motor Company expected to sell to IBM about $1 billion of its accumulated tax credits and depreciation deductions, thereby generating something like $800 million in cash. Chrysler did the same with General Electric.[22] The implication, if not the policy, was clear: the government had decided to keep all U.S. auto companies alive.

• *Regulatory relief*. Actions had been taken by the end of the preceding year which would save the industry about $585 million over the following five years.[23]

• *Antitrust*. Change was in the wind: the Justice Department had lifted the prohibition against information-sharing within the industry regarding emission-control devices.

• *Assistance to the unemployed.* This difficult question remained largely unaddressed in the spring of 1982. In that same spring, Ford and GM were signing preliminary agreements with the United Automobile Workers in which the union agreed to restrain labor costs. In return for these concessions, the companies promised—among other things—not to close any plants simply to buy cheaper parts from outside the country. This was a key issue for the UAW: in 1981, domestic producers had drawn on foreign plants for about $2.5 billion worth of parts, ranging from engines to brake discs.[24] The industry's increasing reliance on foreign parts had had a dramatic and negative impact on domestic employment.

One experienced observer of the industry described its managers as suffering from "culture shock." The industry, he continued, "doesn't understand what happened. Its leaders are mystified. Today there is no real focus of responsibility either in government or the industry. No intellectual mechanism is in place to assemble, clarify, or analyze the facts. The control of the industry is with Japan."

Other researchers are now preparing volumes on the solutions to the problems of the U.S. auto industry; I shall not presume to do so here. But it is possible to use the two models described earlier in this chapter to outline the possible alternatives. How might managers in the industry proceed, given community needs, political realities, and credible sources of authority? There are really only two choices.

APPROACH NO. 1: TRADITIONAL. On the basis of traditional ideology, managers could say, in effect:

> My company is the property of its shareholders and my primary obligation is to them. They are the principal source of my authority. Also I pay taxes and obey the law. Regardless of any understandings I may have with the union, I have a higher duty to make this company profitable. That means expanding overseas operations where costs are cheaper and importing back into the United States, reducing the domestic work force as rapidly as I can.
>
> Community needs—the national interest—will be best served by my becoming competitive in the marketplace as soon as possible. In the light of worldwide overcapacity this may mean that I would diversify out of automobiles and get into something more profitable.

If this strategy does not work, my company will declare bankruptcy and expire gracefully. The stockholders will suffer, but that is a risk that they understood when they bought this company's shares. The banks and the workers, too, must understand that this is the best way—the American way.

This approach has at least the advantage of consistency; it has a certain ring of nobility, as well. It might be the course that our top managers—say, Philip Caldwell and his colleagues at Ford—would prefer, in their heart of hearts, but it is assuredly not one which Congress or the UAW is likely to allow. And Caldwell is, in fact, ambivalent. He has already argued persuasively that the nation needs a strong auto industry; to secure it, he says, a national industrial policy is necessary to assure "employment, industrial strength, and competitive products at reasonable prices. . . . The adoption of [such a policy] requires a change among key segments of our society—government, business, labor, finance, the media, and relevant social elements."[25]

APPROACH NO. 2: COMMUNITARIAN. The second approach more accurately reflects Caldwell's public statements, and perhaps represents the most likely outcome. Assuming this stance, the manager would say:

My authority no longer comes from shareholders. I am equally or more responsible to those who work for me, and to the various communities which my company affects. If workers and the communities through government do not give me authority, I do not have it; I cannot manage.

My company will be aligned with the community need via a cooperative relationship with government—a partnership. The sooner that happens, the sooner my authority will be clear and my industry can begin its recovery. I look to government in consultation with industry, labor, and the banks to define community need clearly and explicitly.

Some observers of today's economy regard the decline of the U.S. automobile industry as harmonious with both the laws of nature and of global comparative advantage. Nothing, they say, should be done to frustrate the natural flow of things. According to this camp, if products can be manufactured more efficiently in East Asia or Brazil or Mexico, they should be; manufacturing should relocate there. Such changes are viewed as being the continuation of "progress" toward a "post-industrial society" in America, in which the service sector becomes even more overwhelmingly predominant. (By 1981, services such as transportation, wholesale and retail trade, finance, insurance, real estate, government, legal affairs, hotels, and auto repair already employed 73% of those Americans engaged in nonfarm work.[26]) But others, like Bruce Scott, call such a view "an elegant rationalization for failure to maintain a competitive industrial base."[27]

Should the United States assume the posture of a "service island" in a manufacturing archipelago? Given the trends outlined above, it would seem that any other outcome will require an active intervention. If we choose not to intervene, we will in effect be choosing to deindustrialize.

Approach No. 1 above suggests that such decisions should be left to company managers. (They would, of course, be required to act with no intra-industry cooperation.) But are all possible outcomes under this approach acceptable? If General Motors decides to move abroad, will the UAW and the broader community accept that decision? How—and at what stage in the process —do we estimate the consequences and the costs of such a development?

Approach No. 2 suggests that the question has unavoidable political and social ramifications that extend beyond the legitimate scope of private decision-making. Government, in consultation with business and labor, would decide what the community need is; agreements would then be reached which could ensure the most effective implementation of that decision by the companies. The implementation would have to accommodate two key goals: efficiency and competitiveness, both aimed at lowering costs.

The politics of our contemporary situation suggest that even if Approach No. 1 were desirable, we will probably be forced by circumstances into some version of the second. If that is indeed the case, industrial managers, as well as bankers and union members, might find their interests best served by the adoption of the second approach explicitly and expeditiously. Their first order of business would be to persuade the government to take upon itself the task of defining a coherent and reliable set of community needs. In the case of the auto industry, it seems certain that any such definition would entail considerable sacrifice by both management and labor.

The second approach says, in effect, that the automobile companies exist to serve and satisfy the community's needs. To adopt this approach, we must return to Robert Dederick's landscape of needs, and determine the procedures by which these various needs can be ranked and balanced. There are obvious and inevitable contradictions on that list: jobs, high wages, competitiveness, antitrust, trade balances, national defense, tax revenue, clean air, and so on. The community cannot have them all; it must make choices.

Government alone can't make these choices, or ensure their implementation. It will require the help of industry to sort out the inherent myriad complexities, and the cooperation of labor to assure acceptance of the final package. It will require the cooperation and the counsel of the banks to work out the necessary long-term financing. But only government, finally, can make the necessary decisions and take the initiatives. In this complicated partnership, government must be the senior partner.

In conclusion, it must be reiterated that this role for government is inconsistent with traditional ideology. The Reagan administration, for example, has explicitly renounced it, even though its Justice Department has implicitly recognized that the community need is at times better served by consolidation and concentration, rather than by competition for its own sake. In this and other instances, the government is plagued by its own schizophrenia: it practices communitarianism while it preaches individualism.

If consolidation of the automobile industry is in the national interest, and the antitrust laws are set aside to allow that process to occur, then there will surely be a demand for another means of defining community need, and the industry will have to be aligned with it. This will entail, among other things, a substantial effort to retrain and relocate the workers—probably over a million—who may lose their jobs.

If industry managers, as well as unions and banks, see their interests best served by this second approach, their initial order of business should be to persuade government to define clearly, coherently, and reliably the community need—that is, to assume explicitly its communitarian function. Managers must be able to inspect their own ideological assumptions, and fully and clearly understand the implications of their interests. They must be aware of the creedal passion that they will experience; they must be willing to argue boldly for the long-term interests of the nation. (This argument may well lead to the elimination of some of their jobs, since four U.S. auto companies may be more than necessary.) They must accept and manage radical changes in the structures of corporate governance, such as has already begun, with the UAW sharing in a variety of managerial decisions.

In short, more change—and the courage necessary to foster that change—will be required.

4

The Costs of Ambivalence:
Roosevelt to Reagan

Although the U.S. government has long had an active, extensive, and for the most part coherent policy towards agriculture, it has steadfastly refused to initiate any such policy towards industry. There are, of course, thousands of policies which affect industry, but for ideological reasons the federal government has preferred not to view them coherently, and American business leaders have traditionally encouraged this incoherence. As a consequence, government policies affecting industry wax and wane according to the dictates of particular demands and interest groups. In periods of general crisis, however, the costs of incoherence have occasionally forced government and business into a position of coherence and cooperation. As noted in the preceding chapters, antitrust policy has also been allowed to deviate from a state of Lockean purity in the name of community need, such as combating depression and fighting world wars. If the gathering evidence proves true, our coming effort to achieve economic growth and competitiveness in an increasingly fragile ecological setting will be another such effort.

These departures from tradition have been pragmatic. The ideological transition which they reflect has been unwanted, and therefore ignored. As a consequence, many such departures have tended to be impermanent and suspect, vulnerable to subversion by the forces of tradition. Let us examine some contemporary departures in the light of their predecessors in our recent history.

In March 1982, sixteen major U.S. electronics companies were exploring ways in which they could cooperate to compete more effectively with the Japanese. Some fifty executives from leading semiconductor and computer companies met with government, trade, and defense representatives to discuss the formation of a cooperative, which came to be called Microelectronics and Computer Technology Corporation. William Norris, chairman of Control Data Corporation and the organizer of the meeting, told the participants that cooperation was necessary to counter Japan's "erosion of the U.S. position in semiconductor memories, and parallel efforts to become predominant in computers as well." The joint research and development collective was seen by the press as "unprecedented" in its size and breadth. "We are here," said Norris, "to start a process which will lead to a solution of a major problem for our industry and our nation."[1]

The group, which a year later had dwindled to ten companies, fully recognized that joint activity of this sort raised serious antitrust questions. By combining their efforts to serve the community need, they were running afoul of a basic tenet of the American ideology: that competition *per se* is good, and that anything restraining competition is bad. A historical perspective becomes immediately pertinent.

Norris's proposal presupposed not only a degree of cooperation among companies in an industry, but also a cooperative relationship between government and business. Such an approach, as noted, is a clear deviation: our traditional ideology presupposes and contributes to an adversarial relationship between government and business. Such contributions are sometimes indirect. For example: the concept of the limited state— which originated in the political arena, and not the economic one —resulted in the size and purview of government being small. But as Alfred Chandler has pointed out, business was not similarly restrained, and large hierarchies were formed in business (especially in the railroad industry) before they existed in government. In 1890, when railroads employed more than 100,000 people, the total military forces of the United States consisted of only 39,000 men. In 1928, more people worked for U.S. Steel or General Motors than for the government in Washington.[2] Civil service in the United States was relatively small until the 1930s.

As business power grew with the rise of the great trusts of the late nineteenth century, reformers looked to government to protect the nation from manifest abuses. An ideological justification for this intervention—subsequently implemented through the antitrust laws—was found in the Lockean concept of competition. Big business was suspect because it restrained competition, and thereby frustrated the invisible hand in the marketplace. In particular, it frustrated individualistic proprietors, whose prosperity—however elusive—was the embodiment of the American dream. In addition, the Lockean emphasis on due process for the individual and contractual relationships among buyers and sellers, as well as employers and employees, contributed to an adversarial and ultimately litigious society.*

Nevertheless, since well before World War I, the United States has experimented with a variety of ways of organizing big business and its relationships to government, in order to define and fulfill the national interest more effectively. The experience of World War I showed the nation that it could achieve remarkable results through planning. Afterwards, especially under the leadership of Herbert Hoover as Secretary of Commerce in the 1920s, a variety of efforts were designed to encourage business to organize into associations to collect and disseminate information, and to standardize work in order to promote efficiency and competitiveness. Historian Ellis W. Hawley wrote that Secretary Hoover "looked at the economy as a kind of giant association, with himself sitting in the center as chief of the association bureau."[4] Hoover was searching for a way to align the authority of government with the competence of business, in order to "reduce the irrationalities in the system that in his view were threatening progress."[5]

* Warren Davis, an official of the Semiconductor Industry Association, indirectly blamed litigiousness for his industry's competitive difficulties with the Japanese, noting that the nation's production of electronic engineers is down to 17,000 a year, far fewer than the Japanese, while lawyers accumulate at the rate of 33,000 a year.[3]

From this modest beginning, though, his efforts soon confronted the antitrust division in the Justice Department—the
keepers of the Lockean faith—who feared that the statistics-
gathering that Hoover was urging would promote monopolies in
industry. Small business in particular felt threatened by Hoover's
"associationalism."

The interplay of history and ideology presents many small iron-
ies. Hoover's initiatives blossomed during the New Deal of
Franklin Roosevelt in the form of the National Recovery Act of
1933, under which a set of industrial associations was established
to rescue the country from the ravages of the Depression. Liber-
ated from the bonds of the antitrust laws, these associations
would function as industrial "governments," in collaboration
with organized labor, under the loose supervision of the National
Recovery Administration (NRA).

The NRA was the brainchild of Gerard Swope, president of
General Electric, who felt that the proper coordination of production and consumption would provide jobs and increase purchasing power. Swope and others conceived of the NRA as a charter
for a business commonwealth—a rational, cartelized business
order, in which prices, profits, and wages would be assured, and
markets planned, so as to avoid the waste of overcapacity, promote efficiency, and spur economic growth. A broad cross-
section of American leaders, including business and labor,
supported the plan as a way to start an upward spiral out of the
depths of the Depression.[6]

In addition to its planned elements, though, the NRA was also
perceived as a means to enable marketplace competition to work
more effectively. From the beginning, therefore, it was rooted
both in individualism and communitarianism. It was ideologically
schizoid. Neither government, business, nor labor wanted to address the ideological confusion directly; all chose to see in it what
they wanted to see. There was a refusal, says Hawley, "to accept
[the two] ideological systems intact and then stick to given positions."[7] Indeed, ideological symbols were used to mask self-
interestedness; thus power prevailed—for the most part that of
business—without legitimacy. Confused government deputies,
many of whom had been recruited from the ranks of business,
unguided by any clear definition of community need and unaware
of the ideological traps in their path, gave way before business

pressure. Labor discovered itself poorly served and smelled "the advance guard of fascism."[8] Those antitrusters who had hoped for more competition found the marketplace becoming increasingly restricted by big corporations.

The NRA was thus a contradiction in terms from its beginning. "Its proponents wanted to permit agreements that would violate the Sherman Act, yet they could not admit that they would permit monopolies or monopolistic practices. . . . The incompatibility between the goals of the planners and those of the antitrusters was glossed over and the buck passed to the administrators."[9] As a consequence, the goals of neither side were met. To compound the ideological problems, the plan simply did not work. Consumers complained of higher prices; unemployment was scarcely dented; small business felt abused by the large companies. It was seen as "a big business racket."[10]

Roosevelt admired the antitrust views of Louis Brandeis, seeing him as a champion of small business. At the same time, Roosevelt liked the idea of partnership between government and big business. His loyalties to two competing ideologies prevented him from serving either one well.[11] In May 1935, when the Supreme Court struck it down, the NRA died unlamented. The move by business toward a tentative communitarianism had foundered on the rocks of government ambivalence. There was a partnership, but business was unwilling to accept government as the senior member; government, for its part, was unprepared to insist. "It combined the worst features of both worlds, an impairment of the efficiency of the competitive system without the compensating benefits of rationalized collective action."[12] Its failure, only two years after it had begun, was due primarily to ideological ambiguity: government had neither discerned nor resolved the ideological contradictions inherent in the act.

We can understand the failure of the NRA as exemplifying the difficulty of departing from an existing ideology without a credible substitute to sustain the transition. It is in some senses an extreme case, but in others quite typical. The aggressive and unproductive invocation of the old ideology is a case in point. It is not surprising that those who initiate ideological departures— whether politicians or business leaders—invariably profess loyalty to the status quo in order to camouflage their movement away from it. Sometimes the camouflage is necessary and useful:

it was during the administration of Franklin Roosevelt, for instance, that many of the most significant departures from Lockeanism were made and solidified. But the consequences should not be ignored. Roosevelt, like his successors, was essentially unmindful of the ideological implications of what he was doing. (Locke was bypassed so that problems could be solved, often in a most non-Lockean way.[13]) The public had not been party to the transition, and in a key sense, therefore, the transition had not occurred. After the great unifying efforts of World War II and the Cold War, we came unprepared to the disappointments and creedal crisis of the 1970s.

But a review of the manifestations of communitarianism since the 1930s gives some idea of how far we had strayed. The Depression persuaded Americans in general (and FDR in particular) that the old models of government, business, and labor were deficient. The promises of individualism were not being met. Because survival, justice, economy, and other values were not being acceptably implemented, the old ideas began to give way. At General Motors, a bastion of the ideological status quo, the rights of property were weakened when Michigan Governor Frank Murphy refused to send in the National Guard to protect the company's property during the sit-down strikes of 1936. The company's legitimacy was also eroded, as Alfred Sloan had anticipated, by the dispersion of ownership among many thousands of shareholders. Finally, the individualistic contract was collectivized, and the National Labor Relations Act assured unions the right to exist, to organize, and to bargain.

Marketplace competition, already shown to be inadequate to the task of keeping rats and insects out of hot dogs, began to demonstrate other failings. In the 1930s, it proved inappropriate as a device to control the great oil companies, whose worldwide capabilities, however distasteful ideologically, were seen as essential to the national interest. The oil companies—partnerships, among themselves and with government at the state, national, and international levels—were clearly essential to securing a place in the Middle East, to holding market share and to stabilizing prices, to assuring adequate flows of oil during World War II, and to keeping Iran free of Soviet influence in the 1950s. The Justice Department's predictable complaints about antitrust violations were put aside in the national interest.

Concurrently, the role of government was expanding to ensure the welfare of the poor and the unemployed, to provide housing, to promote agriculture, to plan the war effort, and subsequently to generate a national consensus for the rebuilding of war-torn Europe and Japan in order to resist Soviet imperialism. This was a massive agenda, in both relative and absolute terms. It was conceived and implemented with no explicit ideological change.

During the 1940s and '50s, of course, a succession of communitarian enemies—Germany, Japan, and the U.S.S.R.—provided us with "virtuous" purposes. But those very purposes—winning a war, containing an enemy, leading a large group of nations in a troubled world—added to and solidified the change, begun in the 1930s, in the domestic role of government. Government was becoming the source of our national vision, the definer of our needs in the world and at home. It was becoming huge and pervasive, far removed from our conception of what it ought to be, but we refused to recognize the implications. If government was in fact to define and implement community needs at home and abroad, it had to assume simultaneously the task of weighing those needs, setting priorities, and acting coherently. Only one factor spared us from facing this reality: during the twenty years following World War II, the nation's economic strength was so vast and unchallenged that we could do essentially everything that we wanted, without counting the costs. There was little necessity to establish our priorities and work efficiently to achieve them.

The time of reckoning came in the late 1960s. There were two mutually aggravating and potentiating elements to the calamity: first, the accustomed behavior of the great institutions—big government, big business, and big labor—collided with hard economic reality; and second, those institutions, especially government and business, had gradually fallen into ideological illegitimacy. A creedal passion period ensued.

In retrospect, the economic realities seem straightforward. Government expenditures were escalating sharply to pay for both the Vietnam War and the Great Society antipoverty programs. Increasingly, revenues were coming not from taxes, but from borrowed or printed money. The results were twofold: inflation, and a deterioration of investment by American business. The year 1969 marked our first trade deficit with Japan, and a falling behind in our competition with Germany as well. As inflation climbed, so did unemployment. By the early 1970s there were the makings of stagflation, a new phenomenon. The great American industrial machine, which had been the source of such unprecedented political and economic might, was running down. Government and consumers alike were spending wildly, and investing little.

After a decade of relative obscurity, OPEC emerged with a vengeance, and the rapid rise in the price of oil only exacerbated the difficulties. Rather than facing the reality of increasingly expensive energy, the government sought to soften the blow. By control of oil prices, the inevitable adjustment by the automobile industry and the economy as a whole was delayed. The country is still feeling the consequences of that exercise in escapism.

Simultaneously, new perceptions of the environment were forcing themselves upon the nation. Air and water, like oil, were not free goods, or even inexpensive. With the belated realization that Americans were contaminating their life-support system came reaction and overreaction. In response to crisis and interest-group pressures, government regulation proliferated. This was a massive intervention in the so-called "free-enterprise system," but, because Americans were so averse to the concept of planning, the intervention was incoherent and fragmented. Inevitably, government was unmindful of the needs of the *whole* community; it was overactive and underplanned.

By 1980, it was plain that America could not afford all that it was trying to do. Unfortunately, however, the other element of the calamity of the late 1960s—the growing illegitimacy of our institutions—came into play as soon as any effective solutions were proposed, and effectively prevented us from coping. The nation was awash in creedal passion. The Vietnam War played an unforeseeable role in this drama: being neither a "good" war nor one we could win, it served as the flash point for the smoldering resentment against big and authoritative government.

Compound this with the general ineffectiveness of government economic policies (and the corruption of the Nixon White House, seen as being in cahoots with Big Business), and the vigor with which Americans attacked their institutions is understandable. It was a holy war, waged in the name of the old religion, a monumental subversion that no foreign power could have accomplished so well. "The ideological challenge to American government . . . comes not from abroad but from home," says Samuel Huntington, "not from imported Marxist doctrines but from homegrown American idealism." [14]

As government was evil, so were business and labor. Business had departed from the notion of property rights, and, despite feeble attempts at shareholder democracy, could not be made to return. It had transgressed against the antitrust laws, and some of its elements—like Big Oil—had conspired with government in doing so. Leviathans in limbo, they were attacked from all sides for polluting the environment, dehumanizing the individual, and corrupting the body politic at home and abroad. Most of all, they reeked of ideological illegitimacy. Their failures and transgressions had changed the game. Now, big was bad; small was beautiful. Battered and drained, reeling before the changing whims of government regulators and OPEC oil ministers, and the resolute onslaught of the Japanese and the Germans, American business had lost its nerve.

Labor had fared no better. Representing a decreasing share of the work force, insisting upon ever-higher wages for already well-paid members, heedless of its impact on the economy as a whole, the American labor movement was perceived as selfish, and in some quarters corrupt. To compound its problems, it was not even managing to keep its members satisfied. Auto and steel workers, benefiting from the cost-of-living escalators built into their contracts after World War II, were being paid about twice the national average for manufacturing workers; even so, they were plainly not happy. More and more money was channeled through the contract apparatus, but that apparatus bought less and less productivity and competitiveness each year. Collective bargaining, that great American innovation, was increasingly suspect. For the first time since before World War II, there were popular cries to weaken the unions.

So there was backlash against all that had evolved since the 1930s, a backlash that reached crisis proportions in the last decade. Leaders of government, business, and labor reverted to the old hymns in the hope of regaining their lost legitimacy, but the result was discordant. Let us return to our review of the government's activities, with particular attention to its role in the creedal crisis of the 1970s.

One of the common themes running through the speeches of Presidents Nixon, Carter, and Reagan, especially in the early years of their respective administrations, was disdain and disrespect for government. Without exception, they were contemptuous of the very bureaucracy they had been chosen to lead. Reagan's caution in 1982 to the National Association of Manufacturers was typical: "Feeding more dollars to government is like feeding a stray pup. It just follows you home and sits on your doorstep asking for more." [15] (But a year earlier in his State of the Union message, Reagan had spoken of the need for this pup to provide "effective and coordinated management of the regulatory process." A year later, in the 1983 State of the Union address, he would assert that this versatile animal had to "take the lead in restoring the economy.")

A decade earlier, Richard Nixon generated political capital by warning against the evils of government and extolling the virtues of individualism. At the same time, however, he saw the need for a coherent government that could think intelligently about national choices. "The critical question," he said in his 1970 State of the Union message, "is not whether we will grow, but how we will use that growth. . . . At heart, the issue is the effectiveness of government." Speaking to the heart of the ideological problem, he added, "As a people we [have] had too many visions— and too little vision." [16]

After the 1972 election, Nixon set about to act on his perception that the blunt tools of fiscal and monetary policy at his disposal were insufficient to solve the nation's growing difficulties. Perhaps buoyed by his overwhelming electoral victory, he was determined that the White House should establish priorities and set a course for the nation, no matter what Congress and the burgeoning interest groups might want. It was an impressive exercise of power. He had already imposed wage and price controls and raised tariffs; now he placed loyal agents in the various departments and agencies of government. He strengthened the lines of control from the Office of Management and Budget, and impounded funds appropriated by Congress for programs he did not like. In short, like the sovereigns of old with whom Locke's ideas had first done battle, Nixon set out to exert the prerogatives of the executive against the power of the legislature. Congress, emboldened as much by scandal as by ideology, rallied its forces in defense of Lockean principles.

The fall of Nixon and the Imperial Presidency had immense implications for the American ideology. Rather than identifying and protecting the elements of Nixon's presidency which would have been pertinent to the nation's needs, Americans sought refuge in their tattered ideological security blanket. They avoided tackling the pressing problem that Nixon aptly illustrated: the ability of the executive to use its power—a power which is immense, essential, and ideologically out of control—effectively and legitimately.

Gerald Ford's presidency represented an ideological hiatus. Because his executive authority was crippled by Nixon's excesses, Ford was unable to pursue any significant objectives. In 1974 Herbert Stein, then chairman of Ford's Council of Economic Advisors, acknowledged that America might "need an economic planning agency like the Japanese or the French." [17] But the cloud of illegitimacy still hung over the White House; its authority was too dubious to allow for any such bold initiatives.

Jimmy Carter campaigned successfully in 1976 by promising to win a war—the destruction of the Imperial Presidency—that had already been won. From the fields of rural Georgia, Carter brought with him a fervent brand of the old ideology, deeply religious in nature. As the leader of a group of committed "outsiders," he saw his task as the seizure of Washington from the bureaucrats and its return to the people. In many of his early speeches, he sounded more like a self-appointed savior, come to rescue Americans from the talons of their government, than the head of that government. Reality intruded only gradually in the Carter presidency. Once at work in the White House, Carter performed like the good engineer that he was—a tinkerer in the ship of state's engine room. For many months it was far from clear who, if anyone, was on the bridge. But eventually the real world closed in, as it had upon Nixon, and Carter was forced to take the helm. There were problems aplenty by the time the President addressed himself to them: the pressures of international trade, the energy crisis, Soviet aggression, and the failing economy.

Surprisingly, given Carter's late start and short tenure, several important initiatives were undertaken in his administration. Oil was freed from price controls, and Americans finally began to conserve it seriously. The apparatus of the Office of the Special Trade Representative was strengthened, and scored a number of successes under the leadership of Robert Strauss, Alonzo Mc-Donald, and Alan Wolff. For the first time, the United States had an effective procedure for conducting trade negotiations with the rest of the world, a procedure which assigned to government the role of achieving a consensus with business and labor for the definition and fulfillment of the national interest in the world economy. A tripartite committee in the steel industry was also formed, which worked less well, but at least provided practical experience and a useful precedent. One of Carter's last proposals was the establishment of a National Reindustrialization Board, intended to bring the principal players in American industry together with government and labor. The board would specifically attempt to set national priorities and rebuild America's lost economic strength.

On balance, however, Carter's presidency was a failure, in large part because his view of the presidency was for too long inconsistent with reality; he was for too long loyal to the traditional ideology. Typically, and in a manner eerily reminiscent of his predecessors, his failure was misinterpreted. Like his predecessors, Carter had come to the belated realization that a basic reorganization of government was necessary. Perhaps reacting more to Carter's style than his substance, Americans gave way once more to their creedal passion; again the nation found itself with—judging from appearances—a Lockean in charge.

It is premature to evaluate the Reagan administration, but it is clear that its early years were marked by a debilitating ambivalence. By 1983, the costs of that ambivalence, both for the nation and for Reagan, were mounting.

Budget-cutting seemed at first a certain winner. It appealed to the two opposing camps simultaneously: the Lockeans wanted to reduce the role of government as a matter of principle; the communitarians viewed economy as necessary for fighting inflation and for cleaning up many ineffective government social programs. This latter group soon became disenchanted, however, when it became clear that no replacements for the old programs would be offered. In the terms of the last chapter, the administration was failing to define clearly a community need. Many were also doubtful about the President's definition of that need with respect to military expenditures and the national interest in revolutionary Central America. (Soon, budget-cutting became more myth than reality in any case, as federal spending actually increased from 23% of GNP to 24.2% in 1982, and the federal deficit pushed upward toward an estimated $200 billion in fiscal 1984.)

The Reagan administration also undertook to downplay affirmative action—a program, as noted earlier, designed to achieve equality of result. Lockeans found this retrenchment appealing, but were for the most part concerned that equality of opportunity would be subverted by an abandonment of school integration unless a substitute plan for equal but segregated education was implemented. Here the President had drifted into an unwonted communitarianism, and found himself drawing fire from all sides. Having deemphasized equality of result, and having failed to ensure equality of opportunity, Reagan was by default an advocate of hierarchy. Although there were reasons enough to support hierarchy—for example, using limited resources to guarantee that schools trained the best and the brightest, in a manner consistent with the community's need—it was understandably controversial, especially for those who felt themselves to be stuck at the bottom.

Capping rights and emphasizing duties was generally appealing to both Lockeans and communitarians. But controversy was predictable when the poor appeared to lose more of their rights than the not-so-poor, while simultaneously being reminded of their duties, in the reiteration of themes like "workfare."

The 1982 annual report of the President's Council of Economic Advisors (CEA) is worth examining for its exceptional ideological didacticism. Indeed, that very didacticism emphasizes the report's other major flaw: it is fraught with ambivalence. Many previous CEA members had been economics professors, and therefore conscious to a fault of their educational responsibilities, but the 1982 triumvirate—Murray L. Weidenbaum of Washington University, William A. Niskanen of the University of California, and Jerry L. Jordan of the University of New Mexico—were especially preoccupied with the importance of "right thinking." Their view on the role of government, and their analysis of the best means of controlling business and the most promising route to individual fulfillment and self-respect, are well worth pondering. But first, it is necessary to place the report in its own context: the CEA's view of the nation's economy in 1981.

The first year of the Reagan administration constituted an economic roller coaster. In the opening quarter of the year, the real gross national product (GNP) grew an astonishing 9%. In the second quarter it declined 1.6% and then rose slightly in the third quarter. The crunch came in the fourth quarter, when the GNP plunged more than 5%. Average growth for the year came out at 1.9%, a far cry from the 4.2% forecast by the President when he took charge in January.[18]

Given the needs of the nation, perhaps most alarming was the 10% decline in business investment in the fourth quarter, accompanied by a 22% drop in residential investment during the year as a whole.[19] The CEA offered no explanation for this deterioration, but it is fair to assume that business was concerned about a lack of demand for its products and discouraged by the very high cost of borrowing money. The prime rate was at 20% during most of 1981, held there both by the Federal Reserve's tight money policies and increased government borrowing to meet the rising federal deficit.[20] Federal spending grew a healthy (or alarming) 15% in 1981, only slightly less than the record-breaking rate of 17% in 1980.[21] The CEA projected a $107-billion federal deficit (including off-budget activities) in fiscal 1983, the highest as a percentage of the GNP since at least 1958—and yet substantially lower than it eventually turned out to be.[22]

Inflation, as measured by the GNP deflator, climbed almost 9%, somewhat less than the previous year, while almost 9% of the work force—roughly 9 million persons—were unemployed in December of 1981. Only 41% of the unemployed were receiving unemployment insurance.[23] Almost one out of every two black teenagers was looking for work.[24]

In spite of the rising unemployment, however, labor costs increased almost 10%, while productivity (output per hour) continued its long decline.[25] Figures that generally do not turn up in

CEA reports showed that the employment costs of unionized workers rose a full percentage point more than those of non-union workers, adding to the public's growing impatience with unions.[26]

Declining productivity contributed to the general deterioration of U.S. competitiveness, manifested in a $28-billion merchandise trade deficit, of which roughly $15 billion was with Japan.[27] But the CEA suggested that we not take the deficit too seriously. In 1980, the report noted cheerfully, the merchandise trade deficit was more than balanced by a $36.1-billion surplus in services, reflecting mostly dividends from U.S. foreign investments, interest on U.S. bank loans, and the like. The economists were also optimistic about the amount of foreign investment coming into the United States: "If foreigners purchase more U.S. real and financial assets in the United States—land, buildings, equity, and bonds—then the United States can afford to import more goods and services from abroad."[28] (Conspicuous by its absence was any analysis of the implications of these massive flows: the half million or so workers in the automobile and associated industries who were idle, the several hundred thousand steel workers who could not find employment, the consequences of becoming a service island in a manufacturing archipelago, and the ultimate control of our basic resources. What foreigners put in, after all, they could take out.)

One of the few bright spots in the economy was the reduction of imports of crude oil and refined products, from 8.3 million barrels a day in January 1980 to 5.5 million in December 1981.[29] This cannot be considered a "pure" victory, however, since it was difficult to know how much of this resulted from an enlightened ethic of conservation and how much from recession-related belt-tightening.

So much for the conclusion of 1981—gloomy even by the CEA's reckoning. What of the future? Prospects were seemingly more heartening. "The current recession is expected to end early in 1982, followed by a resumption of growth by mid-year."[30] The rebound was to be led by consumer goods, housing, autos, and defense. Real GNP would increase by 3%. Business investment would climb 7% in 1982. But the economists included one caveat:

the Administration would still face "the problem of convincing
the public that the Federal government will be steadfast in main-
taining its new economic course."[31]

Unemployment was expected to remain at 9% in 1982, but
some unusual demographic changes would mean that the unemployed would tend to become older. "Between 1980 and 1990 the
number of 18-year-old males will fall by 19 percent, from 2.1
million to 1.7 million, with the bulk of that decline occurring
before 1985."[32] At the same time, the armed forces would be
increasing their ranks by 10%, offering incentives to raise the
quality of recruits. A scarcity of competent young males available to industry was therefore thought to be in the offing.

The CEA's confidence in "the new economic course" deserves closer scrutiny. Would business increase its investment
by the predicted 7%? Where would the investment go—into the
declining industries of the present, or into the export-oriented
enterprises of the future? Would the tax cuts result in investment
or consumption? If consumption, would it be of Toyotas or
Chevettes? If investment, again, where would it go?

These questions naturally raise the question of credit allocation, about which the 1982 report was exceptionally provocative.
In 1981, $361 billion was raised in U.S. credit markets. Of this,
$86.5 billion resulted from federal activity: loan guarantees to
ailing giants in the steel, automobile, and other industries, housing loans and guarantees, subsidies to farmers, and the like. The
CEA decried the fact that "increasingly political judgments,
rather than marketplace judgments, have been responsible for
allocating the supply of credit."[33] In addition to limiting these
tainted supplies of credit, said the report, "the Administration
strongly supports efforts to formalize a Federal credit budget and
to incorporate it into the budget process."[34]

Again, more questions are raised than are answered. Could
this be the birth of a procedure whereby the government set
priorities for credit allocation? If so, according to whose plan?
Was it more important to provide funds for the embattled semiconductor industry than for a house in the suburbs or a fast-food
chain? The administration's frequently expounded free-market
credo would seem to suggest that such thoughts would not be

entertained, but what of the Congressional debate that would surely rage on the subject of a "federal credit budget"? And what about the upcoming orders from the Defense Department? Would there not be pressure to channel some of those funds to the twenty counties in Michigan that were in the grip of a true depression? But what could the unemployed in these counties make? If they made trucks, could we use or export them? On these questions the CEA was silent.

It did, however, have an interesting view on one aspect of credit allocation, namely the leasing provision of the Economic Recovery Tax Act of 1981. The act provided for an "accelerated cost recovery system" for business, shortening the period in which corporations could depreciate their assets, thus reducing corporate income taxes and presumably encouraging investment. The leasing provision enabled companies without taxable income —i.e., without profits—to sell their tax breaks to those that were profitable. The automobile companies that were losing money could, for example, sell their tax relief to IBM, thus enabling IBM to reduce its tax bill. This scheme, said the economists, "should enhance efficient allocation of capital across industries and across firms within the same industry. The fundamental principle underlying the leasing provisions is that investment incentives should be equal for all businesses in a given industry and across industries." [35] But was this not, in fact, a straightforward federal subsidy to the losers—to those who had failed to make it in the marketplace?

One cannot help but be concerned about the discrepancy between the "fundamental principle" stated above and another one presented later on in this report: "Market forces, rather than government bail-outs, will be relied upon to make appropriate adjustments" to the withering effects of international competition.[36] If the President's top economic advisors are not identifying and coping with these discrepancies, who is?

The economists were thoroughgoing in their opposition to what they referred to as the "troublesome 'neomercantilist' view" that the United States government should develop a strategy for improving its competitive posture in the world economy, contending that if the government simply refrained from interfering in the marketplace and enforced the trade laws, all would be well. They failed to address, however, the practical difficulties—past and present—inherent in enforcing the trade laws. They also failed to mention the obvious: that we were being trounced by the Japanese in every arena of competition the Japanese chose to enter, at least in part because of the remarkably efficient relationships among Japanese government, business, and labor. Given the administration's explicit laissez-faire strategy, how would it counter mounting pressures for subsidies and tariff protection, as the human and economic costs of unemployment mounted? Would the principles of free trade and the limited state prosper in a world where those principles were not practiced? Could we force the world to play by our rules, or would we be forced to play by the world's?

This is the context within which William Norris and his microelectronics cooperative will have to operate. It is also the context within which the American automobile industry will perish or survive. It is an environment which remains ideologically hostile to innovation. Ed Clark, who received close to a million votes in 1980 as the presidential candidate of the Libertarian Party, chided the administration for forcing the Japanese to restrict auto exports to the United States. Writing in *The New York Times*, he said, "What claim can the United States make to being a free country if one cannot do such a simple thing as buy a car without government interference?" [37]

And yet history is now repeating itself: the Japanese government announced in January 1982 that it would spend $45 million over the next three years to begin research on "fifth generation" computers. These are to be a new family of machines designed specifically for "artificial intelligence" (AI) applications. AI (a new type of computer software designed to process ideas and knowledge, in addition to numbers) promises to be as significant an innovation as the computer itself. "It will change the way we work, the way we learn, and even the way we think about ourselves," said Nils J. Nilssen, director of AI research at SRI International. [38] In 1982, it was unclear what role the United States would play in its development.

American banks, dangerously overcommitted to a number of less-developed countries, were doubtless wide-eyed at the

CEA's view that the U.S. government and the International Monetary Fund have been overly generous to the poorer nations of the world. The report asserted that both bodies needed to toughen up: there had been "too much emphasis on resource transfer and not enough emphasis on resource development through private market mechanisms."[39] But if we were to encourage Mexico and Brazil to expand their production of steel and automobiles, we presumably would have an obligation, implicit or explicit, to buy the output. What then of our domestic producers of these goods? Would we condemn them to slow death by the iron laws of comparative advantage, after having ourselves promoted that advantage? If so, what would we do with the newly idle? They are an increasingly expensive burden nowadays. Would we tolerate bigger deficits to help Brazil and Mexico, even indirectly?

Continuing on the subject of the developing world, the CEA said that bilateral assistance was preferable to multilateral assistance. It argued that donor countries should "control" where their funds went, and how these funds were used.[40] There is a long, and for the most part lamentable, history of attempts by the United States to control aid to the poor world bilaterally.[41] All nations of the world might have been better served if the economists had read that history before suggesting the weakening or abandonment of the multilateral institutions which have been so painstakingly constructed over the last twenty years.

Chapter Six of the report examined "reforming government regulation of economic activity." The CEA estimated that the regulatory expenses of federal agencies in fiscal 1974 had amounted to $2.8 billion, and that they had risen to $5.5 billion by fiscal 1979. The biggest spenders in 1981 ranked as follows: Environmental Protection Agency, $1.3 billion; Department of Agriculture, $1.2 billion; Transportation, $971 million; Labor, $539 million; Nuclear Regulatory Commission, $435 million; and Health and Human Services, $347 million.

"Concern has grown that many of the decisions of regulatory agencies are economically inefficient," said the report.[42] In keeping with this concern, the President (in Executive Order 12291, issued February 17, 1981) ordered all agencies to develop a benefit-cost analysis when promulgating regulations. He also

required that the Office of Management and Budget "review"—
that is, approve—all new rules. The CEA proposed three major
principles for such an evaluation:

1. Regulations should focus on "a clear national problem."
2. Benefits and costs should be considered in designing them.
3. Business should have maximum flexibility in the way it
meets federal standards.

These guidelines are meaningful only after one has arrived at a
functional "benefit" and "cost." In this regard, it is useful to
look at how the CEA defined "efficiency." An "efficient economic system," it said, "is responsive to individual wants; that
is, efficiency is defined in terms of each person achieving his or
her own goals." [43] But what of the multitude of instances where
one person's pursuit of a goal infringes upon another person's?
If you make Chevettes and I want to buy a Toyota, our goals are
fundamentally in conflict. If your manufacturing process pollutes
the water I drink, we may not be able to resolve this conflict
independently. The report recognized that these problems exist,
but suggested that the government should take a strictly limited
approach to them. (One rationale for such a strict limitation was
that government tended to be "overly responsive to interest
groups." [44])

Given the fact that the issues of health and safety which have
emerged to challenge the community in the last decade were not
likely to resolve themselves, what was the probable outcome of
the administration's new approach? There would be greater centralization of decision-making in the Office of Management and
Budget, where costs and benefits would be weighed and a course
of action decided upon, insulated as much as possible from contamination by interest groups. Such a procedure might well be
more "efficient," to the degree that it was more authoritarian,
but it could also produce a crippling backlash from those who
emphasized democratic processes. The irony was that in the
name of limiting the power of government, the administration
was in fact augmenting it, while also making it less democratic.

Under the heading "Principles Guiding the President's Economic Program," the CEA made this pronouncement: "If the
primary concern is the welfare of the poor, the most efficient

form of transfer is probably cash rather than benefits in kind (i.e., public housing, food stamps, and medical care). Poor people given money can best determine for themselves what goods to buy. If they are given goods and services instead, their ability to learn to make their own choices is limited."[45] To some this rhetoric may have an appealing ring; however, we must contemplate the real problems of many of the poor. The unemployed steelworker in Gary, Indiana, like the teenager in the South Bronx, needs expensive training; he then needs help finding a job, probably far from where he lives. Can he accomplish this sequence of tasks independently with a small cash handout? If not, the CEA's plan would probably relegate him to a life on the dole. His children might well fall into the same trap.

"Efforts are being made at both the Federal Trade Commission and the Department of Justice to reform the enforcement of the antitrust laws to make them more consistent with the promotion of economic efficiency."[46] As noted in earlier chapters, it would be difficult to argue that these efforts were not long overdue. The national interest—in its current form, achieving competitiveness with the Japanese—often requires precisely the traits of bigness and collaboration among firms which Judge Learned Hand condemned as "inherently undesirable." The economists would have served us well by going a little further down this road. Had they done so, they might have helped illuminate the fact that what appears to be evidence of a drift toward individualism is, in fact, part of a broad movement toward communitarianism.

We arrive again at William Norris's sensible idea for cooperation among U.S. electronics firms. The proposal reflects an ideological departure from tradition, and must therefore be explicitly justified by a new ideology—specifically, by an acceptable definition of community need concerning competitiveness in semiconductors and computers. This is ideology in action: if government does not make such a definition explicit, build a consensus behind it, and establish the parameters of cooperation to implement it, the Norris initiative will be vulnerable to the charge of illegitimacy, and to erosion by its enemies.

Happily, the Reagan approach to antitrust (as indicated in the CEA's report and the decisions of William Baxter, head of the

Justice Department's Antitrust Division), is consistent with the aims of the Norris proposal and with the basic tenets of communitarianism. (One senses, though, that they would be uncomfortable with the conclusion.) The administration is clearly more concerned with community need than with extinguishing any incipient restraint on competition. But its task would be made easier if it grasped the necessity to define that need in an acceptable and legitimate way.

A case in point: Pennsylvania's Republican Senator Arlen Specter was greatly angered when, in January of 1982, AT&T was freed to enter new businesses while divesting itself of its twenty-two local operating companies. Specter questioned the process whereby community need had been defined in that case, implying critically that it had resulted from private discussions between the company, the White House, and the Defense Department, at which Baxter was not even present.[47] It was not the outcome which bothered Senator Specter; rather, it was the process by which the result was arrived at. Others were less sanguine about the outcome in this case; their objections, combined with Specter's, illustrate the ideological complexities inherent in the situation.

Charles L. Brown, the chairman of AT&T, was very much concerned about the implications of the breakup. "We think it was absolutely the wrong decision, having in mind the long-term telecommunications interests of this country," he said in an interview in May 1982. "But in fact the United States has no telecommunications policy; we desperately need one. So compared to the uncertainty and the chaos that preceded the Baxter decision, it was the best alternative that AT&T had available."

Perhaps a historical perspective would be helpful in understanding Brown's conclusion. AT&T has traditionally been guided by the national interest, as defined by government in cooperation with the company. From the days of its founder, Theodore Vail, it conceived of itself as an efficient regulated monopoly, rendering uniform service at the lowest cost throughout the country. It prided itself on being the best telephone company in the world. Under the terms of the 1934 Communications Act, which for many years was its charter, the company had what it called "system integrity," an end-to-end control of (and responsibility for) telephone service in the United States.

With the advent of new communications technology in the 1960s, the Federal Communications Commission broke into system integrity, allowing competitors to hook up to AT&T's system and benefit from it. At the same time, the Justice Department, in the name of promoting competition, prohibited the company from competing back: it was deemed too big and too strong to be allowed to "throw its weight around." Thus, the company was hamstrung, caught in limbo between competition, regulation, partnership, and charter. The definition of community need contained in the 1934 act had atrophied in the face of technological change, and no new definition had taken its place. The result was confusion. In the 1970s, the U.S. share of the world telecommunications market eroded, and concern grew in the Defense Department and elsewhere that the nation was no longer preeminent in this critical field.

The Baxter decision, splitting away the local companies, left AT&T with four main components: its Long Lines (long distance) network, a regulated system; Western Electric, its manufacturing arm; Bell Labs, its research group; and a new subsidiary, American Bell, authorized earlier by the FCC to provide communication services. Brown's task was to shape a new organization that embraced two quite different cultures, one of which was, as before, regulated; and the other of which was exposed to the unaccustomed winds of competition. His overriding concern was, as he put it, "to make sure that the performance of the company conforms to what the public expects of it, as we have done in the years up to now. Inarticulate as some of the objectives of the public may be, our job is to discover and fulfill them.

"The crucial question," Brown continued, "is, What is the long-run national interest in telecommunications which we are dedicated to serve? It is not our job to define that interest, and certainly it will not emerge from the kind of contest between plaintiff and defendant which we have had for so long in the courts. Surely it is not the job of the assistant attorney general to make that policy. Will it emerge naturally from marketplace competition? I have my doubts. If the United States is to be preeminent in this enormously complicated field, investments must be made in research and development which will have little, if any, immediate pay-back. It seems to me that there must be some way that government can identify those things which are truly of national importance in telecommunications. Then business and labor can work together to conform to the national interest."[48]

By 1982–83, Reagan's economic policies had boomeranged, returning to strike the very business leaders who had once so enthusiastically supported them. Mounting government deficits, as a result of tax cuts and increased spending, when combined with strict control of the money supply, drove interest rates up to unprecedented levels. Unable to borrow, consumers could not spend, and business was therefore not inclined to invest for production. A downward spiral resulted.

The decline was exacerbated in two ways by the influence of foreigners. First, high interest rates induced them to buy dollars, which drove up the value of the currency and made American exports abroad more expensive, thus punishing their producers. Second, the high-priced dollar made imports cheaper and more competitive in the American marketplace, again punishing U.S. producers. The President, most would agree, could not be accused of being antibusiness; rather, he failed to understand the realities of the world within which he was creating policies.

Ideological confusion has long reigned in America. Only recently has it become too expensive to tolerate. What was missing in the policy statements of the Reagan administration was any coherent sense of the position of the United States in the world community. It was not surprising that President Reagan did not seek to provide us with a vision of where we are going in the world, given his clear preference for domestic issues. His very focus on domestic concerns, though, was a delusion; as the Japanese have learned, most domestic issues—particularly in the economic sphere—are actually international issues writ small. William Norris's proposal, and Charles Brown's analysis of the AT&T settlement, are only two examples of many which could illustrate the point.

The example of AT&T also demonstrates the pertinence and complexity of ideological analysis. Even with an appropriate, if underdeveloped, sense of a community need outweighing a Lockean dictate—that is, the need for some forms of collaboration in industry, which could produce more good than competitive free-for-alls—the Reagan administration had made two mistakes. First, by failing to achieve a consensus, it had jeopardized the legitimacy of its selected course of action. And second, by acting on an underdeveloped definition of community need, it had jeopardized the nation's competitive posture in the telecommunications field.

Obsessed with individualism, or an approximation thereof, the authors of the Economic Report were blind to the communitarian activities which the government had already undertaken, and to those which it would need to undertake in the near future. The seeds of communitarianism were there, though; even in the germinating stage, they confused the President's advisors. It was this confusion, more than any specific policy, which boded ill for the future.

5

Choice and Necessity
in Business/Government
Relations

The effectiveness of the U.S. economy in the 1980s—and thus the welfare of the nation generally—depends significantly on the creation of a more realistic interface between government and business. Several steps are necessary: we must inspect old assumptions about the roles of government and business; we must avoid wishful thinking and the romantic lure of Lockeanism, recognizing what is in fact happening and must happen in the face of mounting crisis; and we must construct new justifications for the most promising of the new ways, fine-tuning institutional practice with these new justifications to assure both legitimacy and efficiency.

Although each recent American president has extolled the virtues of the traditional ideology, the American government—which began as a close approximation of Locke's "limited state"—has blossomed, perversely, into a huge and interventionary government, which by the 1970s was spending close to $5 billion a year regulating free enterprise.[1] Estimates of the annual cost to business of this ubiquitous regulation ranged from $63 billion to more than $200 billion. Our traditional predilection for fragmentation and incoherence in government meant that much of this regulatory effort was contradictory, and marred by unanticipated trade-offs, emanating as it did from the twenty-six separate federal agencies created between 1965 and 1975.[2]

EPA regulations, for example, mandated the use of low-sulphur oil; in practice, this meant increased oil imports from the Middle East, which further skewed the American trade imbalance and increased our defense vulnerability and related military costs. The steel industry, hemorrhaging badly from the wounds inflicted by foreign competition, was beset with more than five thousand separate regulations, many of which were inconsistent with a variety of community needs. The pattern was repeated many times: responding to crisis and interest-group pressures, the federal government flailed at an ever-longer list of grievances. The general perception of the 1950s—that Americans, in the person of their government, could do anything they set their minds to—had by the 1970s become a dangerous and debilitating illusion. For the first time in recent memory, it appeared that choices had to be made.

Tentative steps were taken in that direction. President Ford's Executive Order 11821, issued in 1975, required agencies to certify that the inflationary impact of major legislative proposals and agency rules had been evaluated. The Office of Management and Budget was placed in charge of the procedure. President Carter, in turn, called for a semiannual listing of all regulations; he ordered OMB to establish criteria for determining "significant" regulations, and also set up a Regulatory Council, under whose auspices all agencies were supposed to think and act coherently. President Reagan went even further, empowering OMB to weigh the costs of a regulation against its benefits, and to assess the cumulative impact of all regulations—on a particular firm, on a group of firms, or on an industry.

"Each individual regulation may look good by itself," said Jim J. Tozzi, deputy director of OMB's Office of Information and Regulatory Affairs (OIRA) in 1981, "but when you add them all up, and you relate the totality to macro-economic concerns, they may not look so good."[3]

In those few words, Tozzi both defined the task and suggested its appalling difficulty. How is the executive branch to weigh the costs and benefits of hundreds of government policies on business and the economy? Tozzi and his staff have not pretended to possess the data or the analytical capability necessary for the task. Where these resources exist, they are divided among several agencies and the industries they regulate. Nor was Tozzi's staff guaranteed access to such resources: agencies are understandably jealous of their prerogatives and of the mandate they have received from Congress; and business, conditioned to an adversarial relationship with government, has in many instances been unwilling to share its competence.

Said Tozzi:

> I see lots of people: interest groups, environmentalists, the Nader people, business, labor people.
>
> Industry in particular has a lot to learn about how to deal with the executive branch of the federal government. They're not very good at presenting their case. Most of them use their Washington attorneys and the last thing I need is more lawyers to talk to. The lawyers come in here on a toxic waste issue, for example, and they say, "Under Section 812 of the Act you can give me a variance." I know that. I helped write half the damn laws and virtually all of the regs. What I need is data. I need to know what the impact of a rule will be. Why is it a bad rule? What will the effect be? When the CEO comes in here, we generally get on fine. He tells me his problem and I understand it. He gives me supporting data and evidence. That's what I need.
>
> Industry has to learn to put itself in my shoes, how to look at things from the point of view of a government regulator. They have to understand our problems better. There is big room for improvement here; I mean unbelievable room.[4]

Even at a preliminary stage in our investigation, several important conclusions can be drawn. First, the national government, incoherent by design, is being forced by necessity into coherence. Where competition in the marketplace is inadequate to define community needs—in such areas as safety, health, housing, income, and jobs, for example—the government has found it necessary to establish such a definition, and to produce conscious trade-offs weighing costs and benefits. This has caused growing strains among the agencies of the executive branch, as well as between the executive and the Congress, which in many instances initiated the policies and the laws to implement them. The process has also sharpened the question of whether the definition and implementation of community need ought to occur on the federal level, or on the state and local levels.

Second, it seems clear that a question of great contemporary interest—that is, Should the United States have an industry policy?—is largely irrelevant. If we define industrial policy as the sum of the governmental programs which affect the conduct and performance of industry, our country has such a policy and has it in spades. We need to recognize this fact, and ask the more pertinent questions that it suggests. Does anyone know what our industrial policy is? Are the several components of our industrial policy consistent with each other? Is the policy compatible with business vitality and economic health? Is it reliable over time? Is it realistic, given an increasingly competitive world?

Third, it seems clear that the people who are actually making "industrial policy" in the United States are our top-rank career civil servants. Jim Tozzi, for example, worked in OMB under four presidents, trying to make the regulatory process more coherent and more efficient. "I was thinking about what we were doing now a year and a half ago," he said in November of 1981. "I set up this office and trained the people. When President Reagan came in with David Stockman, they had a well-trained staff ready to go."

Tozzi is only one heartening example of many dedicated and capable career government professionals; we will meet more of them in the course of this investigation. Suffice it to say here that no group will prove more important to the remedy of the American disease.*

Finally, government policies will be increasingly important to the vitality of business. Nothing that occurs in the Reagan administration or its successors will alter this. In these circumstances, it seems unlikely that thoughtful corporate managers will continue for much longer their current adversarial approach toward government, in which lawyers, lobbyists, and public-relations people call the shots. Success will depend rather upon a partnership, in which business, in cooperation with other elements in society, helps government to define, design, and implement a strategy to promote the national interest. Companies will need to think of their relationship with government in terms of strategy —a coherent set of goals and policies extending over time—and

---

* Jim Tozzi resigned from governmental service in the summer of 1983 to become a consultant. He hopes to help corporations improve their relations with government.

these strategies will be a major responsibility of chief executive officers.

"We're working away from the concept that business and government are natural adversaries," said former DuPont chairman Irving Shapiro in 1982. "We have to create a climate in which business and government people can sit down together—with labor representatives, too—and talk about the issues for which an agency is responsible, offer facts, offer alternatives, try to fashion remedies that work. Business must always recognize that the final decision is with government; but government can't make a good decision without the help of business. I would guess that more than half of the leadership of American industry now sees the issues this way. The trend is really moving quite quickly. The thing that persuades me the most is that those who are taking over as CEOs of major corporations all tend to see government-business relations as I have described them."[5]

Alexander Trowbridge, president of the National Association of Manufacturers, offered a football analogy to define effective government-business relations. "I think government is the coach and business the quarterback. The coach is responsible for setting the general goals and direction, and the quarterback's responsibility is to slug it out on the field in order to get there." But Trowbridge is less confident than Shapiro about an end to adversarialism. "I don't think we can shift from the traditional adversarial notion of government-business relations to Japanese-type cooperation. Most business people would, I think, reject any notion of industrial policy or government planning such as is followed in Japan and Europe."[6]

Perhaps it is not unfair to give Shapiro the last word on the subject:

> I start from the premise that the concept of adversary relationships *has* to be abandoned. There is really no choice. We are being forced.
>
> People who run government agencies really have very much the same value system as we in business do. It's just that they don't have access to the same facts. There is no dialogue, and without that, there can be no solution.
>
> I don't think it's controversial to say that it is the role of government to define the national interest. I would agree that we don't have the mechanism to do it, and we keep proving that year in

and year out. But if government isn't going to define the national interest, who is?

Somebody has to define it. I can't accept the premise that it can just float out there in the air and somehow or other be perceived.

I would like to have a few thoughtful men and women from government, business, and labor in a back room who would forget current events entirely and think about the future. I want them to identify the problems of the future, do some long-term thinking and flush up some ideas for us to focus on as a nation. Is that such a radical idea? That's exactly what a good business executive does.

In summary, then, we need an industrial policy; more precisely, we need a consciously designed industrial policy, rather than an ad hoc construction. We need a bureaucracy in place to implement it, and most evidence suggests that our industrial leaders are prepared to assist in its design and implementation. In this chapter and those that follow, I shall describe a variety of crisis situations that reveal the problems in finding the most effective relationship between government and business, and point to some choices to be made. Before doing so, though, it is worth considering industrial policy, and the nature of business-government relations, in general terms.

Our ideological distaste for the concept of industrial policy has meant that the host of governmental programs or policies affecting industry has not been considered systematically, or as a whole. It is not so much that we have been unable to think coherently as it is that we have until recently scarcely tried; we have chosen not to. Such a role for government—or rather, the explicit formulation of such a role—runs directly counter to our traditions. Recently, though, OMB and other government entities have been driven by necessity to consider the totality of the effects of government policies on industry. There is, it seems to observers on both sides of the fence, no choice: the federal government must formulate industrial policy, must make the inevitable trade-offs, and must define the national interest and fix priorities. It has done so in the recent past—albeit surreptitiously—and will continue to do so in the future.

The question, therefore, is not whether government pursues an industrial policy at all, but whether it makes that policy explicit and conscious, or instead avoids predictable ideological problems and makes policy implicit, ad hoc, and inadvertent. In making this choice, we must realize that the costs of the latter approach are high.

During its first hundred days, for example, the Reagan administration announced a sweeping program for economic recovery: "supply-side" tax cuts to stimulate industrial activity, a series of actions to assist the auto industry, and seventy-nine specific regulatory actions aimed at implementing the President's promise to "take government off the back of business."[7] Were these the elements of a national industrial policy? Yes and no. As Robert A. Leone and Stephen P. Bradley have pointed out, "each of these policies has major long-run implications for U.S. industry."

> Supply-side tax cuts, for example, stimulate investment and, conversely, discourage consumption, with attendant consequences for the overall composition of industrial activity. The policy of "voluntary" auto import restraints sets a major precedent and likely forecasts substantial changes in the entire political and institutional machinery by which frictions in international trade are to be resolved—not only for the auto industry but for other industries as well.[8]

It is a partial policy, a policy which fails because its proponents have declined to think systematically. If we continue with Leone and Bradley's example, we soon discover that quantitative restrictions on Japanese car imports discourage Japan from competing on the basis of high volume and low price, and instead encourage its manufacturers to go after the high-margin, luxury small-car market. "This, in turn, penalizes those domestic producers who sought out this market as the mainstay of their future profitability."[9]

One of the less controversial of the seventy-nine regulatory changes was the postponement by the Secretary of Energy of a determination of energy-efficiency standards for major home appliances, ostensibly for competitive reasons. Fifty separate state governments were thereby encouraged to develop their own standards, causing special difficulties for large companies who rely on economics of volume and distribution to keep costs down. Those manufacturers of high-priced, fuel-efficient appliances who were counting on a continuing commitment of the government to energy conservation were disadvantaged; those who were unmindful of energy efficiency—a community need by almost everyone's reckoning—gained a reprieve.[10]

The subject of taxation and tax subsidies deserves a closer look. Although the administration assumed that its 1982 tax policies would allow the marketplace to determine where funds for business investment would go, the reality was that government's involvement in procurement, research and development, and other activities had a significant impact on the nature and direction of business investment. For example, more than half of all aircraft and communications equipment produced in this country is purchased by the federal government. Similarly, the government consumes one-fourth of our annual production of engineering and scientific instruments, and a third of all electronic tubes.[11] The government finances more than 33% of all U.S. industrial research and development, and employs something like 35% of the nation's scientists and engineers.

This reality naturally has a direct bearing on the evolution and direction of major lines of American industry. In effect, public money shapes and nurtures many of our largest industrial concerns, which also serve as the receptacles for billions of dollars of private investment. Should the government take into account its own long-term impact on the domestic economy, and on U.S. competitiveness in the world economy? Should, for example, grants and contracts designed primarily for military applications also be considered part of a U.S. strategy toward commercial markets? The deterioration of our competitive stance in the world market is inexorably forcing these questions out into the open.

Many mirrors can be employed to reflect these issues. In 1980 the federal government was tied in one way or another to more than $300 billion worth of benefits to specific industries. This figure constituted about 14% of the GNP.[12] Included in this substantial total were loan guarantees, loans, subsidies, and insurance. (Not included, of course, were the costs paid by consumers as a result of import barriers and restraints, which either raised the cost of imports or made them unavailable.) These federal funds flowed in a variety of directions, following the ever-shifting dictates of a swarm of interest groups. "The government, for example," Robert Reich points out, "now spends five times as much on R and D for commercial fisheries as for steel, and provides $455 million in tax breaks for the timber industry but none for semiconductors."[13] Many subsidies, furthermore, are channeled to industries—such as housing—that are sheltered from international trade. These are funds that are thereby denied to new enterprises competing in world markets.

After reviewing numerous such examples of de facto industrial policy, Leone and Bradley suggest three simple rules for its conscious design. It should *complement* the strategic interests of domestic companies. It should be *consistent*. (They note, for example, the contradiction between federal emission-control policies and fuel-economy standards.) And it should have *continuity*, minimizing the incidence of abrupt and costly shifts of emphasis.

Henry Schacht, the chairman of Cummins Engine Company, agrees:

> The nation badly needs an industrial policy. We, the business people, fight it as some communistic, socialistic, all-encompassing thing we can't have. I think the business community has been doing the country a terrible disservice.
>
> I view the government as the systems manager. It should not implement; it ought to manage the system. It is the only place where you can gather the competing demands of the society to make some rational sense of them, to provide the leadership, and to set the incentives.

It seems self-evident that properly constructed industrial policy should focus as much on encouraging economic growth and innovation as on helping ailing industries to adapt to competitive forces. In fact, one of the costly failings of our de facto industrial policy has been its tendency to subsidize—and thereby to protect from world competition—large, politically powerful industries, such as steel and autos, at a time when they should be encouraged to shrink, concentrate, and modernize. The result has been described succinctly as a sort of "lemon socialism."[14]

The message is clear: since many government policies affect the health of the economy, it is time for government to abandon its pretense of ideological innocence, and to think coherently about the effects of those policies. This statement seems platitudinous, but only until one contemplates its implications. Who in government will start the thinking? Which agency? Will Congress be the catalyst, or the White House? Will the initiative be wrested away from the interest groups? And how will it be possible for this reform to take place unless business cooperates with government, supplying essential data and analysis?

Our rich adversarial tradition makes it extremely difficult for business to cooperate in this context. Such cooperation is, of course, ideologically suspect. There are few proven procedures for making it work, and a growing number of professionals in Washington derive fame and fortune from the exacerbation of adversarialism, rather than from the skillful construction of cooperative frameworks.

Robert Reich, while director of policy planning at the Federal Trade Commission from 1976 to 1981, compiled a list of these professionals. They include: approximately 12,000 Washington-based lawyers who represent business in the courts and before regulatory agencies; 9,000 congressional lobbyists; 42,000 trade-association officials; 8,000 public-relations specialists; 1,200 specialized journalists; 1,300 public-affairs consultants who help business vis-à-vis the regulators; and 3,500 business-affairs consultants, who help the regulators vis-à-vis particular industries.

"Together with the 15,500 lawyers, lobbyists, and public relations specialists within regulatory agencies and large corporations, these intermediaries comprise a virtual industry of their own," says Reich.[15] This formidable array of well-paid go-betweens has an obvious vested interest: they seek to fan the flames of adversarialism, keeping government and business officials apart by exaggerating the dangers for both sides inherent in any given issue. It is a "vicious circle [that] has been broken only at times of genuine . . . crisis, but the level of crisis sufficiently compelling to engender real business-government collaboration has grown ever higher as the intermediary industry has increased its size and effectiveness."[16]

Some crises, of course, still manage to reach that rising threshold. For example, in the late 1970s, the Environmental Protection Agency, in cooperation with a number of companies in the steel and chemical industries, devised a means of reducing the implementation costs of the Clean Air Act. Under the new procedures, industry was given greater latitude in achieving the goals of the act, the result of many months of cooperative effort between government and industry officials.[17] Support came from the highest levels: shortly before his inauguration, for example,

President-elect Reagan declared that "both business and government will have to . . . lay aside old hostilities and assume a new spirit of cooperation and shared responsibility."[18]

But it is small comfort to have to rely on ever-larger crises to overcome the efforts of the professional adversarialists. As stated earlier, our goal should be to determine how to lessen the amount of crisis required for change. Concurrently, we must also examine the ideological implications of new cooperative procedures, so that they may be legitimate as well as efficient.

The pre-1970 relations between the American governments—federal and state—and the five major American oil companies (Exxon, Gulf, Texaco, Mobil, and Socal*) is a classic example of an effective partnership for the fulfillment of community need. It was, however, ideologically illegitimate. Without doubt, the "partnership" violated the Lockean tenets of the antitrust laws; furthermore, by being both inexplicit and surreptitious, it was unacceptable according to communitarian norms.

Despite the blatant illegitimacy of this arrangement, we lived comfortably with it for two reasons—there was a clear national consensus about the definition of community need (controlled supply and price of oil abroad, and cheap energy at home), and the partnership had the capability to fulfill it. In 1973, both the definition and the capability dissolved. Illegitimacy boiled over and the U.S. oil partnership disintegrated, to be replaced in some instances by arrangements with other governments. Since then the country has paid the price of this disintegration, and in the 1980s, the companies also began to pay. The partnership needs to be renewed, and sooner or later it will be. It will not happen, though, until its terms are made explicit, and the various needs of the different relevant communities are clearly defined.

Since those definitions will be based on the realities of both past and present, let us look more closely at the roots of the oil

---

* With British Petroleum and Shell, they comprised the so-called "Seven Sisters."

partnership, and the causes of its dissolution.[19] In the early 1970s the United States began to feel the impact of basic changes in the control of the world's oil supplies. The principal oil-producing nations, especially in the Middle East, had banded together a decade earlier to form the Organization of Petroleum Exporting Countries (OPEC), but it was not until 1973 that they became a major force. In that year, OPEC nations imposed a four-month embargo on sales to the U.S., raised the price of oil to about six times what it had been in 1970, reduced production, and acquired control over the rights and assets of U.S. oil companies within their borders. As a consequence, consumers experienced shortages, high prices fed inflation, and the ignominious posture of the United States was made stunningly clear: it was dependent for half of its oil on foreign powers which were at best unpredictable and perhaps hostile.

Americans were understandably distressed. Energy, long taken for granted, had not only become dramatically more expensive, but its sources had become uncertain. As they turned down their thermostats and waited in gasoline lines, consumers tried to assess culpability. Who was to blame for this mess? The Arabs, perhaps. But what about the oil companies? It was difficult to ignore the fact that the profits of the major international oil companies had never been higher. Was this perhaps a crisis precipitated for profit?

A historical perspective might have served the nation well in this first moment of doubt. At issue were questions of control that have marked the oil industry since its birth in America in the 1860s. Plagued by overproduction and falling prices, the industry by the fourth quarter of the nineteenth century was a perfect focus for the organizational genius of John D. Rockefeller. In 1883, he gained control of the crucial bottlenecks in the flow of oil—first railroads, then pipelines—and through the formation of the Standard Oil Trust brought order to chaos. "The day of combination is here," Rockefeller said prophetically. "Individualism has gone, never to return."[20]

In so doing, he helped to provoke the antitrust movement, and inspired the unending series of Congressional investigations that have dogged the industry ever since. Legislation also resulted; the Sherman Anti-Trust Act of 1890, for example, included the following two major provisions:

Sec. 1 . . . Every contract, combination in the form of a trust or otherwise, or conspiracy, in restraint of trade or commerce among the several states, or with foreign nations, is hereby declared to be illegal. . . .

Sec. 2 . . . Every person who shall monopolize, or attempt to monopolize, or combine or conspire with any person or persons, to monopolize any part of the trade or commerce among the several states, or with foreign nations, shall be deemed guilty of a misdemeanor. . . .

In 1911, the government used this cudgel to break up the Rockefeller empire: Standard Oil Trust was divided along geographical lines, creating Standard of New Jersey (Esso, now Exxon), Standard of California (Socal), Standard of New York (Socony, the progenitor of Mobil), and others.

Ever since, government and industry have been alternately absorbed by oil shortages and overproduction; in our recent history, there has either been too little or too much. Shortly after World War I, for example, the director of the U.S. Geological Survey ascertained that the United States was running out of oil. The situation could "best be described as precarious," he said.[21] More than a decade later, though, the powerful Texas Railroad Commission was established to control production, thereby avoiding gluts and price wars.

It was in the 1920s, during a period of perceived shortages, that the American oil companies first looked to the Middle East, where the French and the British already had large investments. With the explicit support of the American government, Exxon led the way to Iraq, to be followed by Gulf and Mobil. As Charles Hamilton of Gulf described it, "representatives of the industry were called to Washington and told to 'go out and get it.' "[22] The objective seemed to be twofold: to gain access to new oil reserves, and to establish a U.S. political presence. With respect to the latter, curiously, the State Department was assigning the bulk of the diplomacy to the oilmen.

The development of the Middle East's vast oil fields only exacerbated the recurring problems of overproduction and price-cutting. To cope with this situation, the major oil companies—Exxon, BP, and Shell—met secretly in 1928 at Ashnacarry Castle in Scotland, and agreed in principle to a system of price maintenance based on the U.S. price of oil.[23] This agreement (which was not fully revealed until a government investigation in 1952) was only the first of many, and established a pattern of behavior that would come to concern the Justice Department. In 1941, for example, Justice sued Exxon for conspiring to control the transportation of oil through pipelines, and for making restrictive agreements with I. G. Farben, a mainstay of Nazi Germany's war effort. This was for many a shocking revelation: amid cries of treason, Walter Teagle, then Exxon's chief executive, was forced to resign in 1942, and died shortly thereafter.[24]

In the 1930s, Socal and Texaco, newcomers to the Middle East, obtained huge concessions to establish a joint venture— Aramco—in Saudi Arabia; by 1939 the Arabian oil fields were pumping. Even then, however, the U.S. government had no representative in Saudi Arabia; all negotiations were carried out between the country and Aramco.*

During the same period, Gulf found its way into Kuwait. This time the U.S. government was helpful in ironing out difficulties with the British, who were already there; the American ambassador in London was Andrew Mellon, a Gulf founder whose family held a quarter of the company's shares.[26]

By 1943 Texaco was growing fearful of increasing British influence in Saudi Arabia, and persuaded President Roosevelt to allocate lend-lease funds to that country. At the same time, Roosevelt was preoccupied with the specter of insufficient oil for the American navy. He therefore authorized the establishment of a government Petroleum Reserve Corporation, intended to buy a controlling interest in Aramco. The idea—surely rich with ideological implications—was quickly scuttled, however, in the face of the oil company's express refusal to sell.[27]

In 1954 Texaco and Socal organized the construction of a trans-Arabian pipeline, known as Tapline, to carry Arabian oil to the Mediterranean at Sidon, Lebanon. Before it was finally closed down in 1975, the pipeline was a focus of recurrent controversy. The companies received U.S. government permission to use large amounts of steel, which angered other industrial

---

* Exxon and Mobil joined Aramco in 1948 when they were freed from the so-called Red Line agreement with BP, Shell, and the French national company (CFP). The five had agreed to form the Iraq Petroleum Company in 1928, and not to seek concessions in the former Ottoman Empire—including Turkey, Jordan, Syria, and Saudi Arabia—except through the company.[25]

consumers of that then-scarce resource. And Tapline became a target for guerrillas and a source of tension in the Arab-Israeli conflict; later, it served as an instrument of boycott, and as a bargaining chip for Syria against the United States. It was, in effect, a government foreign-policy commitment that existed outside any stated policy, and free of any meaningful control.

The year 1948 saw two events that were to have a substantial and long-term impact on U.S. relations with the Middle Eastern oil-producing nations. First, Exxon and Mobil joined Aramco, forcing that already powerful entity into the full light of the antitrust laws. The industry awaited the government's response. Said Mobil's chief counsel at the time: "I cannot believe that a comparatively few companies for any great length of time are going to be permitted to control world oil resources without some sort of regulation." [28]

Second, the Venezuelan government initiated a chain of events which led directly to OPEC and the events of 1973. It demanded a 50-50 share of oil profits and equity partnership with all foreign oil companies in Venezuela. Although the oil companies at first resisted this notion of partnership, they gradually perceived its major advantage: it provided the best available security against the regular attacks of Venezuelan nationalists.

In 1950, in the wake of Venezuela's action, the king of Saudi Arabia announced that he wanted a better deal from Aramco, but the company was reluctant to revise the existing arrangement. Enter the U.S. government: Assistant Secretary of State George McGhee, a Texas oilman, devised a plan to please both the king and Aramco, and to protect Saudi Arabia from the "Communist menace." Additional funds for the king would be regarded as foreign income-tax payments, and thus made deductible from the company's U.S. tax bill. In the first full year of this so-called "Golden Gimmick," the U.S. Treasury lost $50 million in oil-company taxes. The State Department was pleased with the arrangement, however; it allowed the United States to provide what amounted to foreign aid to Arabia without having to go to Congress, where pro-Israeli sentiments were considered bothersome.

Other companies were soon allowed to make the same tax deal as Aramco. This arrangement was a substantial inducement for the oil companies to invest abroad, rather than in the United

States. As a result, by 1973, the five "American sisters" were making two-thirds of their profits abroad, and were paying no U.S. taxes on those earnings.[29]

In 1952 the United States became concerned about Communist influence in Iran, where an eccentric new leader, Dr. Mohammed Mossadegh, had taken power, casting out the young Shah and nationalizing British oil holdings. The Departments of State and Defense and the CIA devised a plan to remove Mossadegh, put the Shah back on the Peacock Throne, and keep Iran (and Iranian oil) "free for democracy." A first step in this plan involved the creation of a consortium of the Seven Sisters plus France's national oil company—an explicit vehicle for collaboration. Coincidentally, this was the precise historical juncture when the Federal Trade Commission chose to publish the results of its lengthy investigation of the oil industry. It revealed for the first time the "sisters' " various arrangements since Ashnacarry to divide the market, share pipelines and tankers, and maintain price levels. An ideological furor arose, and in January 1953, the Justice Department accused the five American sisters of antitrust law violations. The timing could not have been worse for the proposed "Iran Consortium": this was patently another example of the sort of collusion that Justice was suing to eliminate.

So now the government's house was divided: State and Defense found themselves squarely pitted against Justice. They argued that the companies "play a vital role in supplying one of the free world's most essential commodities," adding, "American oil operations are, for all practical purposes, instruments of our foreign policy toward these [Middle Eastern] countries. . . . We cannot afford to leave unchallenged the assertions that these companies are engaged in a criminal conspiracy for the purpose of predatory exploitation."[30]

Justice countered: "It is imperative that petroleum resources be freed from monopoly control by the few and be restored to free competitive enterprise. . . . Free private enterprise can be preserved only by safeguarding it from excess of power, governmental and private."[31]

President Eisenhower, like Truman before him, sided with State and Defense, making it clear that the battle against world Communism took precedence over ideological antitrust considerations. (Community need, in other words, was clear.) A coup was engineered; Mossadegh was replaced by the Shah, and a consortium of the Seven Sisters was formed to handle Iran's oil. When the smaller independent American oil companies complained subsequently, they were assigned a 5% share of the take.

By the late 1950s the influence of the American oil industry in Washington was at its peak. Two Texans—Lyndon Johnson, the Senate Majority Leader, and Sam Rayburn, the Speaker of the House—were in key positions; a friendly Arkansan, Wilbur Mills, was chairman of the House Ways and Means Committee; and President Eisenhower was being advised by many experienced oilmen. All were enthusiastic supporters of the industry; all supported the industry's interests, including the crucial and controversial tax deduction referred to as the "depletion allowance." (First enacted in 1926, it allowed oil companies to reduce their taxes by 27.5% of their gross income to take account of their wasting petroleum assets.)

But all was not well in the industry: soon the independent companies, having received a boost through their participation in the Iran Consortium, began expanding, and their increased production helped to create yet another oil glut. As a consequence, Exxon felt compelled in 1960 to reduce the prices it paid to Middle Eastern producing countries. There was a predictable outburst, which coalesced in the formation that year of OPEC. Its explicit goals were to prevent the companies from unilaterally setting prices, to give the producing countries a greater share of oil profits, and to allow those countries' governments to participate in the ownership and control of oil company assets.

In the face of the OPEC challenge, the oil companies sought and received from President Kennedy assurances that collective action by them in negotiations with the producers would not be construed as a violation of the antitrust acts. Again, a particular definition of community need was affirmed: the antitrust laws would not be allowed to stand in the way of the nation's access to oil supplies.

Despite OPEC's internal conflicts—for example, between Iran and Saudi Arabia—the organization gained in strength and cohesiveness throughout the 1960s. The oil companies felt compelled to present a united front, and on several occasions sought a reaffirmation from Washington that the government approved of their collaborative bargaining with OPEC. Each time the affirmation came. Curiously, the industry continued to serve a quasi-diplomatic function: obvious tensions were exacerbated by the 1967 Arab-Israeli war, and spokesmen for the industry warned Washington of the dangers inherent in the government's pro-Israeli policies.

In the early 1970s, the independents bypassed the established order and made separate deals with the new radical government of Libya, buying oil at substantially higher prices than were being paid to other producing countries. The other companies soon followed suit. In Washington, meanwhile, many of the old friends of oil were dead, retired, or discredited. A new generation of congressmen, more representative of big-city voters than of oil states, was in power. Although the oil companies contributed generously to President Nixon's election campaign, the old association was gone. A new, combative relationship—between the government and the oil companies, and between the oil companies and the consumers—was taking its place. (Indeed, by 1974, John J. McCloy, attorney for oil companies since World War II, would be lamenting that "It seems that it is only in the United States that an almost masochistic attack on the position of its own oil companies persists."[32])

In 1972 OPEC demanded not only more money but greater financial participation—51% by 1983. Walter Levy, international oil consultant, predicted in *Foreign Affairs* that the companies would "become completely subservient to their host government." Maurice Adelman of MIT went further; he accused them of being simply "agents of a foreign power."[33]

By 1973 the Arabs were determined to use oil as a weapon in the fight against Israel, and that October, when a new war broke out, their opportunity arose. An embargo was imposed on sales to the United States and other nations friendly to Israel; the price of oil went to $11.65 a barrel, a quadrupling in two months.

The consuming nations were caught with no oil policy. As Anthony Sampson wrote in *The Seven Sisters*:

> Faced with a united OPEC, the consuming governments were thoroughly disunited, and quite unable to agree on a basis of rationing. The sisters were thus landed with the job of serving as a kind of temporary world government, for four or five months, to reallocate the world's oil. Or as one of their executives put it: "We became the world's slaves, beaten, abused by all and loved by none."[34]

The companies, it should be noted, performed their delicate, difficult task with what has generally been regarded as consummate skill and fairness.

As long as the embargo was on, consumption of oil in the embargoed nations dropped markedly. During the first quarter of 1974, gasoline consumption was down 7.7% from the previous year, instead of increasing at its historical rate of 7%. As suggested earlier, though, this decline in consumption was not accomplished without pain and irritation. American drivers, as they waited at the gas stations, had plenty of time to contemplate the oil companies' unprecedented profits, announced in the spring of 1974. Explanations that the previous year's gains had been low, thereby curtailing badly needed funds for investment, did not suffice. Oil executives were hauled before indignant senators and asked a variety of questions about their business. These questions they only partially answered; one company executive claimed the requested information was "proprietary." Senator Henry Jackson was "flabbergasted." In retrospect, his confusion was understandable: the old ideology had long since been abandoned by both government and the oil companies; a new one had not yet replaced it.

In the course of convening hearings on the Multinational Petroleum Companies and Foreign Policy, Senator Frank Church said:

> In part, the industry and the government have no one to blame but themselves. They have enveloped the government-industry relationship with a curtain of secrecy which inevitably has led to the most far-reaching suspicions. The first imperative in any inquiry into the causes of the energy crisis is thus to set aside, finally and definitely, this curtain of secrecy and allow the American people to understand what were the basic decisions which have a bearing on the present crisis, how these decisions were made, what were the alternatives, and what the effects have been.

In the executive branch, predictably, there was an uncomfortable ambivalence. Treasury Secretary William Simon said in November 1974, "I can think of no single change that would improve the outlook for the world economy more than a substantial decrease in the price of oil." A year later, Secretary of State Henry Kissinger suggested that there should be a "floor price" below which the industrialized countries would not allow oil to be sold, so that new investments in alternative energy sources would be safeguarded and encouraged.[35] Sheikh Yamani, oil minister of Saudi Arabia, responded, "You contradict yourself."[36]

Domestically, things weren't much better. President Carter was determined to encourage conservation by raising the price of oil. This controversial definition of community need, once acted upon, exacerbated existing tensions: the companies became the beneficiaries of "windfall profits" on existing reserves. Congress, smelling blood, insisted on taxing the "windfall." When the companies objected vociferously, Carter accused them of trying to engineer "the biggest ripoff in history."[37]

And so, by the mid-1970s, opinion polls showed the oil companies to have hit bottom in public esteem. Partially because of their own actions, and partially as a result of circumstances thrust upon them, they had lost the confidence of the American people. The Federal Trade Commission, as well as many in Congress, wanted to break them up in the name of competition. Others wanted to regulate them, but this was virtually impossible, since only the industry possessed the relevant data. Senator Adlai Stevenson advocated the establishment of a Federal Oil and Gas Company. (This, like Roosevelt's Petroleum Reserve Corporation, would have constituted a charter route to legitimacy.)

The embattled oil companies took on these and other challenges in an impressive display of adversarialism, best symbolized by the Op Ed Page advertisements sponsored by Mobil. They also diversified extensively out of oil: Mobil bought Montgomery Ward, Exxon entered the office products field, and so on. But by the early 1980s, the industry was in deeper trouble. Exxon abandoned a major commitment to the development of shale oil in 1982; other companies groped uneasily. Oil prices were softening in the face of the industry's oldest enemy, glut; the other traditional enemy—shortage—was plainly in the wings.

As America entered the 1980s, it was unclear whether the incoming president shared his predecessor's definition of the nation's energy needs: high and stable prices to encourage long-term investment, in both conservation and the development of domestic energy sources. Proclaiming his intention (later deferred) to abolish the Department of Energy, President Reagan seemed to be saying, "Let the market determine the price"—a stance which, when combined with political realities, had bedeviled the industry for over a century.

Ambiguity was rampant in both industry and government. The definition of community need was unclear, which led to uncertain corporate strategies, which meant that precious time was being wasted. The first two oil shocks (1974 and 1979) cost the United States and other industrial countries an estimated $1.2 trillion in lost growth; it was this economic drag that Americans were experiencing in 1982 in the worst economic decline with the highest unemployment since the depression of the 1930s. The probability of another shock was real, and its consequences portended to be even more grave.[38] It had been supposed that an increased oil price would expand domestic supplies, safe from foreign disruption. But this had not happened. In 1982, the United States was producing 10% less oil at $33 per barrel than in 1970, when domestic oil sold for $3 per barrel.[39]

What conclusions can we draw from this history? First, we can infer that the partnership between the oil industry and government will eventually be renewed. Like partners in a minuet, they need one another. The only question is, How much crisis will be needed to precipitate the new relationship? Second, it seems clear that, unlike the old days, the partnership this time will be overt. Third, government—not the industry—will be the senior partner.

An intriguing question can be posed at this point. Assuming that the best defense is a good offense, why has not the industry publicly and vehemently insisted that the government articulate an energy policy? Can it doubt that sooner or later, in this administration or the next, there will be such a policy, and that the industry's investment plans—indeed, its future—are dangerously hypothetical until and unless a reliable policy is set out? Have some lingering Lockean notions of free enterprise and the limited state colored their perceptions and their judgment, dissuading them from doing what their planning departments have surely told them is essential? Perhaps; or perhaps the companies have concluded, after a decade of public abuse, that a partnership with government is unworkable. If so, they misread history. It has not been partnership that has caused their difficulties; it has been the nature and management of that partnership.

Looking to the future, the major international companies may well decide, in their revised relationship with government, that the relevant community for them is the world; that oil, like money, is a world commodity, and that the governance of its flow should emanate from a global source such as the International Energy Agency. As in international banking, where the role of the International Monetary Fund is of increasing importance in the control of money flow, so with oil—the tension between strictly national interests and global need will surely increase. This tension will tend to hasten the renewal of the government/industry partnership; if we are clever, we can employ this and other pressures to devise an efficient and legitimate partnership. Reality—including ideological reality—demands it.

Oil, we have learned, is very much like money. Indeed, the two are intimately related, as events in the 1970s demonstrated. The oil-consuming nations were forced to borrow massive amounts to pay for this increasingly expensive resource; the loans were arranged by the great private banks of the U.S., Europe, and Japan, which competed with one another for an ever-larger share of the lucrative business. In their race for market share, however, the banks sometimes were less than careful about the ability of the borrower to repay. Not surprisingly, then, the 1970s were marked by the threat of national defaults—by Turkey, Zaire, Indonesia, and others. In the early 1980s, several countries in Eastern Europe were in worrisome shape, as were many small borrowers in Africa, such as Zambia; in our hemisphere, so were Mexico, Argentina, and Brazil. A new pattern emerged: the threatened banks sought and secured the help of their home countries. These countries—having little choice—worked with the International Monetary Fund to bail out the banks and prevent massive defaults.

For example, in August of 1982, Mexico announced that she could not pay the interest on her $81 billion of foreign debt, about half of which was held by major U.S. banks and loaned to both the Mexican government and to private borrowers. There was nothing new about Mexico's plight: for ten years or more (except for a brief interlude in the late 1970s when oil revenues were high), Mexico had been spending more than she earned in international markets. She had to borrow the foreign exchange necessary to service her debt to the banks. But the banks continued lending, since the business was good, oil money was swelling their coffers, and no bank wanted to risk rocking a boat which was already close to swamping. Finally, banks assumed that when push came to shove, if Mexico were unable to meet her obligations, Washington would help. This assumption proved correct. When Mexico threatened to default, the U.S. government quickly came up with $2 billion, in the form of advance payments for crude oil and credits for grain imports.

At least one positive aspect of this pattern can be identified— the issue at stake is clearly defined. If Washington is expected to save American banks from their bad loans to politically important countries, should not the American government have something to say about the bank policies it is tacitly insuring? International lending to nations like Mexico, Brazil, Turkey, Argentina, and Poland is now inseparably tied to U.S. foreign policy, but the procedures for managing this tie are weak and fraught with ideological confusion. As my colleague Philip Wellons concludes: "A look at the dispersion of authority among the Departments of State and Treasury and the independent regulatory agencies, the Federal Reserve Board, and the Comptroller of the Currency reveals that the U.S. government agencies are simply not organized to use the banks for political ends except at the highest levels, and then only in such emergencies as the Iran Crisis."[40] A familiar question arises in this new context: How big a catastrophe must occur before our international banks and the U.S. government begin to think coherently about the national interest, and devise a strategy to implement it?

Myer Rashish, when he was Undersecretary of State for Economic Affairs, told a group of New York bankers in November of 1981 that things had to change.

> The sheer weight of international lending in private markets will not allow us to go our separate ways. Both government and bankers should recognize that in formulating policy toward international lending, there are areas of shared interest which may call for close cooperation, as well as areas of potential friction which may divide us on fundamental questions.[41]

Noting the key role played by private banks in financing the balance-of-payments deficits of developing countries, Rashish stressed the importance of encouraging those countries to adopt "sound economic adjustment policies." By that he meant austerity: the governments had to spend less and the nation had to earn more, by becoming more competitive, by consuming less and investing more.

But who can tell a sovereign country like Mexico to tighten its belt—to cut wages, restrain social spending, end corruption? Certainly not Citibank, or Chase, or the U.S. government. There is, however, a partial answer: the International Monetary Fund, the world's lender of last resort, has shown itself to be extraordinarily adept at doing just these things. Quietly and effectively, in countries as varied as Sri Lanka and the United Kingdom, the IMF has said, in effect: "If you don't shape up, you won't get any more money from us or anybody else."

The IMF's critical role was in jeopardy in 1982 because the Reagan administration expressed an unwillingness to expand its pool of money. This was truly an odd and dangerous turn of events. At the very juncture when the international financial system most resembled a house of cards—and a shaky house of cards, at that—the United States backed away from the one international agency which had shown itself to be capable of holding that system together. Combined with Washington's actions in Mexico, this posture indicated that the U.S. government preferred to undertake bail-outs on its own—an expensive prospect of questionable effect, since it was unlikely to be as effective as the IMF in forcing economic sense on the debtors. Predictably, by the end of the year the administration had been forced, grudgingly, to accept at least some increase in IMF funds.

It would be naive to suppose that U.S. banks and government officials do not discuss their mutual concerns regarding politically important countries. The banks are certainly apprehensive as their market share erodes in the face of competition from European and Japanese financial institutions, which operate in close cooperation with their home governments to promote both the trading interests of domestic companies and their government's foreign policy. The governments have reciprocated. Japan, for example, requires only low reserve requirements, thus encouraging Japanese banks to lend at low margins; in the United States, an array of domestic regulations has badly constrained U.S. multinational banks.

Similarly, our government officials do from time to time request the banks to make, or curtail, loans to specific nations. The freezing of Iranian assets was only one example, but there surely have been others. According to Wellons's analysis, however, these relationships are ad hoc; they are not part of any continuing and coherent strategy. Rather than being part of a national strategy aimed at minimizing crises, they spring only from crises; they therefore breed uncertainty and waste.

In the summer of 1982, European, Japanese, and U.S. bankers, concerned about the huge international debt, were pulling back on loans to poor countries. The threat of a breakdown was mounting. "There's an increasing level of concern just about getting through the next year or so," said one U.S. official familiar with the global lending scene. Some 45% of the $300 billion in international banking loans was coming due that year, he noted. "If there's a panic reaction anywhere," he said, "it could lead to an implosion of the system."[42]

Concern was heightened by the disclosure of Securities and Exchange Commission documents indicating that Citibank had been circumventing government requirements on lending limits and reserve holdings. Karen M. Lissakers, an authority called to testify before Congress on the matter, said, "The overriding issue demonstrated by the documents is the ability of banks . . . to deliberately subvert the rules and policies of sovereign governments. While banks and funds move freely across national borders, bank regulators and government authorities do not." The documents showed that Citibank had apparently dodged the regulations by routing billions of dollars in loans through such countries as the Bahamas, Monaco, and Panama.[43]

"Getting around tax and monetary regulations is bad enough," said Richard Dale, a leading specialist on international banking at the Brookings Institution, "but getting around so-called prudential regulations—that is most dangerous." Dale also noted that SEC documents revealed "a basic philosophical contradiction" in Citicorp: belief in the "free market" on the one hand, and on the other a reliance on the Federal Reserve Board and other government agencies to allow "nothing untoward to occur" in the international banking market.[44]

When questioned about cases such as those presented in this chapter, business executives invariably agree with my line of reasoning. Theoretically, they confirm, a carefully designed co-operation between business and government would be better than the inexplicit, ad hoc, often surreptitious approach that is prompted by a sequence of critical events. In general, they admit that cooperation would be more fruitful than the adversarial approach that our ideological and legal traditions have inspired and condoned. But, these same executives ask, how can we trust government? It is subject to unpredictable changes at election times; it is overly responsive to the demands of conflicting interest groups; it lacks the competence to understand business's complex problems. We can, they conclude, do better ourselves, going to government only when we require its help.

This argument has a certain pragmatic appeal, but its fatal flaw lies in its unacceptable ideological implications. Where questions of community need—or the national interest—arise, government must (and eventually will) intervene. It will do so whether it has the competence or not, because it, and it alone, has the authority. It may of course intervene by rigorously enforcing the antitrust laws, in effect permitting the marketplace to determine community need. But increasingly, as we have seen in the case of oil, such a procedure is inefficient and unacceptable. In those circumstances, some combination of government—involving Congress and the executive branch—must decide community need, with or without the help of business. This is what Jim Tozzi of OMB and others like him in Washington have been doing. (It should also be noted that there is considerably more continuity in their work from administration to administration than is generally recognized.)

Business has only two choices. It can work with these evolving mechanisms of government to make them more effective and efficient, and to help them gain the competence and understanding they require in order to exercise their authority wisely. The alternative presents bleak prospects: it can neglect, combat, or corrupt those mechanisms, inviting continuing uncertainty and deterioration.

6

Defining Community Need
in the United States

The prosperity, safety, and health of the American community require that the current no-man's-land between government and business be better mapped, that new paths be marked out and bridges constructed. There is little disagreement about this basic principle. Controversy arises, though, when a given ideology is invoked to justify such a change. Our experience tells us that there are two possible negative outcomes: the ideology kills the innovation, or the inherent ideological implications are glossed over, and the paths and bridges that emerge are illegitimate, frail, and transitory.

In both cases, the central question is this: Under those circumstances in which the sum of consumer desires in the marketplace is not sufficient to define community need, how is this definition to be arrived at? Who is to do it, and by what process?

A related question, as I have said, concerns the definition of the relevant community for any particular need. (This can be a controversial matter, as well as one subject to wishful thinking. Leverett, Massachusetts, for example, voted itself a "nuclear-free zone" at its town meeting of May 1983.) The neighborhood may best define its needs for parks. States may well determine their need for various industries; the multistate region may address issues of water or electric power; the nation may assume responsibility for defense, foreign trade, and clean air. Finally, there is an increasing number of needs that depend for definition upon the will of many nations, both developed and less developed. At each level, there are—or will be—governmental mechanisms of some sort for defining community needs.

By unfortunate tradition, Americans tend to denigrate the competence of their government to make such definitions, except in conditions of major crisis. Even our governmental leaders lack respect for the institutions they lead. (Ronald Reagan, for example, when asked how he would choose key members of his administration, said, "My basic rule is that I want people who don't want a job in government."[1]) Under such circumstances, it is perhaps surprising that government in the United States is as competent as it is. We are, of course, selective in our disdain for government; we often marvel at the quality and competence of officialdom in other countries. We profess admiration for Japan, for example, where employment in the elite ministries is for the most part limited to those who not only are passionately committed to government work, but who also are graduates of the prestigious University of Tokyo.[2]

Perhaps our budding admiration for effective governments abroad is a necessary first step. It is government that will define community need when the marketplace does not—whether sooner or later, whether competently or not. It must; there is no choice. The questions facing us are how it will do so and how well it will do so. Will it be achieved through the pulling and hauling of interest groups in the courts and in the halls of state and federal legislatures, or by the legislatures, in some way relatively insulated from interest-group pressures? Or will it be achieved by the executive, acting in relative harmony with the legislature? And finally, whatever procedure is adopted, will government and business be relatively cooperative in defining and implementing community need, or will they be adversaries?

The prospect of government intervention to define community need in nonmarket situations makes all good Lockeans, whether in government or business, understandably nervous. Government invariably attempts it only when forced to do so by a serious crisis; then, in order to defuse the predictable opposition, it proceeds incoherently, ignoring the manifold tradeoffs inherent in almost every intervention. We have looked at one telling example: in the early 1970s, the federal government controlled the price of gasoline to protect the beleaguered consumer, at least temporarily. This action deferred consumer demand for fuel economy, which in turn delayed the conversion of the U.S. auto industry to smaller cars, and ultimately helped reduce it to a shambles as that conversion grew more and more overdue. Those officials concerned with energy prices were not empowered to make industrial policy—indeed, no such policy was supposed to exist—but the fact remains that they were fashioning a de facto policy. It was bad and incoherent, concealed behind a veil of ignorance and pretense.

To compound this sorry state, government often proceeds from defining community need to implementing it, or to stipulating in impractical ways how it should be implemented. This denies managers in the private sector the flexibility necessary for efficiency. After its early years of straitjacketing rigidity, for example, the Environmental Protection Agency arrived in the late 1970s at what was called "controlled trading" or "the bubble policy," a procedure for allowing business to achieve more effective and less expensive pollution control by dealing with a community's total emissions, rather than individual sources. In other words, business was empowered to manage the implementation of government standards. DuPont, for example, saved $12 million at its chemical complex in Deepwater, New Jersey, by reducing emissions from five large hydrocarbon stacks by more than 97%, in exchange for not having to meet 85%-reduction requirements at two hundred small, difficult-to-control sources.[3]

Of course, as much as government fails to respect the competence of business, business is frequently unrealistic about the authority of government. The Business Roundtable, composed of the chief executive officers of the nation's two hundred largest and most influential corporations, stated in 1981: "More than ever, managers of corporations are expected to serve the public interest as well as private profit." If they failed to do so, the statement went on, public opinion would force "further government involvement."[4] The implication was that unelected (indeed, self-appointed) corporate executives should themselves decide the public interest, and thereby still the bothersome hand of government. Other voices in the private sector have reached different conclusions. In 1981 the Committee for Economic Development said the following about the role of business in urban development: "Although business can provide leadership and even direction, the community interest ultimately is defined through the political process; corporate actions that conflict with this interest can undermine other community efforts." [5]

Let us now review some instances where the answer to our central question—that is, Who decides community need and how?—is crucial to the vigor and effectiveness of the affected corporations. The examples are in one sense widely varied: electric power, toxic substances, urban disintegration, and corrupt practices. But in another sense they are similar: the satisfaction of the public interest in each case requires a more effective conception of government/business relations, in which the competence of business and the authority of government are combined legitimately and efficiently.

If our real annual growth rate approaches the 4% that President Reagan projected for the U.S. economy in the 1980s, there is a good chance that the nation will confront serious shortages of electric power in the following decade. Lead times for the construction of generating facilities being what they are—now on the order of ten to fifteen years—it is rapidly becoming too late to avoid "outages." The problem can be simply stated: state regulation of electric rates, high interest charges, and antinuclear sentiment are making it impossible for the industry to build the capacity necessary to meet the future demand for electricity. This demand is now increasing as electricity takes the place of unreliable and expensive oil; it will continue to increase with the advent of new technologies such as electric furnaces, automated steel mills, microprocessors and robots.[6] The result, we can safely predict, will be chaotic, inefficient, and costly intervention by government, long after it is too late to follow a more satisfactory route.

When it comes to the generation of electric power, there is in America competence aplenty. In a purely technical sense, that is, we know how to do it. The following questions present themselves:

—What is the role of the various levels of government involved?

—What is the responsibility of the so-called private utilities, which now generate close to 80% of the nation's electricity?

—Who will pay the growing bill for electricity generation, now and in the 1990s? Where and how is the decision to be made? Who decides the tradeoffs among safety, clean air, pure water, and the reliability and cost of electricity?

—Is it desirable that the nation's investor-owned utilities be financially strong?

—Should someone be responsible for answering these questions at the national level, or should it be left to the fifty states, or perhaps to a deregulated marketplace?

In the good old days—before 1970—the manager of an electric utility was expected to determine and fulfill the needs of his community for electricity. State regulatory commissions set rates sufficient to allow the company to meet the costs of carrying out its plans, and also to make enough profit to keep equity investors happy and committed. Electric utilities were in a sense expected to plan the communities that they served.

"At Bonneville Power Administration, where I was administrator in the 1960s," said Charles Luce, until recently the chairman of Consolidated Edison, "we used to build in advance of need. That is to say, we built transmission lines and encouraged the Corps of Engineers and the Bureau of Reclamation to build federal dams to tie into those lines." A utility's responsibility included the economic growth of the region it served, and an adequate supply of energy was a prerequisite for such growth.[7]

By the 1960s, consumers of electricity were the beneficiaries of forty years of declining electricity prices. There were predictions—now quaintly dated—of "all-electric living." Environmentalists of the day regarded electricity as an exceptionally clean form of energy, and the public generally believed the assurances of the federal government—the Atomic Energy Commission, in particular—that nuclear power promised even cleaner and cheaper energy in the future. The relationship between rate regulators and electric companies was mutually respectful, if not symbiotic; investors were confident and satisfied. Common stock of utilities sold above book value, and utility-bond ratings had never been higher.

Robert Leone and John Meyer have described the companies' strategies in those golden days: "Expand as rapidly as possible. Preempt your competition by offering inducements to residential and industrial development. Price aggressively to encourage consumption. Construct large capital-intensive generating facilities to squeeze every last economy of scale out of new technology." And it worked. Declining costs kept prices down and customers happy. New technologies improved environmental quality and rewarded investors.[8]

But by 1980 the situation had been turned upside down. Long-complacent customers were outraged at rising electricity prices, and responded by sharply curtailing demand (except, of course, during the peak periods, when electricity was most costly to generate). Regulators were aghast at the frequency of requests for rate increases. Indeed, rates rose so rapidly in the 1970s that they completely offset the decreases of the preceding fifty years. Environmentalists were concerned about the growing use of coal and nuclear power. (In the latter case, once-trusted technologies had become suspect.) And investors were far from pleased, with returns falling well below the rising costs of money. Utility common stock in 1982 was somewhere around 70% of book value, and bond ratings were down in the low A's or high B's—that is, "speculative," or worse.

Utility strategies were turned on their heads in response. Again, Leone and Meyer: "Rapid expansion is neither politically possible nor economically attractive. Preemptive competitive moves merely increase the number of disgruntled customers. . . . To pursue economies of scale seems more like throwing good money after bad than the sound economics it once was. Conservation, perhaps the only strategy now palatable to all your constituencies, is at best a holding action."[9]

Consolidated Edison of New York, under the guidance of Charles Luce, was the first of America's great electric utilities to make this profound transition. Its story is significant for several reasons. First, the rest of the industry has had to follow in its turbulent wake; second, the transition was remarkably well managed, and may be illustrative in a broader context.

The company had been assembled in the 1930s out of a number of smaller pieces by a group of New York's financial giants: Samuel Sloane, William Rockefeller, George F. Baker, James Stillman, Hugh Auchincloss, and George Whitney, among others. It was run for decades by engineers in whom authority and competence were merged. Their job, as outlined above, was clear: to estimate demand, design facilities, raise the funds for construction, and then build and operate the plant. The New York Public Service Commission (PSC), responsible for setting electric rates, was composed principally of benign ex-politicians, many of whom were effectively in Con Ed's pocket.

As the second-largest employer and the largest taxpayer in the city of New York, Con Ed was inextricably linked to the deteriorating fortunes of that city. (Like the city, the utility had a reputation as a repository of patronage and corruption; indeed, its imposing offices on Fourteenth Street stood on the very spot occupied years earlier by Tammany Hall.) The converse was also true: two years before Luce came to his job, Con Ed had been among the villains of the great 1965 blackout that paralyzed the northeastern United States, depriving 25 million consumers of electric power for as long as fourteen hours. A long succession of "brownouts" and other outages followed. The company consistently argued that it needed more capacity, that reserves were insufficient for safety. A swarm of interest groups, however, prevented construction of new capacity, citing various needs for clean air, pure water, natural beauty, the preservation of marine life, and protection from nuclear radiation.

Of these groups, the Scenic Hudson Preservation Conference was perhaps both typical and extreme. In 1965, the Federal Power Commission authorized Con Ed to build a pumped storage station at Cornwall, New York, to be constructed inside Storm King Mountain alongside the Hudson River. In many ways, pumped storage would have constituted an ideal solution to Con Ed's problems: water from the river would be pumped into a reservoir during the night, when Con Ed had power to spare, and used to turn generators during the hours of peak usage. But just as construction was about to begin, a group of wealthy landowners—few of whom bought their power from Con Ed—undertook to thwart the utility's plan. They had the will (and the resources) to retain a tireless stream of lawyers, whose job it was to keep Con Ed tied up in the courts as long as was necessary. Aided by like-minded groups, they successfully hamstrung Con Ed, thereby depriving a much larger community of the power that it needed.

By 1974 these difficulties were compounded by serious cash-flow problems resulting from the escalating price of oil, upon which Con Ed was heavily dependent. Rate increases lagged behind costs: this was partly because New York City, while the beneficiary of Con Ed's tax payments, was simultaneously the company's largest customer, and consistently lobbied before the Public Service Commission in Albany against rate increases.

In the spring of 1974, the inevitable became evident: the company was broke. It could neither borrow nor sell equity. It was paralyzed by a political order that was unable to resolve the conflicting claims of its many subgroups. There was now no entity that could decide community need: whereas Con Ed had once done so, by the mid-1970s it was clear that it no longer could. It might still have the competence, but it had certainly lost the authority, and no amount of full-page ads decrying the utility's difficulties would do any good.

To his credit, Chairman Luce saw that there was only one solution. Government had to coalesce and exert authority; Luce's job would be to urge and cajole it into doing so. State intervention on the generating side of Con Ed's business was a necessity: the company was doomed unless the state accepted its obligation to define community need. Luce's 1974 appeal to the New York State legislature on this basis at first met with hostility and suspicion. Why, legislators asked, should the government rescue the ailing giant? Why should public funds be used to enrich private shareholders? Was this not just another bluff?

The Con Ed Bill, as Luce's proposed legislation was called, authorized the Power Authority of the State of New York (PASNY) to buy two of the company's plants. Implicitly, the bill also designated PASNY to be responsible for providing any additional power which the company might need. The legislature was skeptical, and by April of 1974, the legislation was in jeopardy.

Faced with the very real possibility of bankruptcy, Con Ed's trustees voted to omit the shareholders' dividend: for the first time in history, the company would fail to meet its obligation to its owners. Luce was roundly chastised by shareholders and the industry alike. He had, it seemed, betrayed the cause of free enterprise. He had disrupted the debt-and-equity markets of America; the value of utility securities plunged. Even his supporters, who agreed with him that crisis might be necessary to force change, felt he had gone too far, and relied too much on the instrument of crisis.

Was crisis employed overmuch, or recklessly? In fact, Luce needed the omitted dividend to meet his payroll. To be sure, the dropped dividend—and the ensuing hue and cry—was helpful in convincing the legislature that he was serious. But the Con Ed Bill, as it turned out, passed the legislature in late April by only one vote, on the last day of its session. Any lesser crisis would probably have been too little.

This example may well illustrate a case in which a manager made maximum use of minimum crisis to effect maximum change. By 1983, Con Ed was among the nation's healthiest utilities. By forcing the state to use its authority, Luce had placed responsibility where the authority was. At the same time, he had preserved Con Ed's competence to distribute and market electric power. The infusion of state money for the purchase of plants, the promise that PASNY would worry about new generating needs, and the stagnation of electricity demand in the late 1970s all contributed to the vast improvement in the utility's financial condition. (Growth in plant during this period of rising costs and rate constraints proved to be a serious blow to the balance sheets of other companies.)

As a result, Con Ed shareholders did relatively well. They earned $5.80 a share in 1981, an increase of more than $1.00 over the previous year, and they looked forward to an annual dividend increase of 9% over the next five years.[10] With its new funds, Con Ed was able to experiment with new technologies to do its job better, and also to keep its enormously expensive distribution system in good shape. The future generating needs of Con Ed customers are now clearly the responsibility of the state, a shift which places the responsibility for locating future generating facilities in the same hands as the responsibility for the inevitable political tradeoffs. It removes Con Ed from the political battleground, where it was no match for the disparate collection of interest groups arrayed against it. It forces those groups to take their claims to the state—to the community as a whole —which is, ultimately, the only institution capable of resolving them.

PASNY continues to enjoy the benefit of Con Ed's competence on the generating side of its business, as a result of the cooperative relationship between the agency and the company. Luce regards the fuel cell, for example, as the most promising new technology for the urban utility of the future: generating electricity chemically, the fuel cell doesn't pollute; it requires no cooling water; it uses hydrogen, which can be derived from natural gas or coal. In partnership with other utilities and PASNY, Con Ed is hosting and helping to install such a cell on Fifteenth Street, just off the FDR Drive in Manhattan. Generating about 5 megawatts—a fair-sized unit—its efficiency will be comparable to, or better than, that of larger generators.

Other utilities around the country are now withdrawing from the construction of new electric generating capacity. Indeed, little or no major construction has been begun in seven years; it is simply too expensive. State regulators are unwilling to allow higher rates now to pay for capacity in the 1990s. Environmental and safety norms are still unclear and uncertain. Consequently, increasing numbers of utilities are, like Con Ed, bringing public authorities into the ownership of what they now are operating or constructing. Many of those utility managers who chastised Luce in 1974 for "selling the free-enterprise system short" are now following his example.

In the southeastern United States, for example, Duke Power, Carolina Power and Light, and others have brought municipalities and cooperatives into the ownership of power plants. In the Pacific Northwest, all new base-load power plants will be built with federal financing. Even in Texas, a major utility was reported to be considering buying power from the Tennessee Valley Authority.[11] "Ten years ago," said Luce, "these and other like utilities would have fought to the death any idea of increasing TVA capacity, or any idea of going into partnership with government for generating electricity."[12]

Why are utilities withdrawing from the generating business? The chief reason, as stated above, is financial: costs are too high, revenue is too low, and both are too unpredictable. Citing Con Ed again as an example, its total capital investment is about $6.3 billion. The common equity of its shareholders is about half that —$3.1 billion. A new nuclear plant started today and enduring the predictable delays would be finished—if at all—in the 1990s, and would cost about $4 billion. Such a plant would produce a million kilowatts, one-twelfth of Con Ed's present capacity, including the PASNY-owned plants. "We would thus be risking a sum exceeding every dollar that the stockholders now have invested in our company to build one nuclear plant that would only increase our capability by roughly one-twelfth," said Luce. A comparable coal-fired plant would cost perhaps $2.5 billion, which "is almost all our common equity." Allowable rates of return on equity in most states are not even as high as the interest rates at which utilities must borrow; there are, in short, clear and compelling reasons not to build.

In 1982, fortunately, the industry nationwide had considerable unused capacity, perhaps as much as 30% or 40%. Critics accuse it of having overbuilt during the halcyon days; the industry admits only that it underestimated the degree of conservation which would be prompted by increased oil prices. In either case, we are adequately supplied today; but what of the future? With lead times of ten to fifteen years, will there be enough generating capacity to satisfy demand in the 1990s? Will utilities have sufficient funds to maintain properly the old facilities they are using today?

On both points, there is reason for grave doubts. Even more alarming, there is nobody in the federal government (or, indeed, in government anywhere) who is responsible for determining whether—or where—the lights will go out in the 1990s. We are faced with an institutional crisis, muddled but inevitable, which has the potential to be disastrous for our country.

In March of 1981, perhaps prompted by this specter of disintegration, Matthew Holden, Jr., one of the outgoing commissioners of the Federal Energy Regulatory Commission (FERC), staged a unique (and as far as I can tell, virtually unnoticed) conference. He invited leaders of the utility industry, the investment community, state regulators, consumer representatives, and other interested parties; he called it "An Informal Public Conference on the Financial Condition of the Electric Power

Industry."[13] This was the first time any such meeting had been held, and its "informality" was mandated by the questionable authority of the federal government to sponsor it, as well as by the FERC's inability to do anything about the problem at hand. (The commission regulates only the price of wholesale electricity sold interstate, about 15% of the total generated nationally. The primary responsibility for such regulation lies with state commissions, which jealously guard their authority.)

The conference took place against the backdrop of an ominous report issued the previous July by the Energy Department's Economic Regulatory Administration.[14] The report indicated that, given a projected load growth of something like 3% a year, "adequate electric power will be available in *most* regions through the end of 1989." But this projection assumed the timely completion of hundreds of new generating units. The report found that fifty-three of the eighty-six new nuclear plants "were not likely to be operational on the dates given." Delays also were seen for new coal-fired plants. The report also noted that 12.9% of electric energy is produced in plants burning oil, most of which is imported and therefore subject to disruption by foreign producers.* This is a particularly serious problem in New England, where oil produces more than 54% of the electricity.[15]

The report made no mention of the 1990s, and it was agreed that reliable predictions of demand that far ahead were difficult. Realistically, however, capacity that is to be available by then must be started in the early 1980s. "The fact is that given all of the uncertainties there is a possibility of absolute blackouts in the 1990s, especially in the Rocky Mountain states, the Southwest, the Northern Great Plains, and the South Atlantic," said Alvin L. Alm, former director of the Energy Department's Office of Policy and Planning, and in 1982 head of Harvard's Energy Security Program.[16]

The transcript of the conference reveals a general tone of incoherence and confusion, with agreement on only one point: U.S. electric utilities were in deep financial trouble. But then, as some said, so were many other industries; the clear implication was that in the natural order of things, the weak must perish. The

---

* Oil-burning utilities consume one-sixth of our 6 million barrels a day of oil imports.

consequences of the "death" of a private utility were not addressed, but there was a tacit assumption that somehow the lights would continue to go on whenever the switch was flicked.

Gordon Corey, retired vice-chairman of Chicago's Commonwealth Edison, led off. "The consistent unwillingness" of state regulators to recognize the effects of inflation and to allow higher returns on investment was "making it virtually impossible for utility managers to finance" the capital-intensive and clearly economical alternatives for the production of electricity. "Indeed," he said, "those utility managers who serve their stockholders best may be those who refuse to commit for new generation."[17] And the failure to commit to new construction and coal and nuclear alternatives will, he said, lead to higher costs to customers as oil prices continue to rise, and to absolute shortages in the 1990s. "If things continue as they are, there will be no private electric generating construction program in this country a decade hence. It will either be a nationalized system, or we will not have a system at all."[18]

William H. Grigg, senior vice-president of Duke Power Company, appeared on behalf of the Edison Electric Institute, the industry's association. Although "there have been no new orders for generating capacity in seven years," he said, the industry had $155 billion worth of building in the works between 1981 and 1985. With returns on equity down, bond rates eroding, and the cost of capital high, he did not see how the industry could meet even its current construction commitments.[19]

Spokesmen for investment companies concluded that "the cash flow of this industry has to be increased" if it were to survive.[20] Ann Faber, vice-president of Standard and Poor's financial service, told the grim story of bond-rating decline: in ten years—1970–1980—the number of utilities with an AA rating or better went from 60% of the total to 31%. Worse, 29% had a BBB rating in 1980, compared to 4% bearing that stigma of uncertainty in 1970.[21] The problem, she suggested, was the fault of state regulators.

The regulators, in turn, told of their difficulties in gaining public acceptance for rate increases. "We are fighting a grand conspiracy theory," said Leonard Grimes, Jr., of the California Public Utilities Commission. He spoke of the suspicion on the part of the public that the utilities and the regulators were in cahoots, and added, "Politicians are riding this coattail as a way of gaining popularity." [22]

Other state utility commissioners felt paralyzed in the squeeze between the companies' demand for higher rates and the public's clamor for lower prices. The companies were pressuring for authority to increase returns by including construction work in progress in the base upon which allowable rates were calculated. Consumer spokesmen vehemently opposed these schemes. Why should we pay today, they asked, for benefits which may accrue only decades hence?

Spokesmen for the seven hundred local municipally owned utilities and the thousand or more consumer-owned electric cooperatives that buy power wholesale from the large investor-owned firms argued with equal vehemence against any action that would raise the costs of electricity to them. The troubles afflicting the bulk producers are economywide, they said, not the result of overly strict regulation. When the economy recovers, the industry will recover. [23]

Jack Keane, People's Counsel for the state of Maryland, told the FERC, "The problem is not as severe as the industry thinks it is, or would have you think it is." [24] He argued that the country has only scratched the surface in the field of conservation, and that much more could be done to make more efficient use of the electricity we now generate. Referring to studies made at Princeton, the University of California, and the Mellon Institute, he said that there were "enormous market opportunities for conservation during the 1980s and especially in the 1990s." [25]

Joseph C. Swidler, Washington attorney and former chairman of the Federal Power Commission and the New York Public Service Commission, concluded: "The utility industry cannot survive unless regulators allow rates which are adequate to attract new capital." [26] According to Swidler, the regulatory system worked well enough in the past, when earnings funded new investment, but circumstances had changed. "Who," he asked, "is taking responsibility for the failure now to build for the future, when the result can only be power capacity shortages in the 1990s?" [27]

As to the amounts of money the utility industry would need to do its job, John Sillin, of the consulting firm of Booz Allen and Hamilton, presented some estimates. Assuming a continuation of the current 3% annual growth in demand for electricity and the need for a 20% reserve margin, the industry would have to invest $350 billion by the end of the decade. If it were deemed desirable to reduce our dependence on oil by building coal stations, he added, it would cost another $50 billion or so.

The industry spokesmen and their investment bankers were convinced that nothing like this $350–400 billion could be raised on either the debt or the equity market, and that there would be an acute shortage of capacity in the 1990s.

A solution which neither the industry, nor the regulators, nor the consumers favored was put forth by Dennis Bakke of the Mellon Institute's Energy Productivity Center. Decontrol electricity rates, he suggested; let the utilities charge whatever they want. This, he said, would force conservation and a variety of other fundamental changes that he felt were required.[28] Deregulation would mean that the total cost of delivering electrical services would eventually decline: General Electric would produce a more efficient bulb, new forms of decentralized and more efficient generation—such as solar cells, windmills, fuel cells, and the like—would become more practical, and people would conserve. The marketplace would thus control the rates of the large bulk producers much more effectively and productively than could politically sensitive administrators.

Tellingly, no one attempted to sum up the proceedings. In fact, the staff paper which was written afterwards has not been released, and probably will not be. By 1982 the confusion had, if anything, worsened. The Edison Electric Institute was purchasing full-page ads in leading newspapers trying to persuade state regulators to be more lenient.[29] The Department of Energy was in a shambles. The constraints on the further development of nuclear power were as tight as ever, despite President Reagan's attempts to loosen them. Indeed, a study by Graham Allison and Albert Carnesale of Harvard's Kennedy School of Government concluded that "commercial nuclear power in the United States has reached a dead end."[30] Robert B. Stobaugh even speculated that unless safety and waste-disposal issues were resolved soon, some existing nuclear plants might be forced to shut down during the 1980s.[31]

In the light of these circumstances, the plea of Charles Luce seems painfully obvious: "Sound national energy policy should not allow a situation to continue in which no institution has the clear responsibility for assuring that our nation has a modern, efficient, reliable supply of electric energy."[32]

Joseph Swidler concurred. In an interview, he said: "There should be a federal focus of responsibility, because energy supply is a matter of crucial importance to the national economy, and it is one that the states can't deal with alone. The trouble is that this runs into traditional views about federal-state responsibilities, and it also collides with the deeply held ideology of the present administration: that the federal government should do as little as possible, optimally nothing."[33]

Swidler's preference is for the creation of federally chartered regional power corporations, which would sell power wholesale to the utilities. The regional companies would be subject to federal—not state—regulation. They would be provided the authority necessary to build new generating facilities in their charter.[34]

He opposed Bakke's notion of complete deregulation. "Who would have responsibility for supply under deregulation?" he asked. "What happens to the existing plants? These things can't be moved around like buses or trains. They have no scrap value. Given the time lags in building new capacity, nobody is going to build anything without assured financing."

Supporters of the deregulation idea like it in part because of its ideological purity—letting the marketplace decide, calling on the forces of competition, and so on. It will prove acceptable, however, only if the community need it serves is carefully defined ahead of time. In the case of electric power, that need will not emerge naturally through the workings of the invisible hand. It must first be defined; then a variety of satisfactory ways may be designed to fulfill it, one of which might be competition. The other three possibilities are outlined in Chapter 3: regulation, partnership, and charter.

It is inevitable that government policy—at one level or another, sooner or later—will determine the future of electric generation in America. Swidler's notion that the proper communities to define this need are the nation and regions within the nation makes sense. Leaving the decision to fifty different sets of state regulators (many elected for short terms by voters hard-pressed by rising costs and reduced incomes) seems a prescription for disaster.

If even the industry itself is occasionally willing to grant the likelihood of this outcome, why does it not seize the initiative and publicly demand at least a focus of federal responsibility? For one thing, some companies think that they fare better under state rather than federal regulation. Even though this view may be held by a diminishing minority, it effectively prevents the industry from taking a united position. Other companies suspect the competence of the Department of Energy, but this is a short-sighted and dangerous rationale. If the DOE is indeed incompetent, the industry's responsibility and self-interest lie in enhancing its competence, and in urging it to assume the authority which is now so fragmented and inadequate.

Ultimately, we must understand the industry's current stance as ideological. Intervention by federal authority for this or any other need is anathema to the industry. But we are collectively walking down a dead-end street, which may soon be unlighted. The companies need to examine the pertinence of the old hymns —if not for the nation's good, then for their own.

A final reason for industry passivity is suggested by an industry consultant and economics professor, Charles J. Cichetti. He has concluded that electric-utility managers have been so bludgeoned in recent years that they have lost their will. "The verve is missing," he says. "Sadly, submission to the whims of regulators is increasingly becoming a characteristic of the nation's utilities." [35]

This rings true. In my interviews with managers in other hard-hit industries, I too have found this passivity: the sense of futility, hopelessness, and depression. Perhaps this is the most insidious aspect of the American disease. Leaders do not lead; those with responsibility do not fight. Timidity, born of resignation, discourages change.

In the mid-1970s, the chemical industry also found itself under attack: in its case, for improperly or unacceptably defining community need with regard to a variety of dangerous substances. Conditioned to adversarial relations with government, and relying heavily upon consumer desire in the marketplace as a criterion for product selection, the industry was abruptly confronted by a snarl of difficulties concerning health and safety. Although chemicals were increasingly necessary for contemporary agriculture, industry, and daily living, they were also contaminating water supplies, fouling the air, and killing wildlife. In the simple equation of public discourse, chemicals had come to equal cancer.

As the tangled web of toxicity in the environment was revealed through research and media reports, many companies continued to suppose that they could in isolation make the crucial tradeoffs inherent in defining community need: choosing either dead bugs or live fish, for example. Furthermore, they assumed that this was their given social responsibility—that if they behaved properly, government intervention could be avoided, as the Business Roundtable statement cited earlier had suggested. This assumption grew out of their sense of competence: if they had the competence to analyze chemicals and their effects, then they must also have the authority to decide how safe was safe enough.

Implicit in this assumption, of course, was the idea that thousands of companies making individual—and in their own eyes responsible—decisions would not only arrive at an acceptable definition of community need, but would also devise some adequate means of enforcing it. This was an impossibility. By the end of the decade, it was quite clear that the authority to define community need and to make the necessary tradeoffs was, for better or worse, the government's. To be sure, the government would require the industry's competence to help it make these decisions; the issue was how best to relate the competence of industry with the authority of government.

John W. Hanley, chairman of Monsanto, put it this way: "Our data base of information regarding effects of our processes and products on the environment and health is helpful to regulators; so, quite properly, industry and government are partners in developing regulations designed to accomplish whatever the law calls for. So we now have much more of a collaborative than an adversarial relationship."[36]

To a remarkable degree, this statement reflects a consensus of the leaders of the big ten U.S. chemical companies in the 1980s. What requires our attention is the nature and terms of the partnership: the procedures and standards used—within government, within companies, within the industry, and between government and industry—by which the community need regarding chemicals is being defined and implemented.

These are issues of process and of substance—of procedures as well as priorities. Some will be made manifest in the following case study of one company's decision to support the passage of the Toxic Substances Control Act, and subsequent developments. Others will emerge later. What should become clear, though—Chairman Hanley's comments notwithstanding—is that these issues are far from resolved, and that they will continue to be a subject of controversy in the 1980s and beyond.

In 1975, Allied Chemical Corporation was both a target of lawsuits and an object of opprobrium for its part in what was known as the "Kepone disaster."[37] Kepone, a highly toxic, DDT-like pesticide, had been produced uneventfully for some years at Allied's plant in Hopewell, Virginia. In 1973, Allied needed additional capacity at the Hopewell plant, and invited bids from outsiders to manufacture Kepone. A new company, Life Science Products—owned by two former Allied employees —submitted the lowest bid, and won the contract. LSP leased and converted a gas station near the Allied plant, and began making Kepone in March 1974.

Two months later, Hopewell's sewage-treatment plant broke down, allegedly because Kepone had killed the necessary bacteria. Shortly thereafter, LSP workers began to develop tremors, quickly dubbed "the Kepone shakes." The doctors whom LSP provided through an "informal agreement" diagnosed the affliction as hypertension.[38] But in July 1975, one worker consulted an outside doctor, who was concerned enough to send blood and urine samples to the Center for Disease Control in Atlanta. There, toxicologists found Kepone levels so high that they speculated as to whether the sample might have been contaminated in transit. They notified the Virginia state epidemiologist, who examined several LSP workers. He later said:

> The first man I saw was a 23-year-old who was so sick he was unable to stand due to unsteadiness, was suffering severe chest pains . . . had severe tremors, abnormal eye movements, was disoriented. . . .[39]

LSP was shut down the next day by Virginia health authorities.

In early 1976, a federal grand jury in Richmond, Virginia, indicted Allied, LSP and its two owners, four supervisors at Allied, and the City of Hopewell on a total of 1,104 counts. Allied, if convicted, faced penalties of more than $17 million. Private suits would claim damages of more than $8 billion.

The James River had to be closed to fishing because of the tens of thousands of pounds of Kepone that had escaped and accumulated in its bed. The seafood industry in the Chesapeake Bay area was devastated. In February 1976 the EPA reported finding Kepone in the breast milk of women in Southern states. (It was linked to the use of Mirex, another controversial chemical, to kill fire ants.[40]) A "60 Minutes" TV report dramatized the events. Morale at Allied was low; hiring had become difficult.

The blame for the Kepone disaster was widely shared. Allied accepted its guilt and was determined to take whatever measures were necessary to avoid a recurrence. The government, for its part, presented an array of authorities that was badly fragmented and ineffective. The Virginia Air Quality Resources Board had an air-monitoring facility within a quarter of a mile of LSP, but it did not check Kepone emissions. Virginia's Water Quality Control Board apparently knew that there were serious problems at the LSP plant, but did not choose to shut it down, trying instead to persuade the company to change its ways. In the fall of 1974, an LSP employee had written to the Occupational Safety and Health Administration (OSHA) claiming that he had been fired for refusing to work in unsafe conditions; OSHA accepted the assurances of LSP's owners that there was in fact no problem. The Environmental Protection Agency sent an inspector to LSP in March 1975; he found himself uncertain whether EPA even had jurisdiction over pesticides. (The inspector's letter of inquiry to the EPA regional office in Philadelphia was still unanswered when LSP was closed.)

In June 1976, Allied managers faced two decisions about what to do in order to avoid another "Kepone." First, should the company introduce a new internal company program called Total Product Responsibility (TPR)? And second, should it support, oppose, or remain neutral toward the Toxic Substances Control Act (TSCA) then making its way through Congress?

TPR, as described in an internal Allied memorandum, would

tighten and centralize control of chemical production, and would also extend the company's responsibilities into a new realm: that of ensuring that its customers were reliable, and would use Allied products safely. "A product would not be sold to a customer where it is known that the end use application is not proper," said the program memorandum. "Hazardous products should not be sold to new customers until the capability of that customer is deemed adequate."[41]

TSCA was another new approach to the regulation of harmful chemicals: it aimed at preventing chemical damage to human health, rather than outlining remedial actions to be taken after the damage was done. It also empowered the EPA to control the production of any new chemical. In effect, it argued that when it came to chemicals, the government (more specifically, a new Office of Toxic Substances) had to decide what "safe" meant.

Allied's managers, by and large, hoped for less government intervention, not more; they were especially concerned about regulation as stringent and extensive as TSCA. Their preference, of course, was for TPR: this was the approach that would allow Allied to control its own destiny.

With modest fanfare, TPR was inaugurated. It was not long, however, before its weaknesses became apparent. While the company could and did tighten internal procedures, it was simply not possible for Allied to be totally responsible for its products. The thorniest area concerned customers: were salesmen to give quizzes to their potential customers to determine whether they were competent to use dangerous chemicals? Even suggesting an indefinite responsibility was perilous: Allied's lawyers feared suits from persons injured by an Allied product long after the company had lost control over it. "Product responsibility" was fine, in short, but the concept of "total" responsibility had to be abandoned. It was impractical, misleading, and risky.

But if Allied could not take total responsibility for its products, who would? A protracted examination of this question, conducted in light of TPR's obvious weaknesses, led Allied to change its posture toward TSCA. In cooperation with the other major chemical companies, Allied moved from neutrality toward an active effort in support of the passage of TSCA, lobbying to make sure that it was practical, effective, and comprehensive. In effect, the companies said: "Our future depends upon a timely and reliable definition of community need regarding chemicals. We cannot decide how safe is safe enough. We cannot make the tradeoffs between dead bugs, live fish, tremors, contamination, etc. That is government's task. We depend on the exercise by government of its authority.'' The effort was successful: TSCA was passed by a large majority in 1976.

The problem was that while the government (in the body of the newly formed Office of Toxic Substances, or OTS) finally had the necessary authority, its workforce—fifty-two employees in 1976—did not have the competence to identify all toxic substances, rank them, make rules governing their production and use, and then enforce those rules. Even with the six hundred employees it had in 1980, OTS couldn't begin to do that. Its effectiveness depended entirely upon ready access to the competence of the chemical industry.

Anticipating problems that might result from this new relationship, Allied launched a major effort to change the attitudes of its managers, up and down the line. Government could no longer be viewed as an unwanted intruder. Richard Ashley, Allied's vice-president for chemicals, said in 1979:

> There has been a big change in the last two years, a shift towards obeying the sense of spirit of the law and not just the letter. We are trying to shift from being adversaries to offering cooperation. . . . This isn't just idealism. It's hardnosed pragmatism.[42]

An example: the company had been participating in a $2-million Business Roundtable study of the costs of government regulation. In 1979 Allied withdrew from the study, worried that its participation might give its employees the impression that regulation was bad. Performance evaluations were changed to encourage executives to think imaginatively and cooperatively with government officials about enhanced safety in production and use of chemicals. And Allied managers developed close working relations with the officials at OTS. Joel Charm, director of product safety, said in 1979 of OTS:

> We want to see it become a well-organized unit with staff large and competent enough to do its job. Good organization tends to mean quicker and more competent decisions. We work with OTS on a scientist-to-scientist basis, not scientist-to-bureaucrat.[43]

And, he continued, "We would be reluctant to see cuts in OTS's budget. That would make it harder for them and for us to do our work."

Note the emphasis on "competence." It would be competence, more than any other factor, that would generate respect in the industry for the authority of its new partner in government.

Similarly, in government, the adversarial attitudes that had characterized EPA in the early 1970s had been greatly muted by 1979. The professionalism and competence of the agency had increased, in part because officials at OTS were particularly mindful of their need for industry's help.

Cynthia Kelly, an OTS researcher, was in charge of taking an inventory of all chemical substances in commercial use. The list came to some fifty thousand by 1982. "To develop the inventory," she said, "we held eighteen public meetings with representatives of industry labor, environmental groups, EPA staff, and others. Overall, the process worked well. My impression is that all parties were delighted to discuss, provide technical inputs, and help shape the final regulation. The process substantially contributed to the technical soundness of the inventory regulations, and made all parties understand the balancing that EPA had to perform to reconcile the often competing interests of industry and other groups." [44]

In January 1980, Allied was warmly praised for its new ways. "Federal regulators are delighted," reported *The New York Times*. "The Environmental Protection Agency praises the calibre of Allied's new safety managers and the company's cooperative spirit. The agency even touts Allied . . . as a model for other companies." [45]

Given these close and cooperative relations with EPA and other regulatory agencies, it was understandable why the chemical industry spoke out as bluntly as it did against the policies of President Reagan and EPA. Budget cuts and sagging morale were pushing some of the most capable EPA officials out of the government.

"It's the worst possible thing that could have happened," said the CEO of one major manufacturing company in an interview, "because we're not going to get away from the fact that federal agencies must set national environmental standards. In the late 1970s we were making some real progress, getting high-quality professionals into EPA who were prepared to work closely with the industry. Now the cream of the crop is leaving.''[46]

''An ineffective EPA is not what the chemical industry needs,'' said the industry's journal, *Chemical Week,* in October 1981. The editorial proceeded to reprimand both EPA Administrator Anne M. Gorsuch and the administration for attempting to centralize decision-making, presumably referring both to the agency itself and to Jim Tozzi's cost-benefit analysis in OMB (see Chapter 5). ''Firm management at the top is good. A management attitude that turns off hundreds of competent and dedicated professionals —and EPA has them—is not good.''[47] ''If EPA can't operate, we can't either,'' confirmed Geraldine Cox, technical vice-president of the Chemical Manufacturers Association.[48]

Although the increased centralization of regulatory power in the OMB certainly caused a decline in EPA morale and effectiveness, interviews in the agency revealed that a larger problem was Agency administrator Anne Gorsuch (later Burford) herself.[49] EPA professionals considered her incompetent, both technically and as a manager. Before coming to Washington, she had been employed part-time by Rocky Mountain Bell Telephone Company to secure easements across farms; as a lawyer, she had never managed more than seven people. Early in her tenure she gave the impression that she mistrusted the career employees of EPA—that they were on the ''wrong side'' of some ideological line. (Indeed, like President Reagan and several of his predecessors, she appeared hostile to the institution she had to manage.)

Consequently, decisions that had once been made in a decentralized fashion required the attention of her immediate staff, composed of lawyers and public-affairs professionals drawn largely from industry. Amendments to state air-quality plans, for example—which before Gorsuch's appointment had been routinely handled by regional EPA offices—now had to be approved by her lieutenants. Career personnel felt that she was unwilling to listen or to learn from them.

The EPA budget was cut by 17% in fiscal 1983, even while Congress was effectively doubling the agency's workload. These factors, combined with the administrator's troublesome managerial methods, meant that both regulation and decisions on regulatory relief were long delayed, at great cost to industry. Thus the governmental side of the partnership—constructed so laboriously during the turbulent 1970s—began to deteriorate badly. Washington's capacity to make reliable and timely decisions about the community need atrophied. As a result, in 1982 some state governments began to step up their regulatory activity, often setting stricter standards for industry than the federal government had. California, for example, tightened standards on pesticides and weed killers. New York, Massachusetts, and Rhode Island instilled tough regulations regarding the transportation of hazardous substances. Ironically, Administration officials found it awkward to object to these initiatives: "states' rights" was, after all, an important element in their ideological approach to government—a good example of the debilitating effects of ambivalence.[50]

At the same time, other states—suffering from budget cuts—reduced their enforcement activity. Russell Train, EPA administrator under President Ford, feared that some were trying to undercut each other by scaling back environmental programs to attract industry. "It's clearly in the national interest," he said, "to maintain uniform national standards for large, very competitive industries."[51]

In March 1983, Burford was forced out. Her failure, it appeared, was due to a denial of the ecological reality and to carelessness in her cooperation with business. There was a partnership of sorts, but its terms and criteria were obscure and questionable.

There was little doubt in the minds of industry leaders that, in the words of one, "the pendulum will swing back." The need for national environmental safeguards and health and safety standards will not become less pressing. (It is estimated that some fifty-two new chemicals are synthesized every week in this country.) Large corporations in industries which are intimately bound up in the public interest, such as the chemical industry, will require some certainty about the definition of community need. Although they may well possess the necessary competence, they will not have the authority to make the definition themselves.

They will demand that the process of definition take place on the national level, because compliance with a multitude of different state and local standards would be unacceptably expensive. They will insist that health and safety standards be determined holistically—that is, taking account of the numerous, related aspects of the community need. These include economic growth, employment, and international competitiveness, among others.

Given this large agenda, the concentration of power which has been taking place in the Office of Management and Budget since before 1970 is therefore likely to continue. OMB is the most appropriate agency to coordinate the competing claims of the agencies and departments of the executive branch. The Office of Information and Regulatory Affairs (OIRA) in OMB will continue to play a central role in seeking to make the definition of community need more coherent and consistent.

The definitional process will require high-quality civil servants whose task is to gather, analyze, and interpret data with the help of the related industry. The role of political leadership clearly will be to encourage and defend these civil servants, using their findings to make final judgments regarding community need. At a given time, they may conclude that economic and competitive factors are more important; at another, they may emphasize health and safety. If the role of government is clear and functional, there will be no grounds for the kind of ideological suspicion that characterized the EPA battles of the early 1980s.

The other party in the leadership also has obligations, of course: coherence in the federal government will be fostered and encouraged only insofar as large companies like Allied formulate coherent strategies toward government. Until recently, few companies had even a rudimentary government strategy. Government was seen as a disparate collection of legal, legislative, and executive players, each of whom was to be handled separately. The game was adversarial, and essentially defensive in nature. Business sought only to win skirmishes, defeating a series of ad hoc government initiatives.

These examples of the power and chemical industries emphasize that such an approach has become self-defeating. At Allied, the effect of the Kepone disaster and subsequent developments was to focus responsibility for the company's posture toward the government in the office of the vice-chairman of the board, and to impose upon him the task of coordinating the company's many interactions with the government. (Before this delineation of authority, some of these interactions were managed by scientists and technicians, others by corporate policy-makers through the chemical-industry association or the Business Roundtable, and still others by legislative lobbyists and lawyers in the courts.) Because each level and category was at least perceived to be interrelated, Allied concluded that they had to be centrally coordinated. Other corporations have made similar adjustments, and as industry develops a coherent approach to government, there will be pressure on government to do the same. (There are already some encouraging developments. In a subsequent chapter, we will look at the evolution of the office of the United States Trade Representatives in the White House.)

As the executive branch of the federal government continues the inevitable drift toward centralization and integration with big business, the attendant ideological implications will need to be understood and carefully managed. Otherwise, as in the case of the code makers in Roosevelt's National Recovery Administration, the efforts will fail, paralysis will ensue, illegitimacy will abound.

First, the nature and terms of the partnership must be clearly recognized. Government provides authority and is thus the senior partner. Business brings competence, in terms of information, analytical capacity, practical judgment, and enforcement capability. The two must work together in a spirit of shared concern and commitment.

Second, for such a partnership to be acceptable politically, it must include representatives of other interested groups, such as labor, small business, consumers, environmentalists, physicians, and so on. An important product of the process is a continuing and reliable consensus about the community need that will hold up against attack in the legislature or the courts. For this reason also it is necessary to ensure that the relationship between the partnership and the Congress is well conceived.

Third, while informality and privacy are desirable for some aspects of the business/government interface in the future, it is plainly necessary that its basic elements be formal and public.

Again, the trade apparatus will be interesting to examine in this respect.

Fourth, the devices for the implementation of partnership need careful thought. In some areas, such as defense procurement and space exploration, the device may be the contract. In others, such as electric-power generation, it may be the corporate charter. In those areas where there is a high degree of uncertainty and change, perhaps less formal procedures are desirable.

At this juncture, it is useful to ask whether there exist today any entities which can help accomplish these difficult tasks. If not, are there prospects for any in the near future? A number of researchers at the Harvard Business School have been exploring for some years the usefulness of third-party institutions at the government/business interface.[52] Such institutions have the virtue of reducing the size of government without diminishing its authority, and simultaneously increasing the government's access to a wide range of expertise. Thomas K. McCraw's study of the Securities and Exchange Commission—a body which over the years has enjoyed a singularly high reputation—reveals its "third-party" strategy. The founders of the SEC, "confronted in the 1930s with a moribund securities market and a demoralized investment community," were determined to reform and modernize the system of capital markets in the United States. They chose to do this by "exploiting private incentives for public ends," using third parties wherever possible instead of large corps of federal employees. The accounting profession was "the linchpin of the entire regulatory scheme," certifying the validity of corporate financial data. In addition, the organized stock exchanges and the National Association of Securities Dealers became unusual and effective regulatory agencies.[53]

J. Ronald Fox finds special merit in nongovernmental organizations that help both government and business conduct research, analyze data, and reach a consensus. The Health Effects Institute, formed in December 1980 by EPA and the automotive industry, performs research on auto emissions, and is an active example of such a vehicle for partnership.[54]

A recent OMB proposal would provide government grants to encourage the development of such private standard-setting organizations, which could assume some responsibility for consensus-making. Such an idea is similar to a longstanding practice in Europe, where what the British call "Quangos"—quasi-autonomous non-governmental organizations—have traditionally been the tool with which communities define their safety, health, and environmental needs. These institutions bring together industry, labor, and relevant experts on a regular and continuing basis. After a standard has been set and a procedure agreed upon for its implementation, government is brought in to certify —that is, give authority—to the agreement. (In theory, such a procedure could be used to minimize both the size of our government and the level of its interventions. In practice, of course, such a procedure would run counter to our adversarial inclinations, as well as to the traditions of American managers, lawyers, and politicians.)[55]

Other procedures involve self-regulation by industry, either through the vehicle of association, or through the appointment of public directors, whose express task would be to define the community need as it relates to a particular corporation. Christopher Stone has suggested the appointment of such directors—who he thinks should comprise 10% of the board—by the Securities and Exchange Commission.[56] Both procedures, again, raise profound ideological difficulties: the former would quickly run afoul of the antitrust laws, and the latter would raise hackles by challenging traditional notions of management authority, property rights, and the limited state. Even if the inherent ideological problems could be overcome, there would remain the difficulty of authority: can the general good be credibly achieved by a small, nonelected body of any composition?

This is not the context in which to explore in detail the full range of instruments for organizing business/government relations. My intention is only to suggest that in the face of our inevitable drift toward cooperation and partnership, there are tools available to us; however, these tools all present a variety of choices which are profoundly ideological in nature. These choices can be made effectively only after their ideological implications have been discussed explicitly. They must not be obfuscated, glossed over, or ignored, as has been our tradition.

What does America's ambivalence—cherished, and yet increasingly dysfunctional—cost? Let us look at the brief, inglorious existence of one recent failure at government/business cooperation. The National Industrial Pollution Control Council (NIPCC) was one of thousands of advisory councils that have come and gone since the days of Herbert Hoover. Some of these councils have been extremely successful, especially in wartime, but most have been disappointing. The failure of the NRA, discussed in Chapter 4, illustrates the difficulties resulting from confusion about roles within business/governmental partnerships: business fails to respect the authority of government, and government fails to protect and exercise that authority. Business starts becoming the senior partner; government, sensing itself being corrupted, retaliates, and ignores the competence of business. Creedal passion ensues. The sinners are castigated, and the inexorable is delayed.

Richard H. K. Vietor of the Harvard Business School has carefully documented the coming and going of the NIPCC from 1970 to 1973.[57] In the spring of 1970, Congress had just passed the National Environmental Policy Act. The atmosphere in Congress was one of righteous indignation. Those who considered themselves "holists" were engaged in semireligious battle with the polluters, real or imagined: steel, autos, electric utilities, oil companies, and the like. (It would be a full decade before the public realized that jobs, economic growth, and the trade balance were as much a part of the "whole" as trees and water.) President Nixon proposed a comprehensive antipollution program, and called for a cooperative effort by government and business to design and implement it. He established the NIPCC with the help of Secretary of Commerce Maurice Stans; Bert Cross, chairman of the 3M Company, was appointed to chair it; and some fifty-two other corporate presidents or chairmen were made members. They represented the largest and most influential corporations in America.[58]

The council's deliberations were strictly secret. Only sketchy minutes of meetings were kept. Environmental activists complained loudly, but the members argued that "their work would not be forwarded" by a change in the ground rules.[59]

Writing reports was one of the chief activities of the council's staff, an activity in which it was greatly assisted by various trade associations. Vietor's investigation shows, for example, that "the Western Wood Products Association, in cooperation with five other forest product trade groups, drafted the report of the NIPCC wood products sub-council." In another instance, the American Gas Association prepared the draft of the utilities sub-council report, and the Edison Electric Institute reviewed it before final publication. Seeking the assistance of the trade associations was not a bad idea; however, these reports were printed by the Government Printing Office, bore the imprint of the Department of Commerce, and contained no mention of the contribution of the trade groups. This was a bad idea, and illustrates the rogue-elephant nature of the council, which went well beyond making the competence of business available to government. In at least two areas (timber management and air pollution), "it succeeded in modifying federal policies to the detriment of the environment." [60]

Ralph Hodges, lobbyist for the lumber industry, saw in the council a useful device to gather and employ what he termed "ammunition to fight the imposition of higher standards." The industry was eager to avert a ban on "clear-cutting"—that is, the leveling of virtually all trees in a woodlot. Hodges established a close relationship with Charles Colson, President Nixon's Special Counsel, who persuaded Commerce Department officials "to make a covenant with the forest products people." Vietor estimated that in 1972, "members of the Council's wood products sub-council contributed at least $81,000 to the Nixon re-election campaign. Clear-cutting continued unabated throughout the remainder of the Nixon administration until the courts intervened in 1975." [61]

In addition, Secretary Stans worked through the Office of Management and Budget to force EPA to lower the Clean Air Act standards. Available evidence strongly suggests that the NIPCC was the driving force behind the Department of Commerce impositions on the EPA guidelines. [62]

In this rather extreme case, business and government became "partners," but both neglected the essential terms of acceptability and legitimacy. Business went far beyond rendering technical advice on the basis of its competence, and began corruptly distorting governmental authority, inevitably becoming enmeshed in the Watergate scandals. Members of the NIPCC were generous contributors to the Nixon campaign: the individuals involved donated $707,000, while the corporations they represented contributed $1,112,000. Five of the thirteen illegal corporate contributions uncovered by the Senate's Select Committee on Presidential Campaign Activities came from council members. Bert Cross was involved in 3M's illegal $30,000 payment to Stans in March 1972. Orin Atkins, an active member of the council's petroleum and gas sub-council, explained his illegal contribution (of $100,000) to Ashland Oil stockholders as follows:

> There was a good business reason for making the contribution and, although illegal in nature, I am confident that it distinctly benefited the corporation . . . its intention was to give us a means of access to present our point of view to the executive branch of the Government.[63]

The dismal excesses of the NIPCC brand of government/business cooperation led Congress to abolish it in 1973 and to enact the Federal Advisory Committee Act. The so-called "sunshine provisions" of the act prohibited the secrecy that was blamed for the NIPCC's missteps. Since then, all federal advisory committees have had to operate in the full glare of publicity. It is another good intention gone awry: the provision has had a crippling effect on many advisory committees, forcing some to disband, and others to work outside official circles, in even deeper recesses of secrecy.

As we will see in subsequent chapters, the remedy for the problems exemplified by the NIPCC is not the prohibition of all private collaboration between government and business. It is, rather, to devise procedures and rules whereby the privacy that is often essential to a working partnership can be made acceptable and legitimate.

7

Unemployment, the Underclass, and Urban Disintegration

In the summer of 1982, government figures showed that some 10 million people were looking for work, and that several million more had given up the search as hopeless. One out of two black teenagers and nearly one out of five automobile, steel, and construction workers were idle. These were the members of the workforce officially recognized as "unemployed." In addition, there was an indeterminate number of people, also estimated at about 10 million, who comprised the American "underclass." These people were cut off in a variety of ways from the legitimate economy and its officialdom. While the ranks of the underclass certainly included at least some of those officially recognized as unemployed, they also encompassed many people even more marginal to society—single mothers, high-school dropouts, street criminals, addicts, and the mentally disturbed, among others. This group was disproportionately black or Hispanic, and young. Its members lived in disintegrated communities, cut off

Portions of this chapter appeared in an article by the author and William R. Glass entitled "The Desperate Plight of the Underclass," *Harvard Business Review,* July–August, 1982.

from the world of work, lacking political power, alienated, traumatized, angry, and hopeless.

It was these groups that were most severely affected when President Reagan reduced federal expenditures for welfare, food stamps, education, and job training. The previous October, recognizing government's disengagement, he had called on businessmen to address the problem, suggesting that they "take leadership and responsibility for solving public needs."[1] He had appointed a task force of thirty-five business leaders who were to lead the way toward "a greater public-private partnership." A year later, little had been heard from them. Their silence was understandable: they already had a full plate of problems of their own, and they wondered whether, even with the best of intentions, they had either the authority or the competence necessary to reknit the raveled fabric of industrial America and its decayed cities. They would be doing very well indeed if they managed simply to run their businesses competitively and profitably, perhaps making enough to invest, expand, and provide more jobs.

The business leaders were not noticeably encouraged by the President's notion that their efforts would be supported by "thousands of neighborhood action groups across America," who—once freed from the smothering effects of regulation and welfare dependency—would rise up to attack urban disintegration. (Reagan singled out for praise the House of Umoja in Philadelphia, where David and Falaka Fattah had helped "more than five hundred boys develop into self-sufficient and productive young men." By the summer of 1982, however, even the Fattahs were feeling the bite of government cutbacks.)

Let us parse the problem ideologically and determine our options. An authentic Lockean—now a rare breed, for better or worse—would suggest that the unemployed, the weak, and the destitute have no one to blame but themselves. They must either die gracefully or exist with appropriate gratitude on the charity of the rich. Such charity should, of course, be administered carefully, so as to instill in the poor the virtues of frugality and the will to work.

This, fortunately, is not the option it once was. Although there is something of this approach in the thought of Ronald Reagan and sympathetic social commentators—notably George Gilder[2] —it seems improbable that it will ever again win the support of more than a minor element in our society. Over the last fifty years or so, the idea of the rights of membership (to income, health, housing, and the other supports of life discussed in earlier chapters) has become irreversibly entrenched.

What unaccustomed scarcity *is* teaching us is that these rights are not unlimited. If we are going to lead the free world and simultaneously clean our soiled environment and expand our economy, we must circumscribe these rights. Every communitarian society throughout history has learned the same lesson: just as the community provides its members with rights, so must it also require duties of them. This simple truth has escaped many contemporary American liberals. Manifesting a classic ideological schizophrenia, they have been enthusiastic about the community guaranteeing rights, but they have preferred to leave the definition of duties to the individual.

Today, however, as Americans survey a constricted economic landscape, they perceive a growing number of citizens who are apparently failing—or declining—to define their duties. There is a growing communitarian pressure, to which even President Reagan has responded, for the state to move in and define duties: in the suggestion that "lazy good-for-nothings" must get off the welfare rolls and work, as well as in the "workfare" concept, which proposes that those on welfare work at some useful task (presumably defined by the state). While these demands have a reasonable ring to them, we—individualists as we are—cannot help but feel a twinge of concern as the state intervenes in these personal ways.

There are, in addition, new problems of fairness that such developments present. If the politically powerful tend to be the wealthy, then the state tends naturally to be most concerned about the duties of the poor and the weak. There is the presumption that the rich, by virtue of being rich, have done their duty. The active expression and enforcement of such a policy, as the gap widens and the bridges crumble between the rich and the poor worlds, may precipitate the unraveling of our societal fabric.

Less cataclysmically, but more immediately, assuring everyone the right to survive in a reasonably comfortable fashion, whether working or not, has made unemployment prodigiously expensive. A Control Data study estimated that in 1981 one unemployed person cost the U.S. economy $50,000 a year. With 12 million out of work in 1983, that comes to about $600 billion in a $3.2-trillion economy.[3] In the old days (a scant decade or two ago!) it was assumed that a dose of unemployment would cool inflationary fevers; but today, unemployment is itself inflationary. Transfer payments to the jobless sustain consumption even as rates of investment and production decline. Budget deficits to support the idle rise, necessitating increased government borrowing; interest rates go up, forcing up prices in turn, setting in motion a dismal, downward economic spiral.

It becomes urgent, therefore, to deal with idleness as efficiently and expeditiously as possible. There are only three ways of accomplishing this: government can pay the unemployed to remain so, which even in the short term is no solution; government can put them to work, under coercion or not; or government can encourage (or require) business not to lay people off in the first place, and to hire, train, and employ those who are jobless. The United States is drifting toward this last alternative because it is obviously the most sensible, but we are doing so without any explicit plan or policy. (Here again, it must be noted, the Japanese have long had procedures whereby government, business, labor, and schools work together to minimize idleness. This is today one of the attributes which make their society more competitive. By devoting fewer resources to the unemployed, they are able to direct more investment into growth and innovation.)

There is little doubt about where we are going and where we must go; indeed, these two roads are congruent. There is considerable doubt, however, about how long it will take us, and which procedures we will employ. And in regard to procedures, it is necessary to separate the three targets of this discussion: the unemployed, the underclass, and community disintegration. Although they are clearly interrelated—in fact, they do not exist in isolation—they pose quite separate problems for business and government.

Let us define the "unemployed" as those who have worked, want to work, and are actively seeking a job. Laid-off automobile, steel, and construction workers come to mind. They often belong to a union, or have some other effective political voice.

They are part of the mainstream of American life. They are motivated to seek and accept training, and with assistance might be willing to pull up stakes and move to take a new job. They have the discipline and habits of mind and body that are required to work steadily and successfully. They neither want nor need a dole.

This group would surely benefit from a national manpower plan, through which job vacancies throughout the country were continuously tracked and filled, and federal subsidies to business and labor unions were provided for retraining for specific jobs. They would also benefit from Felix Rohatyn's proposed revival of the Reconstruction Finance Corporation (see Chapter 1), the Herbert Hoover invention that had such a creditable track record during the 1930s. The new RFC would provide low-cost capital to start new enterprises and invigorate old ones in areas of high unemployment. Rohatyn has also suggested RFC financing for inner-city manufacturing and service facilities operated by private businesses, as well as for rebuilding decaying urban transportation systems and other public services. Higher gasoline and other taxes on consumption should be employed to fund the RFC; it should not contribute to budget deficits, nor divert funds from needed private investment. But, as Rohatyn has said, "both labor and business would have to sacrifice; freedom would be abridged. However, both fairness and wealth would ultimately benefit."[4]

These actions require the leadership of both the federal government and big business, working closely with organized labor. Unless such steps are taken, we can expect growing demands for protection against foreign competition, declining American competitiveness as normal economic pressures are artificially deflected from our American enterprises, increased inflation, declining exports, and a stagnating economy. Those whom we have classified as unemployed (and the generations that follow them) will sink into the underclass, from which an economic deliverance is far more difficult and expensive.

Americans have always bristled at the suggestion that they and their fellows might be members of social or economic "classes," in the European sense of that word. Our objections have been justified: the absence of a feudal experience in our history, and the democratic promise implicit in the American dream, have differentiated us from many other countries. There, vestiges of medievalism continue to reinforce the traditional notion of a class: a category of persons with a particular and permanent status in a hierarchical society, a status which—with its inherent rights and duties—must be accepted. Historically, there has been sufficient mobility in American society to justify this cherished distinction. But the 10 million or so people whom we here call the "underclass" have become entrapped in a class structure well within the medieval definition—and their number is increasing.[5]

The members of the underclass live for the most part in disintegrated urban neighborhoods, where they are increasingly cut off from the rest of society. Their situation is very different from that of the traditional immigrant communities, which were tied together not only by a common ethnic heritage, but also by a zealous faith in the institutions of America. For most immigrant groups, the arrival in America marked the end of a cruel struggle, and the beginning of a new life. Even in the Great Depression, which ushered in unprecedented miseries for the urban poor, there was faith that the political leadership could set right the institutional distortions which had created the disaster. And in addition to faith, of course, there were also militant organizations working for the interests of the poor, most particularly trade unions and big-city political machines, which fought successfully to gain access to the larger community.

In today's depressed urban neighborhoods, none of these forces is present. With the exception of a handful of largely symbolic heroes—the priests and other neighborhood leaders featured in sympathetic media—the mass of the urban poor are isolated, contemplating a government which is at best inaccessible and at worst hostile and life-threatening.

The underclass has learned, over the years, to live in a welfare economy. It is a deceptively cruel system: while it provides for their basic needs, it simultaneously raises the barriers separating them from the larger political and economic context. Indeed, the huge flow of federal funds to the urban poor has mainly replaced one form of poverty with another: drug addiction, broken families, loss of initiative and self-respect, and eroded discipline. Education no longer holds the promise of improvement, and the motivation to learn has been stifled. A criminal economy has blossomed, rooted in drugs, vandalism, and arson. This is the poverty of alienation, and it has profound implications for us all: without access to the rewards of the larger community, the underclass feels none of its responsibilities.

The creation of jobs is an important element of any solution, but unemployment itself is not the problem. The proof is obvious —there are many healthy communities in which unemployment is high but the jobless have not lost faith, and the communal ties have not been severed. For jobs to heal the problems of disintegrated communities, they must be part of a systematic reweaving of all strands of the community.

A heavy-handed cut in government spending at all levels might theoretically decrease the size of the underclass, by forcing some of its members to jump across the widening gap into the legitimate economy. Realistically, though, unless the gap is narrowed and avenues of mobility are reopened, the reality of urban disintegration suggests that the more likely consequence will be an acceleration of violence and criminal activity. Crime already has an aura of heroism for entrepreneurial urban youth, who see it as a way both to avoid the degradation of welfare-induced idleness and to gain power, prestige, and income. Unless the incentives and rewards of the mainstream economy are made accessible to these entrepreneurs, they cannot be expected to take advantage of them. The benefits of a general economic upturn may trickle down to the laid-off auto worker, but they will not reach the underclass.

Harry Spence, the court-appointed receiver of the bankrupt Boston Housing Authority, has described conditions facing the underclass in Boston. "The issue is not poverty. The real issue is social membership. People can live poor if they have some sense of participation and membership in the larger community. It is the sense of isolation and total abandonment that produces violence." As employers have left Boston, residents of public housing have lost their jobs, and in some projects, up to 80% are unemployed. Other institutions—unions, political parties, churches—have followed business out. "Without work there is no discipline," adds Spence. "People get up in the morning; there is nothing to do, nowhere to go. Without discipline there is no community."

Lacking any sense of community, many of the projects have become what Spence describes as "neighborhood marketplaces for criminal activity." Their residents are victimized by criminals, in part because police have grown fearful of entering the projects. (Law-enforcement officials are also discouraged by the difficulty of obtaining convictions in courts, where judges—many of whom are suburbanites—have often favored the rights of criminals over those of the victimized poor.) "The sense of abandonment in these communities is total," says Spence. "Fear is pervasive." Lives are lived behind barricaded doors; forays outside the project are mounted only to cash government checks and replenish food supplies. In Boston, a city with great pressure on the remaining rental housing stock, four thousand public housing units stand vacant—uninhabitable, derelict shells.

At the same time, the declining economy is forcing more and more people to seek housing assistance. Already, 10% of the population of Boston lives in government-financed housing. Another seven thousand are on the waiting lists. Rents, which are set at 25% of the residents' income, do not pay even operating costs, leaving nothing for rehabilitation or new construction. According to Spence, "The poor have nowhere to live. They face real homelessness—people living in cars, squatters. This is a new phenomenon."

Spence maintains that the only long-term solution to the problem is restoration of a sense of community in BHA neighborhoods. Economic, social, and political ties must be reestablished between public-housing residents and the larger society. Private industry, religious and nonprofit organizations, and government must work together to reweave these ties jointly; no group can do it alone. "It is pointless for some company to come in here with jobs unless at the same time the district attorney's office, the police, and the municipality in general start to focus on these neighborhoods," claims Spence. "A public-private partnership is essential."

Restating Spence's conclusion, if business is to help the underclass regain full membership in American society, it must work with other groups to reestablish the ties between residents of disintegrated communities and the mainstream society. Interviews with those closest to the communities reveal one undisputed truth: the problems are all mutually reinforcing. They are part of a circle, and the circle must be attacked simultaneously from several directions if improvement is to take place. For example, providing jobs is pointless if employment training, child daycare, police protection, legal help, credit assistance, and other support systems are unavailable. The task is to build a sense of community where there is none, to gather and rejoin the severed strands of trust and confidence, to build a sense of attachment to and participation in the larger community.

Change can be effected only when the environmental circle is approached on a wide arc, using the solution of one problem and the establishment of one tie as a lever to solve and establish others. This, as noted, can be done only with several groups working together, each in its own area of expertise. Corporations can provide jobs and management resources, but they must depend on the school system to train potential workers in basic skills, churches and social agencies to help alleviate the family problems that interfere with work performance, local government to provide police protection and public services for a safe, functional work and community environment, and small-business entrepreneurs to bring commercial services to larger firms and their employees.

Along with a holistic, cooperative approach, any successful attempt to attack these problems must have two general and fundamental characteristics. (Readers who have attended my arguments from the first chapters will surely anticipate them.) First, there must be *competence* to deal with the problems of the underclass: the collection of skills, resources, capabilities, and understanding required to penetrate the circle of problems effectively. Any organization or combination of organizations that would successfully effect change must have the ability required to select, reach, and be trusted by those whom it intends to affect —the disparate members of the underclass, some of whom are less accessible than others. A successful agent of change must be able to establish communication and other links with those who are outside the range of traditional institutions. But to complete the tie, it must also bring access to the resources of those traditional institutions, including jobs, training, political influence, and funds from the government and private sector. Finally, besides an ability to reach and bring together the two groups, competence also presupposes the ability to provide a level of confidence and motivation on both sides necessary for organization, disciplined activity, and new commitment.

Second, there must be *authority:* a decision-making process acceptable to all participants for setting the goals of community change, for determining the course and speed to be followed, and for making the tradeoffs inherent in any change effort. Introduction of any permanent and irreversible change into disintegrated urban communities is as much a political and social process as it is an economic one, and any new access point, however narrow it may seem, will surely threaten the status quo on both sides. Existing wielders of power will anticipate—in some cases correctly—that change will erode their influence. Those who have adopted the stance that any change is threatening will certainly feel threatened.

Attempts to alter the status of the underclass necessarily raise questions of rights and legitimacy: By what right does a company or other organization presume to change a community? In whose interest and at what speed are the changes occurring? According to what criteria are the costs and benefits weighed? The ability to answer these questions is rooted in the authority or legitimacy of the organization undertaking the change. Government is the normal source of community authority, but in many disintegrated urban communities, the legitimacy and decision-making authority of even local government are not recognized by the residents. In many there is an authority void; in others, pseudo-governmental groups ranging from religious organizations to youth gangs are recognized as legitimate sources of authority. Any successful effort to bring the underclass back into mainstream society must be mounted by a source of authority recognized by those on both sides of the new links that are being forged.

The experience of the KLH Corporation, manufacturers of stereo equipment in Cambridge, Massachusetts, illustrates the problems of a competence limited by inadequate authority. In the late 1960s, the company established a daycare center to meet the needs of its workforce, which was composed largely of minority women from nearby poor communities. KLH management, acting on a sense of social responsibility, sought the best advice and assistance available from local universities. The result was often described as one of the most innovative child-care centers in the country. Nevertheless, the parents of the children who attended protested that university researchers did not have the right to determine what was being taught to their children. They argued that only they themselves had that authority, and threatened to close the school down. KLH management ultimately agreed that the parents should supervise the school's activities; the protests ceased, and as of this writing, the school continues to provide high-quality daycare to the children of the employees. In this case, as in many others, experts had the competence to remedy a problem, but they did not have the authority.

Job training, on the other hand, is an example of the exercise of government authority without the necessary competence. In 1981, the federal government spent more than $6.5 billion on job training, but few of the trainees upon whom these resources were spent ended up with permanent jobs. Most of the expenditure turned out to be nothing more than temporary income maintenance. The failure to involve business adequately in the program, and to employ its essential competence, meant an outcome of waste and disappointment.

Business, as we have noted, can help reintegrate the underclass into mainstream America only in partnership with other agents. There are today a multitude of organizations that purport to address the plight of the underclass. Obviously, business must seek out the types of organizations that—as recognized, competent authorities with a holistic approach—can benefit from the competence of business. Five such types can be identified.

1. NEIGHBORHOOD ORGANIZATIONS. Throughout even the worst neighborhoods in our cities are numerous small organizations— grassroots, self-help, private, nonprofit, and religious—that are endeavoring to improve their constituencies' lives, and so restore a crucial belief in the future. (The House of Umoja, mentioned earlier, is one such organization.) Jack A. Meyer, head of an American Enterprise Institute task force studying how the private sector can address the nation's social ills more effectively, observed that "there has been a tendency to write these areas off as wastelands, when they have within them pockets of strength. With less federal money available, it is urgent to leverage what's

left most effectively. We've got to build on the groups that are already active out there.''

Marcy Kaptur, former assistant director of urban affairs of President Carter's Domestic Policy Staff and now a member of Congress, agreed: "You can't move into a community without respect for what's already there. Churches are crucially important. They are one of the few neutral places where all sorts of community people can gather to talk about their problems." She cited the example of Mason Rowell, who runs Guardian Electric Company, a small business in northwest Chicago: "For years he has headed the Industrial Council of the Northwest in that central city neighborhood—sort of a mini-roundtable of small businesses that reinforce each other. They jointly assess themselves for police patrol, surveillance, and street parking improvements which help hold the place together. One of the small businesses, Mrs. Harris' Pies, gives away damaged merchandise every Friday to the local settlement house."

United South End Settlements in Boston is another example of an active and successful local neighborhood organization. USES had its origins in the settlement-house movement of the last century, intended to help new immigrants adapt to American life, but USES has survived and evolved over time as the composition of its neighborhood has changed. Today, USES runs a variety of programs, ranging from daycare for the children of working parents to the provision of low-cost hot meals for the neighborhood's elderly residents. The organization's building is made available to other neighborhood and cultural activities. Just over half of the USES budget comes from state and federal government sources.

According to Frieda Garcia, USES director, "The ability of an organization to attract government money is an important criterion used by private funding sources, such as the United Way, to make their decisions." Garcia anticipates that recent cutbacks in federal funds will increase existing pressures on private donors, and force organizations like hers to maintain their activities on less money. "We have always pinched our pennies to get the most out of the dollars we had," said Garcia, "and we will continue to do that. But we are also going to have to try new approaches. I plan to analyze neighborhood employers to find workers who can pay full price for our daycare. I've also joined the Boston Chamber of Commerce to gain greater access to the business community. We can use their help in many ways, including management advice on running our food operation, and engineering tips on making our building more energy efficient, but our ability to reach out to them is limited by time and resource constraints, which are only getting tighter.''

Such community and neighborhood organizations, having sprung up and sustained themselves even in the environment of urban disintegration, clearly have competence; they have authority with the residents of the community in which they operate. But their reach rarely extends outside their communities to the larger society, where they might find government support, access to a broader capital base, and a marketplace for their products. Contemplated relaxation of federal regulations regarding daycare facilities, for example, may improve their chances for survival, but without ties to the outside, they will remain small and vulnerable. According to Kaptur, ''Small businesses are where the jobs are, but they are frightened. What's frightening is to be alone.'' To serve as effective bridges for the underclass, neighborhood organizations need the assistance of institutions in the larger society that can reach out to them.

2. FUNDS-CHANNELING ORGANIZATIONS. The Local Initiatives Support Corporation (LISC) is an organization founded specifically to direct corporate resources toward grassroots neighborhood organizations. Begun in 1978 in New York City with $5 million in seed money from the Ford Foundation and an equal amount from private corporations, the LISC budget had grown to $25 million by 1982, supporting numerous chapters around the country. LISC is directed by a board of private, nonprofit, and community leaders in each of the communities in which it operates. It serves as an intermediary, directing funds raised in the private sector to support the development activities of local community organizations.

The LISC concept had its genesis in past experiences of the Ford Foundation, which had attempted to improve conditions in the inner cities after the urban riots of the 1960s. According to Mitchell Sviridoff, LISC president, ''Out of that experience, it became perfectly clear that there was no single comprehensive strategy that made any sense. The most that anyone can accomplish is incremental gain. Maybe if the strategy is well managed, one can stop the spiral of deterioration and reverse it, but not overnight." Consequently, LISC is structured to raise corporate funds and direct them toward a variety of efforts where they will have maximum impact. Again, according to Sviridoff, "the only intelligent strategy now is an economic strategy, which will make the most of available resources in the community and build on existing strengths."

LISC packages its funds and makes them available in the form of grants and loans to well-established local organizations involved in development projects. According to Sviridoff, "Community development corporations and neighborhood organizations have proven to be one very effective way of arresting deterioration, reversing the process, and starting growth and development. They also have proven to be the best way of developing competent leadership and management of development programs. A great many things had to be done if the process of deterioration was to be interrupted and reversed. There were difficult political choices which no city management or no private business could make, and which only a locally based community development organization could make."

As an example of such a "political" decision, Sviridoff cited public housing: "The selection of who lives and who does not live in newly constructed subsidized housing becomes absolutely critical, because if newly constructed subsidized housing is totally populated by female heads of households and a large number of pathological family units, it is not going to be very good housing for long. There is no one who can control the selection process or the eviction process more effectively than a neighborhood organization. Unless you can control who lives and who does not live in newly constructed units or rehabilitated units, you are doomed."

LISC relies on the local community-development organizations to provide the necessary authority for the development process. By working only with local organizations with established track records, LISC buys into an authority that has been established, and provides the resources to make it more effective. Necessary competence comes from three sources: the streetwise leadership in the community-development organization; liaison with the larger community, and access to its resources, provided by the LISC staff; and funds and other resources such as jobs and training, provided by private corporations and non-profit foundations.

By serving as an intermediary, LISC assists its corporate clients and boosts the development process through local development organizations. As a conduit for corporate funds aimed at community revitalization, LISC can enhance their effectiveness by directing them to those projects and organizations where they will accomplish the most.

Sviridoff maintains that "the smarts that work in business won't necessarily work here. To assume that they are easily transferable is a naive assumption." This has been one of the chief barriers to the participation of corporations in community-revitalization efforts, as well as to the securing by entrepreneurial neighborhood organizations and businesses of the outside help they need. Sviridoff argues that LISC, or intermediary organizations like it, provide a crucial service in this process, since they are much better at placing corporate community-development funds than the companies themselves, and their quality control over the recipients ensures maximum impact for the expenditure. Sviridoff—who is cautiously optimistic about the potential for such efforts—believes that numerous worthy neighborhood organizations are operating in disintegrated urban communities, and that more funds will be forthcoming if corporations can see that they are used effectively.

In the larger context, the prognosis is less encouraging. The whole process clearly is limited by the amount of funds large companies can afford to set aside for community development. The same hard economic times that prompt government cutbacks constrain corporations; even if they did not, a doubling of current corporate contributions to the community-development process would replace only a small percentage of the cuts that have been made in federal programs.

3. FEDERALLY SPONSORED COOPERATIVE EFFORTS. Private Industry Councils (PICs) were established by the Comprehensive Employment and Training Act during the Carter administration. The purpose of the legislation was to provide employment and job training for the unemployed, and the specific objective of the PICs was to assure private industry participation in the design and

structure of government-funded job-training programs. PICs are directed by a board comprising leaders from the public, community, and private sectors, and they are involved in a variety of activities involving business development, training, and employment.

Ted Small, president of the New York City PIC, described its mission as the provision of training that will allow the structurally unemployed—that is, those without marketable skills—to obtain permanent, well-paying jobs. Toward that end, it first identifies specific job categories in the private sector where there is a shortage of employment candidates. It then starts (or preferably contracts for) a training program in which the structurally unemployed can enroll. Government funds supplement wages during training and an initial period of employment; in return, private employers guarantee jobs for the program's graduates. If a corporation has its own training program, PICs provide a rudimentary training (instructions on punctuality, dress, on-the-job behavior, etc.) and then lobby the company to admit their clients to the program.

Small cited an example concerning skilled machinists: by means of a survey of industrial activity in New York City, the PIC discovered that small manufacturing companies were turning down potential business because of a shortage of skilled machinists. On the advice of potential employers, the PIC set up a machinist-training program (the only one of its kind in New York), which has succeeded in placing formerly unemployed men and women in skilled, high-wage, long-term jobs, while at the same time supplying the scarce resource that has been preventing the expansion of numerous small machining and manufacturing businesses. Small says that there are numerous jobs waiting to be filled, and no lack of persons who are looking for jobs; the bottleneck is in providing proper training in the necessary skills to match the people with the jobs.

Catherine Stratton, the executive director of the Boston PIC, confirmed that government-funded organizations such as PICs can provide needed assistance to private companies while fulfilling market and social needs. "Frequently," she said, "those companies most able to use government help—for new staff, larger quarters, financing—are least able to find that help by themselves. It is virtually impossible for any company to keep track of the broad range of federal, state, and local aid programs, or to determine its eligibility as guidelines and practices change." Through its business-assistance program, the Boston PIC devotes a large share of its resources to alerting companies to available government help, thereby expanding job opportunities for the unemployed in Boston. According to Stratton, "If you start coupling tax incentives with employment training, you are really talking about fairly hefty savings on the wage side. Many companies simply don't have any idea of the availability of this."

Small and Stratton both emphasized that input from the private sector is necessary if cooperative efforts are to achieve their goals. Stratton put it succinctly: "We have little to show for the great amounts of money poured into public-service employment. That kind of thing has never led to jobs in the private sector. Unless employers have a very large share both in the design and the management of training programs, as well as in providing jobs, we don't do very well."

Government, in other words, has the responsibility of providing the funds, but not in isolation: business must also offer experience and competence. In Stratton's words, "When you're dealing with the problem of unemployment of the most disadvantaged and least skilled, it is absolutely unrealistic to expect the private sector to leap into the breach. They will join in when we produce workers who are ready to continue training. An employer's bottom line is profit; it is not social service, not education. Government has a responsibility to provide a basic preparation for working to its citizens."

The training programs run by the New York City PIC are exemplary models of this kind of public/private cooperation. Trainees are prepared for real jobs, which are guaranteed by private employers. Training programs are designed by employers, so PIC trainees have the required skills. Candidates are selected, and subsidized until they reach entry-level productivity by public agencies with the authority and responsibility to help. Stratton maintained that the concept can be beneficially carried over into the public school system: "It's very important that business gets tougher and clearer in articulating its needs and expectations to the school system. 'We will hire your graduates, but only if you're willing to make some changes and meet these standards.' The demands must be public, and business must hold the schools accountable."

John Filer, the chairman of Aetna Life and Casualty and former chairman of the National Alliance of Business, has encouraged both Aetna and NAB to "support, develop, and improve the operation of the PICs." In his view, they offer a widespread, cooperative structure on the community level that is already in place. Even in the many communities where the PIC programs are regarded as less than outstanding, PIC board meetings can provide a rare opportunity for business, government, and community leaders to meet in a private, nonadversarial atmosphere —a necessary first step.

4. SEMI-GOVERNMENTAL DEVELOPMENT ORGANIZATIONS. The South Bronx Development Organization, Inc., like similar organizations in Baltimore, Philadelphia, Cleveland, Chicago, Newark, and other cities, is a nonprofit corporation created to plan and manage community redevelopment. In this case, the target area is the South Bronx, a twenty-square-mile disintegrated urban area which is home to some 500,000 people.

Created in January 1981 to continue and expand the work of the South Bronx Development Office (which was itself established in 1978 by New York City Mayor Edward Koch), the SBDO has received some $2.5 million a year—consisting of federal and state money supplemented by foundation and project grants—that it budgets according to a comprehensive development plan. Although it is substantially independent from city government, it derives its authority from a board of directors whose members represent city hall, the state of New York, the Bronx borough president, and the South Bronx community boards. By bringing in outside funds, jobs, services, and other resources, it serves as an essential intermediary between the residents of the South Bronx and their neighborhood groups, the outside world of city, state, and federal agencies, and the many private and nonprofit organizations that are trying to bring new life to this battered area.

"The key to the revitalization of the South Bronx is the stabilization and revitalization of its private sector economy—the creation of jobs through industrial growth and the strengthening of commercial areas," said Edward J. Logue, SBDO's director. "SBDO estimates a market for a minimum of an additional 5 million square feet of industrial space over the next three to five years. Industrial development at this scale could produce an additional ten thousand jobs. Meeting that objective requires greater availability of space, better crime control, improving the work skills of South Bronx residents, some modest transportation improvements, and simplified and standardized methods of administering government tax benefits and financing. Above all, it requires the creation of a 'shelf' of cleared, prepared and processed sites, and rehabilitated and processed buildings.'' Achieving those objectives requires the coordinated, holistic approach of the SBDO.

SBDO's achievements thus far have been modest, but still significant. It raised $110,000 from the Vincent Astor Foundation and the International Ladies Garment Workers Union for project planning of a 21.5-acre industrial park and nearby housing. The project, Bathgate Industrial Park, was well underway in 1983, with the first building completed and fully leased. The Port Authority of New York and New Jersey has committed itself to developing the next three blocks. The SBDO contracted with City Venture Corporation to set up a technical assistance center for small businesses, worked closely with Ted Small's New York City PIC to develop training programs linked to job placement and economic development programs, and secured the help of AVCO of Los Angeles to conduct a Job Corps youth training program. The SBDO also works closely with the Local Initiatives Support Corporation (LISC) in its efforts to invigorate local community groups.

Asked about the Reagan budget cutbacks, Logue said, "Much of what they are doing is good. We were seriously handicapped by excessive red tape and bureaucracy. Less regulation is great. But we cannot change the South Bronx without federal money. I think a Marshall Plan is what will work here. The federal government should get a plan from us for the development of the South Bronx and then they should let us alone to do it, working with the community groups and private industry."

The SBDO, and development corporations like it, are an attempt to assemble the necessary combination of competence and authority, and to employ the holistic approach necessary to achieve community change. It performs comprehensive development planning on an areawide basis. It provides, organizes, and contracts for competence from outside sources. It legitimizes the application of this competence through political ties both outside and inside the target area.

The creation of a development corporation with close ties to, but independent from, local government is an appealing way to provide continuity in the face of political changes in city hall. According to Leonard Lund of the Conference Board, "Business likes to have a stable local government it can work with, and which it feels is not going to be moving one way one week and another way another week. Business depends on planning. It must have the kind of environment in which it can make plans and stay with them over a period of time." Particularly in those municipalities whose local government structure leads to program changes based on election cycles, an independent development corporation dedicated to community revitalization can be an attractive way to involve business in the process.

5. DIRECT CORPORATE INTERVENTION. Many corporations have tried to address the problems of the underclass through unilateral actions. Most of these efforts take the form either of charity or of an extension of a regular business activity into poor inner-city neighborhoods. The Conference Board reported that a 1981 survey of its members indicated that some of them planned to increase their charitable giving, while many others planned to redirect their giving in response to the President's call for more voluntarism. This redirection entails the provision of resources to others who have the authority and competence to use them for community revitalization.

A number of other corporations have tailored their operations to directly affect community problems: IBM constructed a plant in the Bedford-Stuyvesant ghetto area of Brooklyn; Wang Laboratories has built in Lawrence and downtown Boston; Honeywell has pioneered in training and employing the handicapped; Chemical Bank makes a special effort to hire the underprivileged in entry-level positions; Aetna and Prudential have allocated a portion of their investment funds for higher-risk community-development ventures. Clorox, Kaiser, Bank of America, and Security Pacific in California; Hallmark in Kansas City; Procter and Gamble in Cincinnati; the Business Partnership in Minneapolis; and many others are recognized as leaders in the communities in which they operate. Most of these efforts are successful applications of a single, specialized competence (constructing a manufacturing facility, hiring employees, making investments) in a traditional business area where the company's authority is generally recognized.

At least two companies—the Rouse Company and Control Data Corporation—make a business practice of holistic community development. The Rouse Company has become well known for its success in turning decaying downtown warehouse and industrial districts into thriving commercial centers. (Examples are in Boston, Baltimore, and Philadelphia.) Control Data, through City Venture Corporation (a consortium jointly owned with several other firms and two national religious organizations), contracts to revitalize entire urban neighborhoods, planning and implementing industrial, commercial, and residential development. This latter example, which seems to include adequate amounts of both competence and authority, warrants a closer examination.

City Venture operates in some ways like a community development corporation. It contracts with either the city government or some other local public authority to provide part or all of a comprehensive development plan for a particular neighborhood. It then formulates the plan, along with specific performance criteria, such as numbers of jobs to be created, and subcontracts various tasks to begin its implementation. Working with indigenous local community groups while bringing in outside public and private resources, City Venture manages the development process according to its plan. Like any contractor, it expects to be held to the performance goal it has set for itself. It also expects to make a profit through its efforts.

Like LISC, City Venture had its origins in the riots of the 1960s. Control Data had constructed a factory in Northside, an economically depressed area of Minneapolis, in part as a result of a 1968 riot. The company had learned that normal practices had to be altered significantly to establish the factory successfully. New ground was broken: employees were hired on a first-come, first-served basis; a four-page application form was reduced to a half-page; a daycare center for employees' children was set up; credit was made available to employees, and its proper use was taught. A company lawyer even became an official bondsman, and visited local jails on Monday mornings to bail out employees. The eventual success of the Minneapolis factory led Control Data to repeat the effort in disintegrated neighborhoods in six other cities.* Each new factory was brought up to speed more quickly than the last, until urban plant set-ups were on a par with those in suburban locations managed in more traditional ways.

Through these experiences, Control Data gained knowledge about how to bring economic development to depressed urban neighborhoods. In an effort to make that knowledge more generally available, Control Data founded City Venture. According to Roger Wheeler, a company vice-president, "There is far more learning necessary than I ever would have believed starting out on this path, and I don't believe most people understand what is necessary to make something like this work. It's like everything else: it's complex, it's got a tremendous array of dynamics, many of which are out of your control. There is a tremendous amount to be learned. We've turned that learning into a product through City Venture."

It has also been turned into a market for Control Data products, according to William Norris, company chairman. By meeting a social need such as urban development, Norris claims, a company can develop the products and services that will carry it profitably into the future. "You look out the window and you can see a need, and you say, 'We can meet that need,' " he said. "We have the management expertise and creativity and we can assemble the resources. What we do not have we can gain through cooperation. If we do it right, we are smart enough to make a good profit in the process."

Norris says that responsiveness to social need is Control Data's corporate strategy: "We started in 1967. We did not have all these products and services. If you get involved and your executives begin to see gain as prospective, then you will develop products and services like Control Data did." He anticipates that the need for urban revitalization will become pressing enough to force a massive public investment in it, akin to the funding of the interstate highway system. He wants Control Data poised to take advantage of that anticipated investment; when it occurs, he be-

---

* It cost $2.5 million to bring the Northside Minneapolis plant up to the employee-training level of other plants. The government paid $1 million of that investment, and Control Data's contribution of $1.5 million was regarded as the equivalent of research and development for a new product.

lieves, the company will prosper as much as the automobile companies did from the interstates.

Norris and his colleagues believe that the prospect of profit is the only way to get business significantly involved in dealing with members of the underclass and reintegrating them into the mainstream community. They recognize that business alone does not have the authority to reshape communities, but if it is clear about its objectives, a company can work with other groups to get the job done profitably. Norris conceded that "there is an awareness that business just by itself does not have enough credibility, but if it will get these other sectors involved, then the private sector can speak with a very loud voice." Roger Wheeler added, "There is a natural suspicion that a big company working in a community is going to rip it off. What Control Data has learned is that there is a process by which partnerships between community, government, and business can be formed, and by which answers emerge in ways that have a chance to bring about success."

Altruism has its place in our society, but the greater need is for responsibility. Charity cannot be stretched far enough to deal with the problems of America's disintegrated communities. Money, furthermore, is by itself no satisfactory remedy. The problem is one of organization and management; it is as political as it is social and economic; it requires an intimate partnership of business with government at all levels.

What, then, is the responsibility of business with respect to the underclass? In an earlier day, enlightened managers might have observed the scene sympathetically, increased their level of corporate giving, and gone about their business. Today, though, that is an insufficient response to the social cancer in our midst. The full resources of corporate America are required, most of all its managerial skills and abilities. Those who argue that business should not be distracted from its central task—that is, from producing goods and services competitively in the world economy —fail to see that this worthy goal is unattainable unless the rising costs of societal disease are controlled.

Business by itself is helpless, however. A second element of its responsibility is to abandon its traditional view of the role of government, to overcome its ambivalence, and to urge—indeed force—government to formulate a national manpower policy, and to define community need at all levels. Business should assist government to do what it must do, and then stand ready to make imaginative use of public funds, as well as its own resources, to achieve the ends that have been agreed upon.

In this way the dreadful costs of decay can be curtailed, and the United States can recover its health and strength as a community. As in all that we have discussed, the initial hurdle for both business and government is ideological. On the strength of the evidence, we must conclude that every identifiable success in this large struggle has been characterized by communitarian practice. In the context of contemporary urban disintegration, Lockeans—even enlightened ones—have little to contribute.

New York City is perhaps the most dramatic example. On the brink of bankruptcy only a few years ago, it is now slowly recovering. "A great deal of intervention and business-labor-government cooperation was necessary," said Felix Rohatyn, chairman of New York's Municipal Assistance Corporation. "Labor acquiesced in a temporary wage freeze and a 20 percent reduction in the workforce. Banks provided long-term low-interest loans. The public paid higher transport fares, tuition fees at City University, and, temporarily, higher taxes. The state provided additional aid . . . credit assistance, and budgetary control. The federal government granted a small, but symbolically important, portion of our loans." [6]

Minneapolis, Cleveland, Detroit, Boston, and other cities have also moved toward partnerships, as political and business leaders work together closely and in collaboration with labor. But the movement is slow and the problems enormous. Not the least challenging is the fact that we must struggle against our ideological preferences; we must learn to respond positively to words like "partnership" and "collaboration." We must adopt a set of institutional justifications that are susceptible to inspection and adjustment. The task is to open our eyes to reality, and to do consciously and efficiently what we are being forced to do anyway by the rising tide of crisis.

Americans have begun to understand that the problems of our cities have grown from the inadvertent effects of government policies in the 1950s and 1960s. These policies, desirable in themselves, were disastrous in combination. Federal investment in highway development, along with mortgage guarantees and tax incentives for homeownership, hastened the movement of the well-to-do to the suburbs. Urban tax bases eroded. A massive in-migration of black and Hispanic poor occurred concurrently; they found fewer and fewer jobs, as manufacturing firms also moved to the suburbs. The cities sought new federal programs to compensate for the damage inflicted by the old; these new pro-grams created problems of their own. But the lesson is not to abandon federal interventions; rather, it is to recognize the sys-temic qualities of the problem.

Americans once had faith that there was no problem that could not be solved by the injection of money from Washington. Pov-erty was defined as the absence of money. If rights—to educa-tion, to food, to housing, to electric power—could be assured, duties would take care of themselves. And American business was presumed to be an inexhaustible source of money.

Then came what Ken Auletta has called "liberalism's Viet-nam."[7] Slowly, our attitudes and structures are changing. We are groping for a new way. As we do so, we feel the tension between what we know we have to do, and what the old creed has dictated that we should do. Crisis is strong medicine; it will clear our heads. But prudence suggests that we take as little of this potion as possible.

8

Ethics and Responsibility

The contemplation of the role of business in ameliorating social problems, such as those described in the previous chapter, inevitably raises the larger question of business ethics and responsibility. It is plainly folly for business to claim or accept responsibility for that which, acting alone, it has neither the right nor the competence to control, whether it be toxic substances, nuclear power, or employment of the underclass. If it attempts to do so, and in the process fails to assure adequate government involvement, it will be blamed for the inevitable failure, and it will be defenseless against the charge.

Standards of right and wrong are conditional: they derive in part from time, place, and situation. Earlier, we examined the unchanging values that ideologies express variously. For exam-

Parts of this chapter are drawn from a lecture by the author, "The Connection Between Ethics and Ideology," given at the First National Conference on Business Ethics, Bentley College, Waltham, Mass., the Center for Business Ethics, 1977, portions of which were reprinted in *Management Review*, July 1977, the American Management Association, pp. 10–19.

ple, the Christian admonition to "do unto others as you would have them do unto you" and its Judaic counterpart (to "do justly, love mercy, and walk humbly with thy God") are slightly different representations of a deeper and universal value. As I have argued, the definition, application, and institutionalization of such values often provoke disagreement, and vary widely according to time and place.

For most of us, it is right to be honest, but it is sometimes unnecessary and even undesirable to be completely honest. It is right not to kill, and yet ethical persons regretted the failure of Hitler's would-be assassins. It is right not to steal, but who among us would deny Robin Hood his glory? Right and wrong, we sense intuitively, depend upon the context. Or, as Garrett Hardin put it in his "Tragedy of the Commons,"

> The morality of an act is a function of the state of the system at the time it is performed. . . . A hundred and fifty years ago a plainsman could kill an American bison, cut out its tongue for his dinner, and discard the rest of the animal. He was not in any important sense being wasteful. Today, with only a few thousand bison left, we would be appalled at such behavior.[1]

In the 1970s there was much public concern about the ethics of business, and especially about what was considered the wrongful conduct of the managers of large corporations. (It is significant that the ethical conduct of the corner grocer was only rarely examined.) Was this because the number of sinners in executive suites had suddenly increased? I think not. Rather, it was because the definitions of right and wrong had been changing radically, and in the process had become both unclear and controversial.

Business, it was said, lacked a sense of social responsibility— but what, after all, is "responsibility"? Philosopher Charles Frankel has defined it as "the product of definite social arrangements."[2] From such arrangements are derived the dos and don'ts that constitute the subtle, coercive framework by which a community assesses and controls behavior. Today, the framework is in disarray. While it is perhaps sufficient to enable us to identify clear-cut villainies and to punish the scoundrels who perpetrate them, it is of less help in ambiguous situations. In particular, it has not proven adequate in appraising the actions of many managers who, in their own judgment and that of many of their peers, consider their conduct justifiable and well-meaning, while large segments of public opinion believe it to be inhumane, irresponsible, or corrupt.

In examining this difference of opinion it is useful to bear in mind Frankel's "definite social arrangements." I have defined these as ideology, and have suggested that two things have happened: First, the traditional ideology of America, that of Hardin's plainsman, has become inconsistent with the real world. Second, great institutions have departed from the traditional ideology, contributing thereby to its subversion and replacement.

Corporate America (but not the corner grocery store) has outgrown the ideology from which it and the community in general have traditionally drawn their legitimacy. In structure and practice, the corporation—as well as the government—reflects a new ideology, but one which has not yet been fully articulated. Our ideology is vague and confusing, and we are consequently fearful. Our leaders, therefore, tend to sing the old hymns loudly; indeed, it seems that the more radically we depart from the old ideology, the more lustily we express our devotion to it.

So we are today seeking to derive legitimacy and authority from ideas which are increasingly inconsistent with practice and reality. As we have seen, there are in theory two possible responses: 1) a return to the old ideology, making practice and reality conform; or 2) an explicit recognition of the new ideology, making the best of it, aligning our behavior with it, and preserving what is most valuable of the old. As preceding chapters have suggested, the first choice is impossible. We must do the second. Until we do so, our institutions will lack legitimacy; our leaders will have diminished authority; and the definition of our values will be unclear, and what many consider unethical behavior will abound.

Many of the ethical issues of our time can be better understood if we view them in the light of this ideological schizophrenia.

As observed in Chapter 6, in the aftermath of Watergate came disclosures that scores of America's most important corporations had violated the Corrupt Practices Act, making illegal contributions to political campaigns and payoffs to politicians for presumed favors. Many Americans professed to be shocked: how could this have happened? But our shock was somewhat disingenuous; political payoffs are in a sense a perfectly natural result of the traditional ideology. If the institution of government is held in low repute—if it is, indeed, regarded essentially as a necessary evil—and if its direction is supposed to arise from the pulling and hauling of innumerable interest groups, then it is only natural that those groups will tend to use every means, fair or foul, to work their will. It is, for better or worse, the way the system works.

Without excusing the misdeeds of those making and receiving corporate payoffs, and without in any sense minimizing their ethical flabbiness, we must acknowledge that more important is the systemic weakness that their behavior exposed. Of equal importance is an awareness of the consequences of correcting that weakness and a precise recognition of our choices.

How can we change the system? We might elevate government to a more respected status, acknowledging that it has a central role in the definition of the needs of the community and in the determination of priorities, and that this role requires a certain objective distance from special interests. We might then restrict the practice of lobbying, insulate government from pressure groups, and charge it with the responsibility of acting coherently in the national interest. As we did so, of course, we would have to be aware of the predictable threats which might be posed by a communitarian state: elitism; unresponsiveness; and perhaps an ominous, exaggerated partnership between government and large corporations, which—while displacing the adversarial relationship inherent in the traditional ideology—might evolve too far, into a form of corporate statism that could erode essential elements of democracy.

One of the most important uses of ideological analysis is that it helps to make explicit this range of possibilities, both good and bad. Understandably, those who seek a change in practice are tempted and inclined to obscure or mute that change. Rather than guarding against change, we must be wary of unexamined change. It is perfectly possible for the United States to get the worst of communitarianism unless we are fully alert to the choices with which the transition presents us.

The evolving plight of New York City suggests a host of intriguing ethical issues for business which also have important ideological overtones. In 1976 the Episcopal bishop of New York bitterly chastised the companies that were leaving the city for more pleasant and secure suburban settings. And indeed such a stand deserves a sympathetic analysis, since New York's principal difficulty in recent years has been the erosion of its economic base. In the late 1970s, there were approximately 8.5 million people in New York; they required 3.5 million jobs to sustain themselves, and there were fewer than 3 million jobs available. The result was soaring public expenditures to provide the unemployed with at least a subsistence living, while the tax base depended upon to pay those costs was shrinking.

How should the "ethical" business executive have responded to the bishop's criticism? We must acknowledge that ad hoc contributions to charitable causes are irrelevant to a problem of this magnitude. Private or corporate charity simply cannot address the absence of a half-million jobs. Second, the problem involves the whole of the New York City community. Indeed, it extends beyond New York to the suburbs of New Jersey and Connecticut. Furthermore, although history forewarns us that many will object to the suggestion, New York is in important ways a creature of the nation, and a victim of its demographic flows and pressures.

What is the relevant community in this case, and what are its needs? The answer has proven complicated. In recent crises, the political order of the city, New York State, the several neighboring states, and the federal government have all had to assume leadership roles. The city's bankers and the general public had to realize that their banks were as important politically as they are economically—that they are, in fact, inextricably connected to the political order, and that their distance from it has been part of the problem. Once the relevant community has been defined and the need discerned, action can occur in which business can play a crucial role, as suggested in the previous chapter.

In partial response to the bishop's criticisms, there is in fact little that business can do alone. The solution requires a partnership with the political order—and before that can occur, the political order must become more coherent and more alert to its planning function. Until business recognizes this (as it has, to a certain extent, in New York), it will be blamed—unfairly, perhaps, but blamed nevertheless—for the systemic breakdown that New York has experienced.

As noted in the last chapter, the go-it-alone propensity of business was particularly prevalent at the end of the 1960s, manifesting itself in a heady blend of "social responsibility" and corporate omnipotence. Those were the days of collaboration among powerful white urban business leaders, who were supremely confident that their wisdom and resources could overwhelm the problems of racism, poverty, and blight that plagued the cities. What these men failed to understand—even when the affected communities pointed it out to them—was that they had neither the right nor the competence to introduce permanent changes into the social and political milieu around them. The task of renovating the ghetto was above all else a political one, in which the business leaders could play a role only after the political realities had been faced and dealt with. They were part of a larger system, and it was the system itself that was malfunctioning.

The failure to observe this fact has most often resulted in waste and bitterness. Indeed, some of the most "ethical" intentions of business leaders can lead to ethically unacceptable consequences. I had a friend, for example, who owned a small paper company employing some five hundred workers. It was located on the banks of a turgid New England stream, into which seventeen paper companies dumped their effluent. In the spring of 1969, Harvard Business School celebrated Earth Day, and my friend, who participated, was truly "born again." Infused with a new respect for nature's fragile balance, he went back to work determined to clean up his effluent, and spent $2.5 million doing so.

A few months later I read that he had gone broke, so I asked him what he had learned. He was, it seemed, enveloped in a kind of beatific haze as he spoke of the goal of clean water, and of sacrificing material things toward that end. When I pointed out that the water was no cleaner, he said, "Well, that's those sixteen other fellows upstream."

"How are they going to get the word?" I asked.

"Oh, they will learn from my example."

"Did it occur to you," I asked, "to go to the state, or to the several states bordering the river, or perhaps even the Environmental Protection Agency in Washington and seek strict standards, strictly enforced, so that when you went clean, everybody else would go clean, and the water would actually run clean?"

"Oh, no," he said. "That's not the American way. Private enterprise can do the job. That's the social responsibility of business. We can't have those bureaucrats interfering with doing the job."

There is something noble, I suppose, about the individual who puts principle ahead of profits, but only if he is conscious of what he is doing. If my friend had said to himself, "Before I violate any one of the Lockean Five, I will die or go broke," we would have had to call him a martyr, consistent within his ideology. (We might have suggested some improvements in the tactics of his martyrdom, but we would have had respect for his motivations.) This, however, was not the case; my friend did what he did unmindful of the distortions that the old ideology imposed upon his perceptions and decision-making in a changed context. His stream was no cleaner, and five hundred people lost their jobs. With his ideological confusion so predominant, my friend had no business managing anything.

A final note of caution: when business leaders say that, acting alone, they can solve our community problems, it is usually only the unsophisticated who will tend to believe them. These same converts will be quick to blame business when the problems persist, as they almost certainly will. Anger and confusion—and violence, if the disillusionment is abrupt enough—are apt to follow.

The ethical fallout of Watergate also included the disclosures of large and questionable payments to foreign governments by such corporations as Gulf Oil and Lockheed. Bob R. Dorsey, Gulf's chairman, defended a payment of $3 million to South Korea's ruling party in 1970 as necessary to secure the continued favor of that regime. Senators questioning him pointed out that the company's investments in that country were fully insured by the U.S. government against expropriation, and that United States influence in South Korea was substantial. Dorsey was asked why he had not told the U.S. embassy about the problems he was having with the government. Was a corporate contribution of $3 million to a South Korean political party not the proper concern of the U.S. government? Dorsey's answer, while difficult to take seriously, is still symptomatic of a larger problem:

"Well, I suppose it goes back to a sort of lifetime habit, a lifetime experience," he said, "of having received very little help from the State Department and the American government in foreign endeavors, and very often finding they had little interest and would just as soon not talk to us." Noting that he was not speaking about the embassy staff in South Korea—which he considered "extremely helpful"—he continued: "Maybe I was basically ashamed of what was going on, I do not know. . . ." Later in his testimony, he spoke of American companies abroad and their relationship to the American government, saying, "They were sort of like motherless children, they had to make their own way in the world. . . ."[3]

What is at stake here? First, we must remember the time and the place. South Korea, in 1970, was a government strongly supported by the United States and seriously threatened by a hostile North Korea. South Korean politicians who were active allies of the United States and American corporations had asked representatives of those corporations for money. It was, from their point of view, the price of doing business. In this context, it is understandable why Dorsey—among others—did not turn the Koreans down flat. What is not clear is why he did not feel compelled to go to the embassy and report the matter. The national interest of the United States was clearly involved, as was that of a U.S. corporation. According to his testimony, he avoided the embassy for ideological reasons: he cited, for example, inherent limits on the relationship between government and business, suggesting vestigial assumptions about the "limited state" and "property rights." *

In any case, the issue becomes one of the relationship over time between large U.S. corporations like Gulf and the U.S. government. What should we make of Dorsey's contention that American oil companies got little help from the State Depart-

* There remains the possibility, of course, that Dorsey may be something of a Cold War hero. It is altogether possible that throughout the 1960s, the American embassy was assisting the ruling party, and that Dorsey was the conduit for U.S. government funds. Endless speculation arises: If this was the case, ought we to praise Dorsey for protecting his secret connection? Or ought we still to hold him responsible to some higher standard? This question brings us, of course, to our own definitions of the national interest, and the confidence with which we leave that definition to the institutions of government.

ment? As we have noted in earlier chapters, the record seems to support the opposite conclusion: the U.S. government—in the Middle East, Peru, and elsewhere—has been more than solicitous of oil company interests. We have discerned a covert partnership between the companies and the Departments of State and Defense (although, as stated earlier, there is considerable doubt about who the senior partner was). Looking to the future, and to the enormous importance of the oil companies, banks, and other multinational corporations to the community need of the United States, we will face a rising tide of ethical conflicts unless the terms of the partnership are made explicit and public.

The Lockheed case also raises ethical issues about the government/business relationship. In August 1975, Lockheed, a major U.S. defense contractor, admitted it had made under-the-table payments totaling at least $22 million since 1970. Some of the payments, particularly those made in Japan, were used to promote the sales of the L-1011 Tri-Star jetliner. Difficulties in both the production and sale of the L-1011 had pushed the company to the brink of bankruptcy; in 1971, Congress was forced to bail Lockheed out, agreeing to $250 million in loan guarantees. At that time, Congress established a Loan Guarantee Board with broad powers of supervision over Lockheed.

But four years later, Lockheed's management was defending its array of questionable foreign payments, arguing that they were necessary to consummate foreign sales, especially of the L-1011. The company also argued that such practices were "consistent with practices engaged in by numerous other companies abroad, including many of its competitors, and [were] in keeping with business practices in many foreign countries."[4]

Daniel J. Haughton, then chairman of Lockheed's board, told the Senate Subcommittee on Multinational Corporations that French competition in wide-bodied aircraft was especially serious. He submitted as supporting evidence a newspaper report that the French Defense Ministry had indulged in a variety of payments and "sweeteners" to make France a major arms exporter. Haughton's point was clear: in the interests of Lockheed's shareholders he had to do the same.[5] Was Lockheed acting in the national interest, or in its shareholders' interest? Haughton said the latter, but his use of the French example suggests that he was thinking of the former.

The central issue in this unfortunate saga was without doubt the relationship between Lockheed and the U.S. government. There were, needless to say, many connections, many of them confusing. Lockheed was, first, a major defense contractor. Second, it was in one sense the adopted child of the Congress, and answerable to the Loan Guarantee Board, of which the Secretary of the Treasury was chairman. Third, it was a major exporter of military aircraft. All evidence suggests that the problems and conflicts inherent in this tangle of relationships were simply not addressed.

The government, with ideological reservations, was prepared to help Lockheed when the company's banks went to bat for it in 1971; afterwards, though, there was little to suggest that the Loan Guarantee Board did much supervising. The board steadfastly (and somewhat mysteriously) refused to allow Congress's investigative arm, the General Accounting Office, to examine Lockheed's books and records, even though the GAO was obligated to do so under Section 7b of the Loan Guarantee Act. The board's executive director argued that the GAO was trying to "bully" and "harass" the company.[6] He spoke—although it strains credulity—as if GAO inspection of Lockheed would constitute an undue transgression by government against the free-enterprise system.

There is evidence that President Nixon and others in the U.S. government were active in persuading Japan to purchase L-1011s; we do not know specifically who, if anyone, in government knew about the $7 million paid to Yoshino Kodama for his efforts on behalf of Lockheed's products there. The payment itself, while certainly a staggering sum, is less the issue than its context. In broad daylight, such a payment would be one issue; in total obscurity, it is entirely another. Clarity and explicitness are, again, essential. The sale of military equipment around the world is inextricably linked to the national interest. It affects our defense posture, diplomatic alliances, and balance of payments. But the clear importance of arms sales demands that these transactions be carried out not by lone corporate agents, working surreptitiously, but through a competent, legitimately authorized procedure.

There is certainly evidence that the U.S. government was aware of industry practices in this sensitive area. For example, in 1974 an assistant director of the Defense Department's Security Assistance Agency sent a letter to defense contractors; he attached an article entitled "Agent's Fees in the Middle East." The article, he said, had been "cleared for open publication" by the Defense Department. The article described the necessity of using an agent to sell in many parts of the world. It goes on to speak of "influence."

> One local agent . . . admitted to the writer that he has three members of the National Assembly of the country on retainer fees for the purpose of obtaining inner circle intelligence and to promote the sales potential of his principal's product. . . . Obviously the agent with the greatest margin of profit or percentage has a distinct advantage over those with a lesser fee in that greater influence can be applied to all personnel in the government decision-making chain.

The government-approved article went on to point out with refreshing candor that influence might not require cash. "Rent-free use of a villa in France or a flat in London with car and servants" would, according to the article, suffice in many cases.

Under the heading "Current Regulations," the article also stated: "The Armed Service Procurement Regulation (ASPR) permits payment of reasonable agents' fees as part of 'cost of sales' on Foreign Military Sales." Finally, the writer cautioned that certain Middle Eastern governments—he mentioned Iran—were trying to tighten up on agents' activities, but concluded that "this lucrative function, developed over the past two thousand years, will not evaporate easily."[7]

If this reflects the government's views at the time regarding foreign payments, it is not surprising that Lockheed's Haughton thought he was behaving consistently with the national interest. His problem, like that of Gulf's Dorsey, was that the interest was not clearly or acceptably defined, and that the role of the corporation in meeting that need was confused.

One final irony and a footnote in this unhappy drama: when the time came to remove Daniel Haughton in 1976, it was the bankers who did it, not the shareholders or the government.[8] Why the right to manage Lockheed at that particular moment should have reverted to the debtholders is unclear, but that was the course of events. The L-1011, the focus of so much of the hubbub, was never a money-maker, and it too was jettisoned, in the fall of 1981.

It is useful to distinguish among the many kinds of "questionable" payments, especially in light of the arguments that may be employed to justify them. In general, we should recognize a difference between paying an official to do (or to do more quickly) what he should do anyway, and paying that same person to do what he should not do. The former can be justified in terms of "greasing" the system; the latter can never be justified in the name of property rights, and only rarely in the name of community need. For example, we can sympathize with the local agent of a pharmaceutical company in tropical Africa who, during an epidemic, pays a customs official $100 to move an urgently needed batch of perishable drugs off a steaming runway. On the other hand, we ought not to condone the alleged bribe by United Brands in 1974 of the Honduran Minister of Economy, intended to bring about a reduction in that country's export tax on bananas. Of course, if the United States were at war, we would not be overly upset if bribery were used to persuade another country to sell us oil or render some other essential good or service.

There are in theory two ways of dealing with the issues raised by the Gulf and Lockheed cases. Congress employed one of them in 1977, passing a law that prohibited U.S. companies from making payments when they had "reason to know" that the payments would go to foreign officials.[9] But theory is often far removed from practice; predictably, after this law had been in effect only a few years, voices were already being heard suggesting that it was in fact operating against the national interest. With some justification, these critics argued that:

• The law was culturally myopic. In many countries, such payments were not only encouraged, they were expected.

• At the same time, in virtually every nation of the world, bribery of government officials was already a crime.

• The law was hurting U.S. companies in international competition, eroding U.S. market share, inflicting further damage on the U.S. balance of payments, and contributing to U.S. unemployment.

• The Justice Department's guidelines defining the terms of the law were ambiguous, and the costs of accommodating these ambiguities were excessive.[10]

A second, more productive approach begins with two questions: what is the community need, and what is the relevant community? In terms of the U.S. community, its minimum need is for a measure of fair play in the world; for a framework of rules, generally acceptable to all trading nations, within which U.S. companies can compete without disadvantage. Clearly there needs to be an international accord about what is "fair."

Community need, however, becomes considerably more complicated when political and diplomatic interests are factored in. It may prove to be in our interests to have certain countries dependent upon America for weapons and airplanes instead of upon Europe or the U.S.S.R. Similarly, the United States might prefer not to be excluded from sources of certain raw materials, such as oil, gold, and strategic metals. In both cases, though, the lengths to which the United States might go to satisfy these needs depend upon a governmental judgment, and that judgment must be based upon a definition of community need.

As for the relevant community, there are clearly two: the nation, and the world trading system. Once the national interest is clear, its fulfillment in the larger context becomes a matter for negotiation or imposition. Corporations may be able to help government define community need, but they cannot do it by themselves. After such a definition is arrived at, they are of course essential to its implementation.

The Foreign Corrupt Practices Act, Congress's 1977 measure, is entirely irrelevant to such a process. Instead of a rigid and unwieldy legal structure, what is required is the capacity within the federal government to think coherently about and decide upon the community need, and then to devise an appropriate set of relationships with business to implement it ethically and efficiently. What is "ethical" in this context is a function of the definition of community need over time; it is neither universal nor absolute. (For example, the Defense Department letter and article cited earlier did not reflect the definition of community need subscribed to by many members of the U.S. Senate after Watergate.) Any reliable definition of community need in the United States must be rooted as securely in the legislative branch of government as it is in the executive. Later, we will observe the importance of this formulation to the success of the Office of the United States Trade Representative, rooted by law both in Congress and the White House.

Until government is properly structured and related to business, we can expect continuing ethical problems resulting from confusion and ambiguity. This by no means suggests that all ethical problems will be eliminated by such a restructuring—obviously, we must remain realistic. In communitarian Japan, where government/business relationships are relatively neat and well ordered, the Lockheed payoff scandals precipitated a major ethical shock, and a subsequent change of government.*

Nevertheless, the ethical problems discussed in this chapter derive to a great extent from the lack of the "definite social arrangements" mentioned at the beginning. And these are a function of ideological realism and clarity. To the extent that ideology is clear and consistent with what institutions are doing and must do to cope with reality, the definition of right and wrong—and thus ethical behavior—is greatly simplified.

Many individualistic Americans are left with a troubling dilemma: if ethical behavior requires a recognition of and adaptation to ideological reality, and if that reality is nearer to communitarianism than to individualism, then "ethical" action becomes for them increasingly impossible. If the ideology of in-

---

* Indeed, the then General Secretary of Japan's ruling party (who in 1982 would become Prime Minister) was moved to record a telephone message denying his involvement; here are excerpts of what you would have heard if you had dialed his number in March 1976:

"Hello, everybody. This is Yasuhiro Nakasone. I'm sticking to my job . . . in good spirits, managing to hold out despite the enormous amount of work I have to do every day. . . .

"I should like to repeat once again that I am totally uninvolved in the Lockheed scandal; and I have never received any hush money. I swear to this in the name of Heaven and Earth. . . .

"The various factions within our party . . . are pestering the executives with complaints, and there is nothing more arduous in this difficult world of ours than to settle such disputes. . . .

"Should our party overcome its present troubles, I am sure that I will be known as 'the admirable Secretary General.' Hence, I am determined to carry out my responsibilities. . . ."[11]

dividualism is *per se* good, they argue, moving to communitarianism is evil.

An indignant alumnus of the Harvard Business School, complaining about an earlier manifestation of these arguments, wrote:

> We are urged: Don't fight it [communitarianism]. Join it. I would argue that to the extent that the business leaders of this country join it they are aiding and abetting the forces of collectivism which will destroy the opportunity of the masses to rise above serfdom. Professor Lodge's message boils down to: Take care of yourself. Don't stand on principle and risk being left out of the new order. Learn how to be a good, obedient manager in the welfare state. I am as well aware as Professor Lodge that the public is merely getting what it is clamoring for. But does that make it right?[12]

He went on to chide me for suggesting that the transition from the old to the new was an inevitable response to changes in the real world, and worried that his alma mater was training managers "for the great socialist future" instead of equipping them to fight for Lockeanism.

If ideology is held to be moral dogma, then ethical teaching and behavior must conform to it. This is the case in the U.S.S.R.: those who depart from the dominant ideology in word or deed are "evil" or "mentally ill." Given the creedlike character of the traditional ideology in America, there is a natural propensity to elevate it to the status of dogma. This seems to me to be as dangerous as ignoring the obvious ethical and moral pitfalls of communitarianism. Slavery, after all, was justified long after it was plainly repulsive under the constructs of property rights and the limited state. Clinging to an outworn and irrelevant ideology can itself destroy morality.

While moral struggles in the name of an ideology can be glorious, they can also be rather miserable, as the later Crusades remind us. And while fighting losing battles has a certain inherent nobility, it is also inherently wasteful.

In conclusion, even though a clear-headed view of ideology and ideological trends does not lead directly to ethical "answers," it can certainly clarify ethical choices. If a community is relying on a definition of community need, one must ask, Who decides what it is? Similarly, if there are rights, there must be duties; who decides what they are, and how they are to be implemented? If government must be involved, how is it to play its role? The alternative is increasingly unacceptable: ideological ambivalence and inadvertence virtually assure unethical, irresponsible responses to these questions.

9

Managers and Managed

Just as the real world is precipitating changes in the roles and relationships of government and business, so too is it compelling inspection of the fundamental assumptions governing the relationship of managers to those whom they manage. These two sets of relationships, furthermore, are increasingly intertwined. It is impossible to perceive labor-management relations clearly without at the same time examining the impact of public policy on those relations.

By the early 1980s, there was little disagreement that U.S. corporate managers, employees, and trade unions would have to change their ways in order to compete successfully for markets, both in America and abroad. There was even a surprising degree of accord concerning the shape and scope of those changes. What was lacking, though, was an explicit recognition of the radical implications inherent in these changes for managers and unions. As a result, we were and are faced with the dangers of ambivalence: of lingering too long with outmoded forms of relationships, of moving to new ones without a full appreciation of their consequences, of failing to manage the transition efficiently and effectively.

The survival of a company in this time of intensifying global competition depends upon its having advantages over its competitors: better management, better research, more technological innovation, better products at lower prices, a better organization for marketing and distribution, and a workforce dedicated to meeting high standards of quality and cost. It is one of those rare axioms that are as true as they are simple: if Japan or France or Mexico can provide better cars, steel, or whatever at lower prices than the United States, there will be fewer and fewer jobs for Americans in those industries. Public policy can mandate tariffs, import quotas, or subsidies to protect or promote the ailing firms, but these measures institutionalize a cost, in taxes or inflation, which becomes increasingly unacceptable politically and self-defeating economically.

In the face of these realities, labor and management in the 1980s were seeking to change their relationship. In a film entitled *Battle for Survival,* narrated by General Motors' president James McDonald, General Motors suggested the stakes: eighty thousand GM workers had been laid off; Japanese cars had taken 21% of the U.S. market; the company, in 1980, lost $763 million; and GM labor costs averaged $19 an hour compared to Japan's $11 an hour. "We need to put aside traditional adversarial relations," said McDonald. "Hundreds of thousands of jobs are at stake."

In response to these troubling statistics—particularly the last —the United Automobile Workers agreed to restrain demands for increases in wages and benefits at GM as it already had done at Ford and Chrysler. Even so, there was doubt as to whether this new restraint would prove adequate to make the U.S. auto industry competitive. Both General Motors and Ford, hedging their bets, announced plans to import small cars from Japan in 1984.

Of special interest, though, was the entirely new form of "dialogue" inherent in these negotiations. In return for the workers' restraint, management agreed to limit its right to close plants and buy from abroad, to introduce profit-sharing, and to move toward some kind of "lifetime employment." Symbolically, Chrysler in May of 1980 had placed Douglas Fraser, president of the United Automobile Workers, on its board of directors. By August of 1982, Chrysler directors were unanimous in their praise of Fraser as a fellow board member. "He's ethical and fairminded, and at the same time it's clear he has the interests of his membership at heart," said Anthony J. A. Bryan, chairman of Copperweld Corporation. Chrysler chairman Lee Iacocca concluded that "Doug Fraser is a super guy" to have on the board,[1] and invited him to stay on after retirement from the UAW presidency in 1983.

Nevertheless, within the union there was ambivalence about its role and mission—that is, about its ideological justifications. Should it fight simply to gain more for its members, or should it seek to share more of the responsibilities of management? In November, when the company and the union undertook to negotiate a new contract, the tension between these two conflicting goals caused Fraser to "temporarily suspend" his attendance at board meetings. "I'm concerned about the perception some people might have had," he said. At the same time, he insisted that he and his fellow UAW leaders continued to believe that workers "should have their voices heard, and their ideas advanced, at the highest levels of a corporation." He cited particularly the importance of union officials' having full access to the company's financial records.[2]

Some managers also felt the strain of this ambivalence. In spite of the changes that were occurring, GM's top management appeared unwilling or unable to grasp the new reality. The old ideology, it seems, was getting in the way. In 1979, when Fraser's election to Chrysler's board was announced, GM chairman Thomas A. Murphy said, "I don't think it makes any sense for him to be on the Chrysler board or any other board. . . . How can a leader of a union sit on the board of a company, and then move over and intelligently negotiate with other members of the industry without some conflict? Directors shouldn't be selected because they represent a certain constituency."[3]

What Murphy failed to perceive was that labor was no longer simply another "constituency." It was, with management, an integral part of General Motors. An incident in 1982 illustrated the point: only days after agreement was reached on the new contract—under which the union agreed to restrain wages—GM management voted itself a bonus. But hours later, when the union heard about it, the bonus was rescinded.[4] In effect, the wages of all members of GM had become rooted in the new consensus, and the old right of management to determine salaries—including their own—had given way.

Agreements similar to those reached in the auto industry were also reached in other industries, such as steel, rubber and transportation, where workers demonstrated their willingness to freeze wages and sacrifice cherished work rules in return for the preservation of jobs and a voice in management. Indeed, in the new consensus, a major factor in future competitiveness was recognized to be the ability of management and labor to restrain costs through worker involvement in decisions that had previously been management's alone.

Again, however, the old ways died hard. In the steel industry, which by 1983 was operating at only 30% of capacity (with 60% of its workforce unemployed), there had been some ten years of experience with consensus between management and labor at the top. The companies and the leadership of the United Steelworkers had agreed in 1971 to automatic wage increases and arbitration of disputes as a means of eliminating the threat of strikes, in part because it had become clear to both sides that disruptions caused by work stoppages provided an important opening for foreign steel producers eager to sell in the U.S. market. But consensus at the top had gone unmatched by any comparable change in relationships at the bottom, where plant managers and shop stewards continued to think and act in the old adversarial ways. By 1983, the labor costs growing out of the 1971 agreement had far outstripped any gains in productivity, and had become a major cause of the industry's lack of competitiveness with foreign producers.

Edmund Ayoub, assistant to the president of the United Steelworkers, saw the problem. "I have long felt that trade unions tend to bargain like ostriches," he said. "We have had our heads in the sand, and the object is to get whatever we can without paying attention to the consequences. But I think that a fundamental change in collective bargaining is occurring. We are being forced to pay attention to the consequences for the industry and the nation."[5]

In December 1982, the USW at Wheeling-Pittsburgh Steel Corporation agreed to slash employment costs by more than $100 million, after having accepted a comparable reduction the previous April. In return, the union gained, among other concessions, an important voice in management: a moratorium on plant shutdowns; a promise that the company would spend all the labor-cost savings on modernization of existing plants, and not on diversification out of steel; and a role in the determination of company financial policies. In addition, the company agreed to reduce nonunion salaries by an amount equivalent to the union cuts. A year later, the national basic steel agreement included wage and benefit cuts expected to amount to $2 billion over the following three and a half years. In return, management pledged to use these labor-cost savings for reinvestment in modernizing the industry.

But as the auto, steel, and other industries contracted and innovated for competitiveness in 1982, there remained the problem of hundreds of thousands of unemployed workers. An embarrassment for both unions and government, they constituted a mounting pressure for trade protection. If that pressure was to be resisted, many recognized, there would have to be some sort of government policy regarding retraining, relocation, and job creation.

These trends, generated by the pressures of reality, represented a radical departure from our historical traditions. This radicality needs to be understood if the new ways are to be well managed.

In the 1920s the right to manage General Motors was conferred, without a doubt, by the owners. They were a relatively small group of identifiable individuals who let it be known what they wanted: a good—indeed, a very good—return on their investment. There was no union. Workers came out of the countryside eager for a job. Management created jobs, setting terms that workers could either accept or reject. Obviously, because the alternative was grim, there was a strong incentive to accept, and once a worker had arrived in Paradise Valley—as the workers' district of Detroit was known—it was hard to get out. Labor relations were thus the fruit of the traditional ideology. The authority of the manager came from the owners. Workers, bound by individualistic contracts, were expected to obey. Government's role was the protection of property and its related rights.

The utility of this model depended in large part on economic factors. The real world of the early 1900s, for example, supported the structure. Times were good; the Horatio Alger genre was sufficiently grounded in reality to persuade the young worker that he could make it to the top one day. By the 1930s, however, the real world had changed in a variety of ways, and old notions of authority changed with it. Ownership became widely dispersed. The Great Depression had arrived, idling a quarter of the work force. Factories had become huge, and work impersonal. As economic conditions deteriorated, a new economic model began to replace the old: adversarialism became the order of the day, with management and shareholders pitted against the union and the workers.

At the end of the 1920s, Adolf A. Berle and Gardiner C. Means were writing their famous study of ownership and control, and suggesting that these two functions were being separated. In short, those who theoretically owned—the shareholders—no longer controlled.[6] Alfred Sloan, as noted in Chapter 2, was also concerned about the implications of the dispersion of ownership for management authority. Owen D. Young, the prophetic chairman of General Electric, told a Harvard Business School audience in 1927:

> I hope the day may come when these great business organizations will truly belong to the men who are giving their lives and their efforts to them, I care not in what capacity. Then they will use capital truly as a tool and they will all be interested in working it to the highest economic advantage. Then an idle machine will mean to every man in the plant who sees it an unproductive charge against himself. Then we shall have zest in labor, provided the leadership is competent and the division fair. Then we shall dispose, once and for all, of the charge that in industry organizations are autocratic and not democratic. . . . Then we shall have no hired men.[7]

Not only did Young suggest that labor should hire capital, but he also delineated the implications of such a departure for corporate governance: worker representation at all levels of corporate decision-making.

Managers, however, were unmoved. Failing to respond to the crises of the 1930s, the automobile industry found itself being organized in 1936 by the UAW, under the leadership of John L. Lewis (and later, Walter Reuther). Unionism converted the individualistic hierarchical contract, rooted in property rights, into the *collective* contract, to be bargained adversarially. Even though the authority of the shareholders had dispersed and the rights of property weakened, managers considered it their primary task to maximize return on investment. The union, understandably, found its mission in seeking more for its members.

While at first the course of adversarialism was difficult, in part because of its unfamiliarity, by the end of World War II both sides had become accustomed to it. In 1948, a new auto workers' contract was signed containing two innovations, which by 1982 had become two of the most significant contributors to the industry's labor-cost disadvantage: the cost-of-living escalator, which promised wage increases commensurate with the consumer price index; and the "annual improvement factor," guaranteeing workers a raise in real purchasing power each year, linked to productivity increases not specifically in the auto industry, but to manufacturing in general. This second linkage was discarded in the 1970s, when productivity increases softened and eventually declined, but for twenty years or more it produced wage increases of between 2% and 3% every year. These two provisions, combined with increases in fringe benefits, had by 1982 nearly put much of the industry out of business.

Ironically, in 1948 and afterwards, management was proud of its collective-bargaining record. Although expensive, it had at least preserved managerial prerogatives, including the semi-sacred right of managers to control. Whatever riches were disbursed through the collective contract—and they were significant—there had been no ground given in terms of worker participation in management. This was, of course, crucial to the traditional assumptions held by managers concerning the derivation of authority. The old hierarchies had been preserved intact, even though they were performing less efficiently. A heavy price was being paid for ideological myopia.

Labor, too, had a vested interest in adversarialism. "I believe deeply in a conflict theory of labor relations," Thomas R. Donahue, secretary-treasurer of the AFL-CIO, told students at the University of Massachusetts in January 1982. "Workers properly want, and are entitled to . . . a larger piece of the pie, whatever the size of the pie. . . . The meek may inherit the earth, but probably not in your or my lifetime."

In isolation, Donahue's comments may seem parochial, but

they do reflect a very real context, in which managers regard unions as adversaries to be outmaneuvered, or better still, destroyed. As recently as five years ago, Heath Larry, former chairman of U.S. Steel and then president of the National Association of Manufacturers, announced the formation of a "Council on a Union-Free Environment," to assist employers "to manage with sufficient skill" so that "employees will find no need to invite the services of a union to represent them."[8]

In these circumstances, it was not surprising that Donahue felt embattled. Union membership was down to little more than 20% of the work force; its influence in Congress was at low ebb; its role and mission in many settings was unclear; and President Reagan, who had been elected in part because of the support of labor, seemed bent on downgrading the stature of the labor movement. He excluded the unions from his inaugural ceremonies, and a few months later exulted at the decertification of the air traffic controllers' organization. There was certainly no life in the idea of joint consultation among government, labor, and business for "the reindustrialization of America," which had been one of President Carter's last proposed initiatives before leaving office in January 1981.

And yet, despite this apparently hostile political and economic climate, it was during the early 1970s that substantial departures from the adversarial relations between managers and unions began to occur. In both the automobile and steel industries (as well as in other, nonunion settings such as IBM, Hewlett-Packard, TRW, and Procter and Gamble), the contractual relationships between managers and workers were gradually being augmented or even replaced by consensual ones, aimed at developing a sense of commitment and community between managers on the one hand and those whom they managed on the other. The process took many forms: team building, organizational development, job enrichment, and—in the steel industry—a no-strike pledge and compulsory arbitration.

In many industries, management and unions were finally becoming aware of their common interest in warding off the growing threat of foreign imports. It was the competitive forays of the Japanese, in particular, that quickened the pace of consensual activity in the 1970s. The United States, once the economic wonder of the world, was being trounced in the marketplace by Japan, as well as a number of other Asian and European countries. What was most disconcerting to Americans was that our disadvantages appeared to be systemic. We were being defeated by our dependence on the weaker of two contrasting sets of relationships among government, business, and labor; in short, we could not compete with a country that was capable of formulating and implementing a coherent national strategy. Said Philip Caldwell of Ford: "Individual United States companies are competing against Japan *as a country* [emphasis added]." New relationships among government, business, and labor in the United States were required if we were to recover.[9] The Japanese were making better products for less money, employing fewer workers, more modern equipment, and more advanced technology.

The grim necessities were becoming clear: the country had to consume less and invest more; companies had to innovate and take risks for long-term gains, instead of settling for short-term return to shareholders; managers had to manage more imaginatively; and workers had to work more productively. Nor were we alone in our plight: Western Europe faced the same situation. What historically has been called "the Christian world" was being forced by competition to suppress old divisions and seek a new sense of community, and to follow the dictum of Pope John Paul II's encyclical *On Human Work*: "In no way can labor be opposed to capital or capital to labor, and still less can the actual people behind these concepts be opposed to each other." [10]

There is growing evidence that relatively well-educated people can derive an enhanced sense of fulfillment from their work, and will work more efficiently, if they have a greater role in the design and control of that work. Today in America there is what Irving Bluestone, former vice-president of the United Automobile Workers, called a "tidal wave" of procedures aimed at ensuring such participation. They vary widely from community to community, industry to industry, and job to job. The procedures have many names, but they are all embraced by the necessarily vague "quality of work life" (QWL). (At Ford, these means and ends are called "employee involvement.") They proceed from the top of the enterprise down to the shop floor, but also from the shop floor up. They are found in some fifteen hundred companies, in many service as well as manufacturing industries, and in both the private sector and the public sector.

Implicit in all of them is the idea that relationships between those who manage and those who are managed are best determined by consensus, rather than by an adversarial contract. Consensual procedures are not necessarily a substitute for the collective contract; rather, they are aimed at problems and issues which do not conveniently fit within the contract form. It remains to be seen whether the evolving machinery of consensus will erode the contract—certainly, that possibility exists. At the same time, there is the threat of erosion of traditional notions of corporate governance. The right to manage in QWL plants comes not so much from shareholders, via a board of directors, as it does from those who are managed. Indeed, in many QWL plants —GM's, for example—the word "management" has been supplanted by the phrase "support team." In such a structure, the effective manager is the one who can assemble winning combinations—"the gamesman," as Michael Maccoby has called him.

How does this approach address our contemporary maladies? The answers are, of course, complex. But simply stated, consensus management not only provides the individual with a greater sense of fulfillment, but also educates him about the reality in which the corporation exists. He perceives the demands of competitiveness that confront the firm, and experiences the necessity of sacrificing for the good of the whole.

Obviously, the idea of consensus carries with it profound implications for both managers and union leaders. It reminds managers, for example, that the interests of the whole must be borne in mind if its goal is to be achieved. Steelworkers are unlikely to make concessions if the profits of their labor are invested in an oil company. If workers must sacrifice for the good of the whole, so must management. QWL programs invite comparisons, for example, between the salaries of the chief executive and the sweeper. QWL plants are characterized by an absence of executive dining rooms and special parking places in the company lot. Managers do not wear ties and coats. These symbols, or rather the lack of them, emphasize the democratic nature of the innovation. Similarly, the role of the union official is subject to thoroughgoing revision in a consensual setting.

Even the most carefully constructed of such consensually managed corporations, however, are not immune to the realities of hard economic times. Indeed, the increased efficiencies resulting from consensualism can themselves be the source of new conflict: what happens to the thousands of workers who are idled after labor and management have cooperated for competitiveness? Along with our longer-standing dilemmas, these questions are also at the core of America's challenge in the 1980s.

In the winter of 1982, some 4.5 million workers faced contract negotiations that entailed the necessity of wage-and-benefit concessions—of forgoing "a larger piece of the pie," to use Thomas Donahue's phrase. Unions recognized that corporate profits, such as they were, had to be devoted to making their companies more competitive. This concession was not given freely: in return, they insisted upon an unprecedented invasion of what had been management prerogatives. They demanded access to corporate financial records to satisfy themselves that management's picture of the situation was accurate. They sought assurances that management would in fact spend the money saved from lower labor costs to benefit the corporation and its employees, and not use it to diversify into other industries or build plants in other countries. They sought a share in company profits, and control over the investment of billions of dollars amassed in pension funds, so that those funds could contribute to the revitalization of communities in which union members lived. In short, they were seeking to participate in what had been purely managerial decision-making, to join with managers in a consideration of all aspects of corporate activity. In some cases, the consideration extended to an examination of the community as a whole.

The first big concession came at Chrysler, in 1979, when the UAW agreed to give up more than $600 million in wages, vacation time, and pensions in order to keep Chrysler going and make it eligible for government loan guarantees. In return, the union gained most of the rights outlined above, as well as a seat on the board of directors for UAW President Douglas Fraser. Ford, GM, Pan Am, and other companies followed suit. There were some indications that, given enough control, workers would be prepared to make even larger sacrifices.

One procedure which may facilitate employee participation in the management of firms is an Employee Stock Ownership Plan (ESOP). It is not a new idea—indeed, there are today some five thousand ESOPs in the United States—but it is gaining new proponents. In 1982 about 10% of America's large corporations had initiated employee buyouts, generally through some sort of ESOP.[11]

Gail Sokoloff's study of the Hyatt roller-bearing plant in Clark, New Jersey, provides valuable insight into the issues of worker control.[12] In this case, approximately eleven hundred workers—both management and labor—used an ESOP to buy the plant from General Motors, in one of the largest employee takeovers in U.S. history. When reconstruction of the company was completed, wages had been cut 25%, restrictive work rules abolished, employment reduced, and workers and managers given equal representation on the new company's board of directors. The measures may sound Draconian, but the point of the takeover was to preserve jobs in Clark. To this end, employees agreed that the plant had to be made more competitive, both in the products it made and in the productivity of its workforce.

The antecedents to the takeover are only too familiar. A militant local of the United Automobile Workers at Clark had driven wages and health-and-safety costs well above the level at other GM plants. The plant had lost money for more than five years, in part because of high labor costs and restrictive work practices. At Clark, for example, workers operated only two machines, while at other comparable GM plants they ran three or four.[13] As early as 1977, the union recognized that its successes might pose a potential threat to the viability of the plant.[14] Roger Smith, chairman of GM, had warned that the company would look increasingly to outside nonunion or foreign suppliers—"outsourcing," as the strategy was called—because American workers had "priced themselves out of the market."[15] At the same time, the plant's principal product, tapered roller bearings used in the rear wheel assembly of cars and trucks, was becoming obsolete as the industry moved from rear-wheel to front-wheel drive. It was no surprise, therefore, when GM announced in August of 1980 that it would close the plant and its 2,500 employees would be jobless unless a buyer could be found.

Clark's union leaders began to plan an employee takeover, seeking help and advice from the Economic Development Agency (EDA) in Washington and from the plant's management. EDA offered advice, but little else. Management hesitated, torn between two perceptions of its role at the Clark plant. On the one hand, they were GM employees, part of the corporate hierarchy. But they were also members of the Clark workforce, and they faced the possibility of losing their jobs or having to move.[16]

Workers were similarly ambivalent about the takeover initiative. For one thing, they feared the loss of their retirement benefits. Furthermore, they distrusted the "radical" wing of the local union that was perceived as being behind the effort. In the words of one union leader:

> You're talking about a bunch of people who all their lives worked for General Motors and now all of a sudden the union's saying, "Let's buy the plant." People become suspicious, regardless of who they trust or don't trust. They don't want to be involved in things like that. They think there's something shady.[17]

These fears found concrete expression. In 1980, a plantwide referendum seeking endorsement of the takeover idea was defeated by a vote of 794 to 788.[18] The union's effort had failed, but the idea remained alive. Early in 1981, a group of fifteen managers met and decided to pursue an employee buyout vigorously. They sent a letter to the 2,500 employees of the plant, inviting them to join "in an intense effort to explore both the depth of interest and the realistic economic feasibility of keeping this company alive." The letter was distributed by members of local management outside the plant's gate on a cold January morning. "Kind of a strange sight to see management people leafletting the plant," one manager observed.[19]

Shortly thereafter, the union leaders agreed to join the management effort, and the Hyatt Clark Job Preservation Committee was formed. It consisted of five management and three union representatives; each side, though, had one vote. In deliberations, both sides had to agree with all conclusions. The committee retained the attorney who had been hired initially by the union.

The reaction of the plant's employees to the joint initiative was dramatically different from that which greeted the union-only effort. Within two weeks, more than 1,100 employees had contributed $100 each to pay legal fees and the costs of a feasibility study by Arthur D. Little (ADL). Management's involvement appeared to have legitimized the idea of employee ownership.

ADL's study concluded that the plant would be economically viable—providing that GM agreed to buy the plant's product for three years, and that there was an increase in machine utilization, an abolition of restraining work rules, a reduction of scrap and waste, strong management leadership to improve quality and productivity, and a substantial reduction in base pay.[20]

What were the reasons for the action of union and management? Job preservation was certainly the principal motivating factor, but other factors emerged. Pride was certainly important: the union claimed that its members could increase productivity 100%, given the right circumstances. (In fact, union leaders openly acknowledged that their "effectiveness" as a union had contributed to the plant's low productivity.[21] "We had over 100 people just working on health and safety; not contributing to the product at all. . . . It was unreal."[22]) The union leaders were convinced that with changes in corporate personnel, structure, and philosophy, great improvements could be made.

Sokoloff also found that managers had a strong "sense of responsibility to the work force as a whole and to the union."[23] One manager remarked: "Some of us thought if we could help the union, it would have a much better chance to succeed. I think it was obvious that they couldn't do it by themselves."[24]

"There's a real affection for this place," said another management participant. "I came right here out of college, worked with this division, and I've been here ever since. There are a lot of people like that."[25]

The Hyatt Clark takeover could not have occurred without the active support of General Motors. The company agreed to buy the output of the plant for three years, and assisted in obtaining the necessary financing. Sokoloff was curious to determine the reasons for GM's eagerness to see the takeover succeed; she found that first and foremost among them was GM's desire "to send a signal" to the UAW International that the company was serious about the need to lower wage and labor costs. GM, she also concluded, "has viewed the Clark employee buyout as a 'pilot project' for future plant shutdown situations."[26]

After protracted and often painful negotiations, General Motors, the Hyatt Clark management, and the plant union finally reached a buyout agreement in July, 1981. The union agreed to the Arthur D. Little prescription, including a reduction in sick leave, paid holidays, and life insurance, as well as a 25% cut in pay. It argued that management should also accept pay reductions (and indeed, some managers' salaries were cut), but in general management claimed successfully that the plant had to pay competitive wages in order to attract the quality of managers necessary for success.[27]

The union's reasoning is very important to an understanding of the event, and to any extrapolation of broader lessons from the sequence of events at Hyatt Clark. The leaders did not believe they were abandoning their principles. "We only have so much money in this plant," said one man. "The question is, how can we best utilize our money? We're not making concessions to our employers. We're making concessions to ourselves. There's a big difference."[28]

To institutionalize this sense of commitment, it became necessary to construct a board of directors that reflected the new reality. It was composed of outside individuals, jointly selected by union and management, and equal numbers of management and union representatives. In ten years, furthermore, the entire workforce will have the right to vote for the board of directors.[29]

In most ESOPs, shares are distributed on the basis of salary, but at Hyatt Clark, the union insisted (and the management eventually agreed) that stock should be distributed on the basis of hours worked. In other words, the stock was available equally to all employees. A union leader put his case this way:

> If you're a college graduate and you've a master's degree in business, then you're getting your extra wages through your extra salary. If I'm a laborer, I'm getting paid for my minimal talents at a lesser pay rate. So the difference in compensation is made over a year in salary. But I should still have the same share of ownership. I'm giving my eight hours a day; you're giving your eight hours a day. You're getting $100,000. I'm getting $10,000. But we're both giving everything we've got, so we both should have an equal share.[30]

For the plant managers, "the exclusive right to manage" was a critical issue, and the union recognized that management had to manage. But the source of management authority had radically changed. No longer did it come from a hierarchy, rooted obscurely in the property rights of GM shareholders. Now it came from the managed. This was the basis of the new trust, and the new commitment upon which the future of the plant depended. The union did not consider that it had given away its power; rather, it had altered its form.

"The *quid pro quo*," said one union leader, "is that we're going to own the company; we're going to control the company. That's a big *quid pro quo*. And that's why it's important to the trade union movement. Because it's power. And that's what the ball game is all about. It's about power and money. We lost the money, but we're going to make it back in power."[31]

The Clark plant today has slightly more than eight hundred employees, one-third its previous size. The moves that it has made to reduce labor costs have attracted sufficient capital to allow it to continue operations and to diversify into new products. But its ability to prosper in the future depends, in part, on the degree to which all of its members realize the profound implications of the changes they have made. They will have to root out any old adversarial assumptions that may reemerge. Managers must act on the conviction that their rights are now derived only from those they are managing. Workers must realize the competitive realities of today's world economy. Both must be willing to sacrifice imaginatively, so that the whole enterprise and the surrounding community will prosper.

The eleven thousand employees of National Steel's unprofitable plant in Weirton, West Virginia, were given an ultimatum in July, 1982: they would have to take pay cuts of as much as 32% over the next four years to keep the plant alive. (National had offered to sell the plant to its employees in 1981.) McKinsey consultants who studied the feasibility of the deal said that in addition to the pay cuts, hourly employment could be expected to fall by seven thousand during the 1980s.[32] When the sale was completed in 1983, it surpassed Hyatt as the largest employee buyout in U.S. history.

In Bolivar, Tennessee, the Harman auto-parts factory achieved considerable competitive advantages in the mid-1970s when management admitted the UAW local into partnership. It was the work of Sidney Harman, company president, and Irving Bluestone, vice-president of the UAW. Together they brought to rural Tennessee what was then the most radical example of union participation in management in the U.S. This effort was particularly successful: the number of Harman employees has grown from 600 at the start of the project to more than 1,150 today.

In 1980, Harman's union encouraged the company to submit the lowest bid on a contract with GM for automobile mirrors in order to save 150 jobs. Afterwards it agreed to necessary wage restraints; the only grounds for dispute concerned the proper spread between the wages of management and the lowest-paid worker. Michael Maccoby, who was active in the design of this experiment, reports that "recently, workers came in voluntarily on the Thanksgiving weekend to set up tools in order to win a rush order from the Ford Motor Company. An eighteen-week changeover program was carried out in five weeks." [33]

Changes in the automobile industry had begun at General Motors in the late 1960s, when that company was experiencing severe productivity problems. Unexcused absences, for example, increased 50% between 1965 and 1969. On occasional Mondays and Fridays, as much as 20% of the workforce failed to show up for work. Grievances and disciplinary layoffs were at unprecedented levels. Drugs, alcohol, and guns in the locker rooms were very visible symptoms of a larger problem.

A local union president in 1970 said:

> Every single unskilled man in my plant wants out. They just don't like it. This whole generation had been taught by their fathers to avoid the production line, to go to college to escape, and now some of them are trapped. They can't face it. They hate to go in there.[34]

At the same time, foreign automobile manufacturers were beginning to capture a larger share of the U.S. market. More and more money was being channeled through the collective contract, in an effort to buy better performance, but the tactic proved fruitless. "Management and the public have lately been shortchanged," concluded GM chairman James Roche in 1970. "We have a right to more than we are receiving." [35]

The union was no less frustrated. In many ways, leaders had lost control of their members. Try as they might to persuade the rank and file that they were getting a good deal in the collective agreement—in fact, their wages were about twice the national average for manufacturing workers, and twice that of their Japanese counterparts—many employees remained dissatisfied and unwilling to respect the discipline of the contract. In short, the authority of management, rooted in property rights, and that of the union, rooted in membership representation, had been eroded. Their relationship, prescribed in the contract, was no longer definable or negotiable by leaders whose authority was uncertain. Both groups, and their leaders, were adrift.

In 1970, Irving Bluestone took over as director of the General Motors department of the UAW, and a year later Stephen H. Fuller left the Harvard faculty to become vice-president of GM for personnel administration and development. Fuller's was a new position at GM: the company had split its labor relations staff in two, assigning responsibility for the collective contract and its adversarial negotiating process to George B. Morris, the vice-president of labor relations, and delegating to Fuller the task of solving the problems of productivity and motivation which had become so troublesome. It was by most accounts a fortunate combination of talents. During the 1970s, Bluestone and Fuller, working separately in their respective organizations, forged what was to be one of the most extensive and successful procedures in America for involving workers in what had been management decisions.

Shortly after his appointment, Fuller said:

> What we are doing is signaling as obviously and as frequently as we can the commitment of top management that it is interested in improving job satisfaction. We are trying to open the doors and give people an opportunity to share in improving the quality of what they do.[36]

Of course, those in management and labor who were accustomed to and dependent upon the contract were doubtful about (if not hostile to) the participation which Fuller and Bluestone were encouraging. But to both proponents and detractors, their efforts were a recognizably different approach, oriented toward consensus instead of conflict.

Speaking of George Morris, the vice-president of industrial relations, Bluestone said:

> I think George felt that any encroachment upon managerial prerog-atives which would be indicated by workers participating in a meaningful way in making decisions on the shop floor was an ero-sion of authority, and the corporation must retain for itself all pos-sible authoritarian control over the workplace.[37]

From both sides of the adversarial fence, shop stewards and plant managers schooled in the traditional notions of contractual proceedings and management rights felt threatened by the changes. There was backbiting; union people feared that they were being coopted by management, and management worried that their rights were being transferred to the union. (The charges that were traded, to be sure, had a somewhat hollow ring; both sides could plainly see that whatever rights and authority might have derived from the old constructs were growing feeble.)

Beginning with joint health-and-safety committees, new-hire programs, preretirement counseling, and drug-and-alcohol-abuse programs, Fuller and Bluestone prodded managers and workers throughout the GM system into joint activities that eventually would improve the quality of the product, scheduling and orga-nization of work, setting of standards, and more. By 1980 it was clear that in order to be an effective manager at GM, you had to be able to earn and retain the support of those you managed.[38] In all significant ways, the right to manage now derived from the managed.

Although the quality-of-work-life program at GM was begun with the commitment of Fuller and Bluestone at the top, its par-ticular form of the QWL program evolved under local control, and differed from plant to plant. Said Ray Calore, president of Local 664 at GM's Tarrytown, New York, plant:

> We as a union knew that our primary job was to protect the worker and improve his economic life. But times had changed, and we began to realize we had a broader obligation, which was to help the workers become more involved in decisions affecting their own jobs, to get their ideas, and to help them improve the whole quality of life at work beyond the paycheck.[39]

This was consistent with Bluestone's conception of the mission of a union, which was "to bring democratic values into the workplace." Donald Ephlin, the UAW chief at Ford, echoed the same notion: "We are going to be working for the expansion of industrial democracy in the plant." [40]

To protect union members from the anticipated exploitation of QWL programs by management—"a stopwatch in sheep's clothing," as William Winpisinger of the machinists' union tartly called them—both sides agreed to six laws governing their application: QWL could not be used to support a speedup or reduce manpower; workers could not be forced to participate; no agreements in the contract would be waived; the elected union representatives had a right to attend any QWL meetings; the program was strictly voluntary; and either party could get out at any time. [41]

One potential snag emerged, which was apparently handled to everyone's satisfaction. In 1979, the union suspected that GM was using QWL as a way to avoid future unionization, especially in some of its southern plants: after all, if workers and managers could control the plant through discussion among themselves, what was the need for a union? Facing the possibility of a companywide strike on this issue in 1979, GM agreed to guarantee union representation at all new plants opened after 1979.

As a result of these and other successes, there seemed little likelihood of movement away from QWL at GM. Significantly, when George Morris retired, his successor as vice-president of industrial relations—Al Warren, a former personnel director at Fisher Body—was one of Fuller's men. "That was a signal up and down the system," said Fuller. [42] QWL had come to stay.

In many ways, however, its future is far from clear. We must restate the questions suggested by Hyatt Clark. Can GM *vs.* UAW truly become GM/UAW? In this context, the views of one GM sander on the assembly line are relevant. Martin Douglas had been with the company eighteen years when he was laid off in February 1982. As he wrote in *The New York Times*:

> General Motors is constantly comparing my wages to those of the Japanese auto worker, but I am sure that GM doesn't want to enter a relationship such as the Japanese firms enjoy with their workers.
>
> GM has never offered to guarantee me a job for life as the Japanese do, or subsidize my housing, or provide me with opportunities for low-cost vacations. Instead, GM wants to cut my pay to that of

my Japanese counterpart and close the plant whenever by so doing it will maximize its profits. . . .

I don't know what the president of General Motors made last year. I do know that in good years, he made close to a million dollars. I don't know exactly what he does each day, but I am sure I have a better idea of his job than he does of mine.

So now he comes to me when times are hard and asks for sacrifices, and I say to him: "You should have come a little earlier when times were good and we could have gotten to know each other. If you had, I would now be more willing to help."[43]

How long will it take to overcome the bitter legacy of adversarialism? Can the sense of participation and control implicit in Bluestone's vision of corporate democracy become a reality? The answers to these questions depend on how well management, labor, and government understand and manage the implications of what is happening. Even Bluestone and his fellow union leaders—the wellspring of some of the most sweeping and radical realignments—are ambivalent about what they have begun. They distinguish, in Bluestone's words, between "managing the workplace and managing the enterprise." Bluestone, for one, prefers to see QWL in terms of the former, not the latter, but he acknowledges that over time, worker involvement in broader managerial questions is inevitable. "In fact," he said recently, "it's happening more quickly than I would have expected."[44]

Glenn Watts, president of the Communications Workers of America (CWA), has made QWL an essential part of his union's national strategy at AT&T and other companies in the rapidly changing electronics and telecommunications field. "Workers must be involved in planning the introduction of new technology or it won't work," he said. "We are definitely moving in the direction of consensus-building and away from the old adversarial relationship." Although, like Bluestone, he was reluctant to suggest that unions would participate in management decisions about the enterprise as a whole, he has concluded that "bit by bit, we're going to get there. I can't at the moment imagine how, but it seems to be absolutely inevitable. Either that or we're going to have chaos in our society, with the people that don't

have fighting to get something from those that have it. It's a
question of timing. It will take time.

"If you look at what quality of work life really means," Watts
continued, "it is a breakdown in the adversarial relationship, a
breakdown in the old notion of authority rooted in property, and
shareholders, and a board of directors, the old hierarchy. The
manager is going to get the right to manage, the ability to manage,
only so long as the people he manages are interested and involved
and prepared to give it to him. The task of management is to build
this consensus, and the role of the union in these circumstances
is one of contributing to the creation of the consensus." [45]

At the same time, Watts was conscious of tradition: "To the
extent that the workers are not the owners of the business, they
play a different role. They've got an interest in the enterprise
and their interest must be protected. But I do believe it can be
protected by the more traditional collective-bargaining process
augmented by quality of work life programs and other such
innovations. I do not embrace the idea that workers ought to
participate on the board of directors, for example."

When others reflect on tradition, they conclude that QWL activities have their antecedents. Thomas Donahue, for example,
has concluded that the collaboration occurring today is no different from similar efforts in the past. Noting that there have always
been committees of cooperation between management and labor,
he said, "Our interest in quality of work life goes back to the day
—probably 200 years ago—when the first trade unionists banded
together in America to seek to improve the condition of their
work." [46] Significantly, though, Donahue goes further: he argues
persuasively that cooperation can work only if the union is
strong. Union strength, he suggests, derives from the contract,
which in turn rests on a basic conflict between the respective
interests of labor and management. The conclusion is paradoxi-
cal: there can only be cooperation if there is conflict.

Phrased differently, the crucial question seems to be: Can the
union be strong if the contract becomes less important? Can the
union find strength in consensualism? In partial answer to such
questions, it is significant that the CWA is finding that its skill
and experience in negotiating QWL programs has become an
important part of its competitive strategy against other unions, in
the communications industry and elsewhere. Recently, for ex-

ample, it organized 35,000 government workers in New Jersey, partly because of its QWL capabilities. If we posit that the needs of workers, companies, and the country lie increasingly in the realm of consensus-making, then the unions that stick to their contractual traditions may disintegrate. The strong union may be the one that learns best how to define a role for itself within the new consensual approach. If this supposition is true—and the preponderance of evidence suggests it is—there is no time to waste on ambivalence; the unions must face squarely the new relationships, and redesign their roles accordingly.

But how can workers with pressing and legitimate short-term needs be expected to take a long-term view of the enterprise? It will take a considerable broadening of perspective, for example, if a union leader in Detroit is to understand the need for overseas facilities: for example, if GM is going to sell cars in Mexico, it must, according to Mexican law, produce cars there. And what of GM's decision—probably a competitive necessity—to buy 200,000 Japanese small cars in 1984? If such strategies are to be accepted, it seems clear that American workers must be in some way compensated: retrained for new jobs, relocated, given a share of the corporation's profits, or some similar arrangement. Obviously, this is not the stuff of contractual bargaining; rather, it must emerge from a widespread sharing of information, a common understanding, and a spirit of partnership.

The role of government cannot be separated from such questions. A clear public policy for trade and investment is essential, and a major responsibility at least for funding the retraining and relocation of displaced workers must fall upon government. It may well prove necessary for the United States to have a national manpower plan, whereby skill shortages and surpluses are identified, and appropriate educational efforts are made to promote the skills that are needed. An ideological caveat, though, is appropriate: such suggestions are greeted with skepticism by many.

Labor, as we have seen, is ambivalent about QWL. Management is hardly less so. Most managers with experience in QWL settings agree to their positive attributes: they are happier work environments, characterized by growing productivity and a flow of good ideas about how to do things better. They promote a sense of teamwork and loyalty, and in many instances, increase the worker's sense of duty. Experience at the Cummins Engine plant in Jamestown, New York, a highly participative environment, shows that peer-group pressure on work teams is a potent deterrent to tardiness and absenteeism. (In fact, consensual pressures have from time to time been judged to be unwholesomely severe.)

But managers, predictably, are anxious about the loss of authority and control that they perceive as inherent in the transition to consensualism. Even though considerable evidence suggests that the power of managers actually increases as they learn to derive authority from those whom they manage, managers who have never done it are understandably anxious. Middle managers and supervisors are especially uneasy; they are literally in the middle. In a survey conducted by Harvard Business School professors Richard Walton and Leonard Schlesinger, one supervisor said, "I'm like one of those lizards that is always changing color, except that I don't have any control over what color I am. When the workers want me, I've always got to be there. When they don't, I have to tread lightly." Another notes that while workers get a good deal of attention, training, and reward from QWL, managers may not: "When things are going well," he said, "no one recognizes how I've busted my butt to get the team working together. But when things go poorly, they let me know right away." [47]

Furthermore, with the greater efficiency of participative systems, it is often feasible to operate with fewer managers, and a legitimate fear of being laid off must be added to their list of apprehensions. This raises an interesting point of representation in our emerging industrial democracy: if workers are organized for participation and representation, and top management has its own organization, it will be necessary to organize supervisory personnel to ensure their full participation.

Innovative managers in participatory systems have sometimes been disappointed that their success in a particular plant was not adequately recognized at corporate headquarters. Some successes have even been frowned upon. Walton has documented this phenomenon at the General Foods facility in Topeka, Kansas. Even though the Topeka experiment was acknowledged almost universally to be an outstanding success, its consensual practices apparently threatened managers at headquarters, "whose leadership style was built on opposite principles." The demands of Topeka managers for independence—for the right to go their own consensual way—created friction among those in headquarters who "simply did not understand the Topeka system. The effect of this friction was to sour the career opportunities within General Foods for most of the original Topeka managers." [48]

In the broader context, the problem facing managers is identical to the one facing unions: if they do not understand the full implications of their pragmatic actions, they will certainly fail to anticipate its full range of consequences, and may indeed induce some of the worst possible outcomes of the transition. How can the two converging camps grasp the full implications of their activities? As I have suggested earlier, the concept of ideology is most helpful. It is not that the changes outlined above are occurring for ideological reasons; rather, they are the product of necessity, of inexorable changes in the real world, and of pragmatic experimentation to find a better way. Without doubt, though, those changes cannot be fully comprehended unless their ideological implications are made clear. Only after managers and union leaders fully understand what old assumptions are being eroded can they see the new choices before them, and act upon them. In the words of James J. Renier, president of Honeywell's control-systems business: "It's not just a matter of technique, but of real philosophies. You can't just put out a memo saying, 'You will be participative, you jerk.' " [49]

The idea of consensus—as opposed to contract—is inherent in the actions of managers and unions as they seek ways in which to restrain wages, close plants, increase productivity, improve employee motivation, and promote "fairness." It was what lay behind Fuller and Bluestone's work at GM, and that of the managers at Topeka. It depends on labor-management trust instead of arm's-length antagonism.

As Donald Ephlin, UAW leader at Ford, said of the 1982 agreement: "It was a problem-solving exercise, not negotiations in the true sense. We had problems that we wanted solved—the loss of jobs and the lack of security that our members have. The supplementary unemployment benefit plan had gone broke; payments had stopped." On the company side, Peter Pestillo, Ford's vice-president of labor relations, was equally revealing: "We make a great effort in this agreement to work toward greater participation by our work force in the business process. I think that's the wave of the future. We use a word deep in the agreement that's simply called 'governance.' "[50] It seems doubtful that Ford and the UAW could have reached their agreement if the company's "employee involvement" program—involving workers directly in management decisions at all sixty-five Ford assembly plants—had not been in place.

Pestillo's use of the word "governance" is significant because it clarifies the debate about that subject. In the past, worker representation in corporate decision-making was considered an aspect of constituent representation, and as such had been denigrated, since it was deemed impractical to involve all constituencies.[51] But today, worker involvement in governance is occurring neither for ideological nor for legal reasons; it is occurring for reasons of efficiency and effectiveness, fueled by real-world events. Managing the effects of the transition, however, requires recognition of its ideological consequences and implications.

Consensual systems are not all good. There is nothing utopian about communitarianism, as even the briefest review of history surely reminds us. As contemporary forces move us toward consensus, it is worth remembering that the idea of contract was invented to protect the individual against the oppressive hierarchy of the Middle Ages. "Group-think" jeopardizes many precious attributes of individualism. But if the trade union continues to derive its purpose and legitimacy from an increasingly irrelevant adversarial notion of contract, the labor movement will be in deep trouble. If it fails to adapt, it will certainly perish, and the individual will in no way be protected against economic tyranny.

In order for labor to adapt, it must appreciate fully its new functions in a consensual setup. Pragmatically speaking, unions are doing exactly that, but pragmatic innovation without ideological renovation is insufficient. In the steel industry, the evolution of consensus between companies and the United Steelworkers of America has taken place in a vacuum; neither companies nor union perceived the ideological implications of what they were doing. The result has been estrangement within the union, between the shop steward on the floor—who continues to embrace the old adversarial idea—and the union leadership, which has moved to a new concept. If consensualism is to work, it must be introduced simultaneously from the top down and from the bottom up. The industry has been belatedly introducing worker participation at the bottom, but the legacy of adversarialism dies hard.

Implicit in QWL programs is the idea of duty. Both managers and workers limit their rights, conscious of their interdependency and the interests of the whole firm. The Ford-UAW agreement, for example, says that nonunion salaried employees must accept the same hardships as union workers in an "equality-of-sacrifice" provision. Local union officials may file a grievance if they think that Ford is keeping too many managers on the rolls while union members are being laid off.[52]

Important questions of corporate governance arise: How are workers to be represented in decision-making at various levels of the corporation? Do they want to be? This, after all, takes time and effort. Where does the company turn if there is no organized representation of workers, as is the case in most U.S. companies? (Phrased differently, could the auto industry, for example, have made the progress it has without a union to reflect worker interests adequately in corporate decision-making, and to make decisions acceptable to workers?) AT&T might want Glenn Watts on its board, his own preferences notwithstanding. If so, can Watts responsibly say no?

The CWA believes that far from being superfluous, a union is as essential in a consensual environment as it is in a contractual one. Its leaders cite two reasons: First, the union forces management to take the new programs seriously. As one GM manager put it, "When you ask a bear to dance, you can't stop just when *you* get tired." Second, the rights of workers—including both those of the contract and those that evolve through QWL programs and the like—are protected.[53]

In Japan, where consensualism has resulted in enormous efficiency, workers at Toyo Kogyo used very similar terms to explain why they need a union:

—"The union is essential to protect the workers from capricious decisions by management."

—"There are times when management tries to force higher output rates even when they haven't made their investment contribution."

—"They sometimes expect workers to do it all."

—"The union must constantly remind management that the worker deserves his share of economic gains that are reaped by the successful Japanese auto firm." [54]

If the American economy is being outpaced by foreign government/business/labor systems that are more effective than our own, as Ford's Philip Caldwell and others have said, it seems that we must either raise tariff walls to protect ourselves from this alien competition, or we must assemble our own tripartite apparatus in order to compete successfully. Since tariff protection cannot be effectively maintained in an increasingly interdependent world, our only choice is a tripartite system assembled in the name of community need. The labor movement has generally favored this approach since 1980; business and government have been somewhat more ambivalent. A great deal of this ambivalence derives from traditional ideological assumptions about the roles and relationships of government and business; it is these assumptions that need inspection.

In 1979, a so-called "National Accord" was established under the leadership of former Secretary of Labor John T. Dunlop to provide a mechanism for cooperation on important national issues among government, business, and labor. Although the Dunlop group had some fruitful discussions and agreed generally on an incomes policy, there was insufficient time to develop the trust and confidence necessary for such cooperation to be effective. In the interim, President Reagan took office, and let it be known that he felt that no such cooperation was necessary, and that "free market" forces would produce economic growth and restore employment. As a result, Dunlop took his consensual efforts outside of government, forming an unofficial "Labor-Management Group" in March 1981. Lane Kirkland, president of the AFL-CIO, headed the labor representatives in the group, and Clifton C. Garvin, Jr., chairman of Exxon, led the management representatives. Focused mainly on national economic policy, the group's statement of purpose read: "The national interest requires a new spirit of mutual trust and cooperation, even though management and organized labor are, and will remain, adversaries on many issues." [55] The situation was less than ideal: there was obviously a serious question as to whether labor and management, without the participation of government, could effect meaningful change. There were, furthermore, legal issues involved.

Unlike European labor law, the American version has generally evolved after, rather than before, managers and unions have experimented with new forms. It has served to recognize and perhaps "neaten up" an established situation. Prior to the 1930s, the law generally sustained the traditional ideology: the fundamental task of government was to preserve property rights, and to protect the sanctity of the contract. Union organization, conflict with management, depression, and the New Deal combined to inspire the Wagner Act of 1935. Based on an adversary model of labor relations, it was designed to foster industrial peace by strengthening collective bargaining and assuring the rights of labor. It strengthened unions, and helped prevent employer interference in their activities. The underlying assumption, of course, was that employers and employees were inherently separate, with different purposes and objectives, and their relationship was best defined as one of controlled conflict. The Taft-Hartley Act of 1947 and the Landrum-Griffin Act of 1959, while they sought to make the conflict fairer and more democratic on the union side, did not alter this basic model.

Today's participative innovations reflect a fundamentally different model. Whereas the old structure tended to assume distrust, antagonism, divergent goals, strict controls, limited responsibility, and limited authority, the new one rests on the opposite premises.[56] The law, however, has not evolved correspondingly. As labor lawyer Thomas Schneider has pointed out: "The purpose of the law is to maintain a strict dichotomy between labor and management . . . to force employers to refrain from any action which will place them on both sides of the bargaining table"; "an employer must leave a union . . . scrupulously alone." Likewise, it strictly forbids an employer from interfering in any way with the formulation or administration of any labor organization.[57] Although Schneider concludes that legislative changes at this point are unwise, his observations highlight the degree to which current trends diverge from traditional assumptions—and the existing legal structure—regarding roles and relationships of management and labor.

If we assume that these trends will continue, and are indeed vital for efficiency and competitiveness, the choices seem clear. First, both management and unions could stick with the old conception of their roles, and the adversarial contract. Management could continue to view its basic task as the maximization of financial returns, and the union could retain the notion that its job is to secure more for the workers. The result is predictable: labor costs rise faster than productivity, causing inflation and a continued erosion of competitiveness; strikes proliferate; the economy suffers. Market share is eroded. Industry disintegrates or diversifies. Jobs are lost. Union membership declines. Both sides are weakened. The industrial face of the country changes, and not by choice, but by accident.

A second and preferable alternative is to encourage and strengthen the innovations that have begun, and to extend and intensify them. This requires a fundamental change on all sides, a recognition of the radicality of what is happening, and a redefinition of the roles and mission of both management and unions. It is unwise to minimize the implications. They affect, as I have suggested, both the very top and the bottom of corporations, and they extend to the role of government and the relationships of government, business, and labor. Any attempt to introduce change unmindful of the full extent of their effects will be frustrated by predictable obstructions, emanating from the old assumptions.

Frustration could lead the United States in a direction which it has thus far avoided—namely, into the rigidities of class conflict. American labor has never been a class movement like its European counterpart. The American labor leader does not regard himself as a leader of the working class, pitted against the owning class; he has rather taken the view that through adversarial bargaining, essentially economic in nature, he can gain political and social justice for his followers. But if in the face of a stagnant economy and competitive losses he fails in this approach and finds himself increasingly unsuccessful in moving to a more promising and profitable conception of his work, he may well be forced into the sort of political and social action embodied in the notion of class conflict.

The futility and damage of such a course were revealed to me during the summer of 1975, when I studied labor relations at the Cowley works of British Leyland, just outside Oxford, England.

Nowhere have the costs of ideological ambivalence been higher than in the United Kingdom. The British suffer from an even more acute and complex form of ideological schizophrenia than Americans, for their disease embraces three conflicting ideologies: two old ones, and a new one that is desperately trying to be born.

First, there is traditional communitarianism, with roots deep in Britain's history. Here the observer detects notions of hierarchy: class, status, feudal rights and obligations, deference and noblesse oblige, kings, queens, lords, and commons. Here, too, is the origin of the idea of government that, under God, plans for the good of the kingdom. (It is also the wellspring of the old idea of the university as an institution that teaches gentlemen about the world and all that therein lies, while steadfastly avoiding the earthy practicalities of specialization.)

In the Glorious Revolution of 1689, this ideology came under attack from Lockeanism, and although it was severely damaged by revolutionary individualism, it was not entirely expunged. The notion of equality gradually displaced hierarchy, but it never did so entirely. A curious dialectic resulted: if there are classes and if there is to be equality, there must also be a class struggle through which the working class seeks its place alongside the owning class. The modern history of Britain can be seen as a struggle between these two sets of ghosts, a painful and costly battle to evolve a third ideology—a new communitarianism—that meets the exigencies of the real world.

In the summer of 1975, the Labour Government had just acquired the shares of British Leyland. The company was broke; the banks could no longer meet its payroll. Anthony Wedgwood Benn, then Minister of Labor, was forced to act quickly. Without even the pretense of a coherent notion about how best to allocate Britain's dwindling resources, he made a crisis-driven judgment that the nation needed an auto industry. At the very least, close to a million jobs were at stake. An angry debate ensued in Parliament, with the Conservatives expressing strong doubts about the ability of the company to increase its productivity sufficiently to meet the demands of competition. They were concerned about the deplorable labor relations, singling out Cowley, where stoppages, slowdowns, absenteeism, and shoddy work had virtually crippled production.

Benn had the votes necessary for the takeover, but he sought to mute his opposition by requiring British Leyland to introduce "industrial democracy" as a way of achieving efficiency and lowering labor costs. The debate did not make the definition of "industrial democracy" clear, but Lord Ryder—who presided over the government's National Enterprise Board, which held BL's shares—said that it meant worker participation in management, and that it was a serious matter: "Any manager will be sacked who does not introduce it enthusiastically."

I went to the Cowley works, where some five thousand laborers were making cars. It was clear that work was proceeding relatively slowly. The Transport and General Workers Union (T and G) at the plant had been troubled for many years by a Trotskyite leadership. Conversations with both sides were illuminating.

The senior shop steward—an elderly man named Reg Parsons —was still a committed revolutionary, although an ex-Trot by that time. "The party takes too much of my time," he explained, "but I'm still a believer." I asked him what Trotskyism meant, and he explained that it involved workers' ownership of the means of production, carefully distinguishing it from the more statist brands of communism.

"It sounds something like 'industrial democracy,' " I said, recalling what I had heard in Parliament.

"Well, you must understand basically I am a leader of the working class, inevitably pitted against the capital-owning bastards."

When I asked him who they were, he pointed to the office where the two young men sat who were trying to manage the Cowley works.

"But," I asked, "who owns British Leyland?"

"The government," he said.

"And who is the government?"

"The Labour Party."

"And what's the most important component of the Labour Party?"

"The Trade Union Congress."

"And what's the biggest union in the TUC?"

"The T and G," he replied.

"But that's your union," I said. "Surely you are nearer the ownership of British Leyland than those fellows up there trying to run this place."

"Look," he said, "I don't know what you're driving at. I'm a leader of the working class inevitably pitted against the capital-owning bastards—have been all my life."

Parsons had only a few years to go before retirement, and was understandably reluctant to change his life's mission at that late date, whatever the reality. But he was not alone in conjuring up old ghosts to justify his actions; the managers of the Cowley works shared many of his inclinations. When I asked them what the trouble was with the plant, they said: "These fellows have had too much carrot; they need some stick."

"Who is going to wield the stick?" I asked.

"We are, of course. That's our job."

"Where are you going to get the muscle?" I continued. "Where does your authority come from?"

"The prerogatives of management. The right to manage comes from property rights. Everyone knows that."

"But who owns British Leyland?" I asked.

"Well, now that you mention it, it's the government."

"And what's the government?"

"The Labour Party."

"And the biggest component of the Labour Party?"

"The TUC."

"And the biggest union in the TUC?"

"The Transport and General Workers." They paused. "You mean it's that no-good Trot down there?"

Symbolism has an important role in reinforcing structures, both outmoded and contemporary. Among the many symbols of the old ways at Cowley were the several varieties of eating places. The workers' canteen had long, bare tables, sporting only a pair of salt and pepper shakers for every twenty workers. One level up, foremen enjoyed smaller square tables, on which were plastic water pitchers. At the top, senior supervisors had the benefits of waitress service, and carpeted floors beneath their mahogany tables. One incident seemed particularly telling: early one morning, as I talked with Parsons in a dirty little office below ground level, we looked up and observed through the high window a shiny black car, driven by a chauffeur, pulling up before the main entrance. Out stepped the plant manager. "There goes the bastard now," said Parsons. In truth, the manager was a decent young man, paid only modestly by American standards, whose perquisites included a company car. The psychological costs of this perquisite in that context were extreme: it would have been less expensive for the company to have doubled his pay and encouraged him to ride a bicycle to work.

At the end of the summer, in gratitude for the company's hospitality, I wrote a summary letter—unsolicited—to headquarters. I reprint it here because I think its suggestions pertain to many industrial settings today:

The old basis of management authority has eroded. Lord Nuffield [the founder of Morris Motors, the Cowley assembly plant] is dead; the old conception of managerial rights deriving from property rights is in the grave with him.

The "Government," for all intents and purposes, owns B-L, but "Government" is an obscure and fragmented entity which has neither the will nor the capability to impart adequate authority to management.

Management must have authority in order to exert the discipline required to make the organization function with justice and efficiency.

There is only one source—as far as I can see—from which realistically this authority can come at the present moment: from the workers via their shop stewards.

That is where the real power lies and it must be recognized. The national trade union organizations are of relatively little use in providing a basis of authority at the moment, because they are abstracted and detached from the workers.

Therefore, the Cowley managers have but one choice: to encourage and to enable shop stewards at Cowley to understand and to use the power which is theirs; to make clear to them that in a real sense the authority of management must spring from their decisions; and to help them make their decisions wisely.

If this reasoning is correct, the workers have the right and the power not only to provide management with its authority but also to decide who management is. I would make this clear to the shop stewards and provoke a discussion of what the characteristics of good and acceptable management are at Cowley, what competence is desirable, etc. I would ask, as it were, for a vote of confidence from the shop stewards.

Happily, it seems to me, many of the shop stewards whom I met seem responsible men who would respond well, if somewhat skeptically at first, to such an approach.

I recognize that this is a radical way to define what "industrial democracy" must mean. But management derives its authority from all those whom it manages; while at first blush this advice might appear shocking to the Cowley managers, on second thought it should appear as merely realistic.

The shock effect would be useful, it seems to me, in gaining shop stewards' cooperation, trust and confidence. If and when management say, "I am working for you—if you will help me," you will have the beginning of a new relationship.

I did not receive a reply to my letter. I did, however, get a Christmas card from the general secretary of the Labour Party that year. The inscription read: "Unity within, the enemy is without."

It appears that changes are occurring at BL, but they are slow and hard. In July 1982 the *Financial Times* reported that all Cowley employees would henceforth eat in the same dining area. "The canteen will be carpeted, however," the paper reported. " 'Some of our executives just cannot get away from the idea they should always have a carpet under their feet,' said one man from the shop floor." [58]

10

Making American Strategy
in a Competitive World

Many American business and labor leaders are acknowledging
that the federal government of the United States must have a
coherent strategy for dealing with the ramifications, both domestic and foreign, of international trade and competition. Priorities
need to be set, and realistic government and business policies
must be designed to achieve those priorities. The pretense of free
trade and *laissez faire* only obscures the fact that all nations of
the world—including our own—have and will continue to have a
host of policies that affect the behavior of business: subsidies,
tax incentives, accounting conventions, credit allocation, trade
laws, monetary policy, foreign and defense policy, environmental policy, energy policy, and many others. Either these policies
are designed coherently, with their overall effects calculated and
balanced; or they are the casual result of disparate interests,
seeking a variety of incompatible goals. Until fairly recently the
United States could afford incoherence; today, the costs are too

Portions of this chapter appeared in an article by the author and William R. Glass
in the May–June 1983 *Harvard Business Review* entitled "U.S. Trade Policy
Needs One Voice."

great. We need to find and employ mechanisms to promote coherence.

In this chapter, I will examine such a mechanism, which—with increased support from government, business, and labor—could become an effective instrument for the formulation of a national strategy to recover lost ground in the international arena. This mechanism is the White House Office of the United States Trade Representative (USTR), headed by a Cabinet-level appointee who supervises a staff of a hundred career officers. A number of other instruments have been proposed to accomplish this task, including, for example, a new Cabinet Department of Commerce and Trade, an expanded Council of Economic Advisors, and an Economic Cooperation Council. But the USTR, working closely with a strengthened White House Office of Management and Budget, has the best chance of effectively formulating a strategy for the United States in the world economy, assuring its implementation, and coordinating the necessary design of domestic policies.

Although it has important ideological implications, this is a pragmatic suggestion. First, the USTR exists; it is in place. Second, it has a successful record of achievement and good relations with Congress, the executive, business and labor. Third, it is focused on trade, an arena in which the need for an American strategy is most widely perceived, and in which the problems of policy incoherence are most dramatically illustrated.

Let us first review some of the empirical evidence that supports the contention that coherence is increasingly critical.

"I support free trade, but also know that it has limits," said Dr. Ruben Mettler, chairman of TRW and head of the Business Roundtable in 1982. "For example, there is a threshold below which it is against our national interest, as well as that of our trading partners, to allow a major U.S. industry such as steel to sink. Our government must develop the capacity to think coherently about what that national interest is, and business and labor have the primary responsibility to aggressively protect that interest by becoming fully competitive in world markets.

"The Defense Department is vitally concerned about shipping

certain products to the U.S.S.R., while the Commerce Department approves those very export licenses. We swing back and forth unpredictably. We are often neither a fully reliable supplier in world markets nor sufficiently restrictive in certain technologies critical to national defense. We need a strategy." [1]

Acknowledging the traditional aversion of business to the definition of the national interest by a coherent government, Irving Shapiro, former chairman of DuPont, said, "I don't think it's controversial to say that the role of government is to define the national interest. We don't have the mechanism to do it and we keep proving it year in and year out, but if government isn't going to define the national interest, who is?" [2]

Charles Brown, chairman of AT&T, Fletcher Byrom, retired chairman of Koppers and head of the Committee for Economic Development, Frank T. Cary, chairman of IBM, Howard Love, chairman of National Steel, William Norris, chairman of Control Data, Henry Schacht, chairman of Cummins Engine, and many other business leaders share these views. [3]

They derive from a realistic assessment of the growing interdependence of the United States with the rest of the world. To summarize data presented in earlier chapters: we are irrevocably enmeshed in world competition, and in many areas we are losing. Our trade deficit in 1983 is likely to be more than $60 billion, about half of which is with Japan. Some 20% of U.S. industrial production is now exported, and farm produce from two out of five acres is sold abroad. One out of every six jobs in U.S. manufacturing derives from exports. Almost one third of U.S. corporate profits comes from international trade and foreign investment of U.S. firms. The share of trade in the gross national product has doubled in the past decade. Considering potential exposure to import penetration, more than 70% of U.S. goods are now effectively in international competition. And more than half of the nation's supplies of twenty-four important raw materials, ranging from petroleum to cobalt, are obtained from foreign sources. [4]

The competitiveness of American business in the world economy is at the center of trade policy. As Bruce Scott of the Harvard Business School has pointed out, competitiveness is a function of a community's allocation of resources and of its political and economic organization. The competition of East Asian countries, for example, is based on a willingness and an ability to save, to invest, and to design a strategy through which government, business, and labor work in concert to abandon fading industries and create new ones aimed at the rich markets of the West.[5]

The pressures on the United States to think strategically are prompting a heightened awareness of relationships among the several components of public policy. For example: high interest rates restrain investment, and create a massive demand for dollars in the world, which leads to an overvalued dollar and an undervalued yen. This in turn makes U.S. exports more expensive, and foreign imports less so. As the trade deficit grows, the economy stagnates and unemployment rises; welfare costs climb; government deficits to pay for them rise; inflation results from public money flooding the economy for purposes of consumption, not production. Rising government deficits require increased government borrowing, which keeps interest rates high. All the pieces of this vicious circle are related. No policy can work which does not recognize this holistic reality. Thus, as Dr. Mettler said: "A sound economic strategy requires that monetary, tax, regulatory, antitrust, and trade and investment policies and practices be framed in a worldwide context."[6]

Thomas R. Donahue of the AFL-CIO added: "We need a framework through which government, business, and labor can arrive at a consensus about industrial policy. It's very clear that nations which can do this are moving ahead of those which cannot. It is folly to pretend that we can live in a world which is so interlocked by trade patterns and rely on a free-market system when that system is regularly deformed and distorted by others. If we continue, we will be allowing other nations to dictate our national policies and direction. Some industries undoubtedly will have to contract. There must therefore be national support structures to phase them out—job retraining, development of other industries in a parallel time frame, and ways of matching workers to new industrial needs."[7]

Before returning to the question of where and how the formulation of national strategy can best be institutionalized in the federal government, let us consider the plight of a particular industry—the steel industry—as an example of a situation which requires strategic attention.

The condition of the American steel industry in 1983 dramatically demonstrated the need for continuing, coherent thought and action by companies, government, and labor. Each of these groups had long pursued its own objectives, and the resultant policies were whipsawing the industry, leaving it unable to meet any of the competing goals adequately. It was becoming clear that we could not have everything: if we chose to pursue social goals, for example, the cost would have to be diverted from the pursuit of economic efficiency, competitive supremacy, and financial return. It was equally obvious that we had no mechanism with which to set priorities among our many objectives. Some policies shaped the environment so that the steel industry achieved social ends; others encouraged financial return; still others favored competitive improvement. The strength of each set of policies varied over time, and the industry, in responding to first one set of government policies and then another, has over the long run failed to satisfy anybody.

By 1983, the industry was operating at 30% of capacity; more than 100,000 steelworkers had been laid off since the 1960s; foreign producers had captured 20% of the domestic market; the industry was retrenching. President Reagan had said in 1980, "America needs a modern, world-class steel industry. My administration will support government policies which enable us to achieve it."[8] Three years later, however, reality did not resemble that ideal.

Labor's point of view was well summarized by Sam Camens of the United Steelworkers of America: "There is no steel company that has any long-term perspective of the needs of the nation. Management is thinking only about the short-term interests of particular companies. They're not modernizing; they're not plowing profits back into new plant. The purpose of the business is to make money—not steel, not product, not services—but money; and every three months they're evaluated by *Business Week*. That's not the way to insure a healthy economy. Somebody has to think about the community as a whole—and twenty years out."[9]

From a broader perspective, it is clear that other countries have been more coherent and persistent about the goals they have sought for their steel industries, and have shaped policy environments accordingly. The results show up in the international trade arena. The Europeans want employment from their industry and are getting it, albeit at high financial cost. The Japanese look for market share through mechanization, and are prepared to pay the price in financial return and employment. Many developing countries desire a steel industry to satisfy national pride and to earn foreign exchange; short-run financial return is unimportant.

In contrast, what the United States wants from its steel industry is unclear. Policies affecting it consistently reveal contradiction, rather than purpose. We have not been able to force other nations to change their objectives; their achievement of their goals has left us increasingly befuddled about ours. Nor is the problem an isolated one; indeed, it has very broad implications. The success of ongoing international trade negotiations clearly requires either an implicit or explicit definition of the nation's interest regarding domestic steel manufacturing. Without such a definition, we will not improve our competitive posture, and we will continue to suffer vacillation, dissatisfaction with industry performance, and waste.

What are the origins and expressions of the steel industry's competing goals? An analysis of statistics provided by the American Iron and Steel Institute for the years 1972–1981 shows that industry managers have sought high financial return under current accounting conventions. Of the four possible goals for the industry—economic efficiency, financial return, competitive supremacy, and social/political contribution—the industry has pursued financial return, essentially through improvements in economic efficiency. This has of necessity entailed sacrificing competitive position and employment.

The effort to improve financial returns has been made by industry management despite recent government policy, most of which—notably depreciation rates and environmental-control laws—has tended to sacrifice financial return in favor of other goals. While management was seeking to improve productivity by closing plants, government was simultaneously requiring increased expenditures on plant and equipment. Pollution-control laws, with their standards based on effluents rather than finances, directly contradicted efforts to improve industry productivity by shrinking the asset base. Between 1972 and 1981, the steel industry was forced to spend $6 billion to control air and water quality, while its overall asset base was declining by $8 billion. These forced expenditures, when combined with slow depreciation rates, retarded the improvements in productivity that were essential to high financial returns.

The lessons of this confused state of affairs seem clear: If as a nation we want management to pursue financial return, we must design policies with that in mind. We must also remember that an effective pursuit of this goal will have negative consequences for other laudable objectives; therefore, policies to encourage any one goal must be accompanied by procedures to handle the attendant negative consequences. If we choose full employment at wage rates consistently higher than productivity increases, for example, we can't also expect big financial returns.* If management is seeking high financial return while government policy pursues high employment, we will end up with neither. It would be more efficient either to emphasize employment with the necessary subsidization, or to go for profit with requisite adjustment and retraining policies to take care of the idle.

The industry's dismal performance figures obscure some very large differences within it. (The large, integrated producers have performed very badly, with seven out of ten recording losses in 1982. The so-called "mini-mills" are more profitable, as are some of the specialty producers.) But government policies—which affect the different segments of the industry in different ways—are often applied across the board. The clean-water program, for example, was designed with large operations in mind. It mandated treatment plants containing bacteria that must regularly be fed large amounts of pollutants—as Robert Leone put it, "The bugs have to eat three times a day." If we wanted to encourage profitable mini-mills, that policy would need to be inspected. Many questions present themselves: Do we want or need a profitable steel industry? What does the President mean by a "world-class" industry? What is the "threshold" to which Dr. Mettler

---

* Real labor costs in basic steel rose 46% between 1970 and 1979; productivity rose only 25%.[10]

refers? With world steel production capacity now exceeding demand, who should reduce their capacity?

In fact, government policy toward international competition has been consistent, but not effective. In general, whether under the guise of antidumping and countervailing-duty laws or trigger-price mechanisms, the U.S. has tried to force other countries to accept our implicit steel policy of seeking high financial returns and high wages without government subsidies. Subsidization by governments, for whatever reason, has been deemed "wrong" by our government, which has attempted to get other governments to behave more "fairly"—i.e., to pursue the goals we are pursuing. Our persistent attempts have been regularly unsuccessful, and the result has been a decline in American market share. As the American steel industry has pursued a high return, markets have naturally gone to those willing to take lower returns. We have few options at this point: we must either reduce labor costs and profit expectations, accept a continuing decline in market share, or seek some form of protection.

In 1982 the U.S. government found itself once again obliged (both by law and by its commitment to free-trade principles) to seek to prevent foreign governments—in this case, our European allies—from subsidizing their steel industries. The Europeans came to the table under the threat of countervailing duties to be imposed by the United States on their imports, but also angered by the dispute over the Soviet-European natural-gas pipeline. With this background, the Europeans sought to negotiate guarantees of a certain share of the U.S. steel market. This represented a departure; the idea of market shares was clearly inconsistent with free-trade pronouncements. On the other hand, it was appealing to both the industry and the government: the industry relished a more orderly marketplace; and the government was eager to prevent its political, diplomatic, and economic relations with Europe from being further soured. A deal was struck in October of that year, whereby the Europeans agreed to reduce steel exports to the United States for the next three years to slightly over 5% of the market, down from 6% in 1982. Given this initial success, it seemed likely that the industry would seek similar deals with Japan, South Korea, Brazil, Mexico, and other steel exporters accused of subsidizing their steel industries.

For the United States, these are relatively uncharted waters.

If this country is to be an effective negotiator in world trade in steel and other important industries, it must know its own interests and priorities, and have some coherent notion of policies for achieving them. Of one thing there can be no doubt: the nation will need a mechanism for developing the consensus necessary to implement those policies effectively.

If management and unions in the major American industries were to design a governmental apparatus capable of formulating a strategy for the United States in the world economy, I believe it should have the following capabilities:

1. It must be able to formulate a single government position, reflecting the views of the executive branch. Recognizing the very different interests and responsibilities of the several interested departments of government—Agriculture, Commerce, Defense, Treasury, State—the ideal apparatus should collect, balance, and compose those various demands into a coherent U.S. position. This is plainly not easy. If we impose strict restraints on European steel exports, for example, the Europeans are likely to retaliate against U.S. farm products, damaging our agricultural sector. Similarly, U.S. exports become prohibitively expensive as the value of the dollar rises in response to the Federal Reserve's tight money policies and high interest rates. State and Defense, for their part, are loath to anger European governments at a time when they are seeking greater European commitments to NATO.

But these conflicting priorities reinforce the point that trade negotiations are inevitable, and that America must know its own mind. They also suggest that the organizing apparatus should not be part of any single department, but should be above them all.

2. It must be able to secure congressional endorsement of a definition of national priorities. This requires congressional participation in the formulation process, and suggests that the constitutional separation of powers between Congress and the executive should be bridged in matters concerning trade and international competition. No trade policy can be effective without the support of Congress, and the actions of that body affect American competitiveness in many ways. Furthermore, relations between Congress and the executive in this area must be continuing, stable, and relatively formal in nature, to ensure continuity through electoral changes.

3. The apparatus must be able to work cooperatively, indeed intimately, with the companies and the labor unions who are on the front lines. The government needs their competence—knowledge, technical skills and judgment—in conducting negotiations, just as business and labor must have the authority of government to set the global framework within which they can plan and prosper. Furthermore, no trade policy can be effective without a consensus between business and labor; both parties must accept it, or they will fight it in Congress and elsewhere. The procedures for securing agreement by business and labor will naturally include bargaining about a wide range of factors, which therefore must fall within the purview of the apparatus. If, for example, government expects the steel industry to accept more foreign competition, it might at the same time ease environmental regulations. If competitiveness requires the consolidation of a particular industry, the apparatus should be in a position to fend off antitrust action, as well as to assure displaced workers of retraining and new jobs. It thus needs to possess a wide reach throughout all government systems and programs, which neither the Administration's proposed Department of Commerce and Trade nor the House Democrats' proposed Economic Cooperation Council would have.

4. Domestic interest groups will—and should—affect the formulation of government strategy. The apparatus must be able to persuade those groups to balance their competing demands with a view to the general long-term needs of the nation. Once a general approach is agreed upon, the apparatus must be the single focus for negotiation of trade agreements between the United States and foreign nations. It is senseless for these negotiations to take place at many different levels in Washington; this only encourages foreign interests to search out the point where our armor is thinnest.

The apparatus must also be able to evaluate and pass through pressures from the international to the domestic arenas. The negotiation of tariff and nontariff barriers with other countries, for example, reaches into all aspects of the U.S. government and economy. Nontariff barriers include, for example, subsidies to encourage exports. But when is a subsidy a subsidy, and when is its purpose export rather than domestic justice? Europeans complain that U.S. price controls on natural gas have kept costs of our chemical industry unfairly low. Is that a subsidy? The leasing provisions of the Tax Act of 1981 were designed to funnel money into the profitless industries of America, including big steel. Did that constitute a subsidy? The free-market enthusiasts in Washington decry credit allocation by foreign government as being unfair; yet the Council of Economic Advisors reported that in 1981 the U.S. government allocated $86.5 billion to private industry and agriculture in direct loans, guaranteed loans, or government-sponsored loans.[11] If credit allocation is to be a matter of negotiation abroad, therefore, our ideal apparatus has to have some role in it at home.

5. *The apparatus must have a superior, independent staff.* Since negotiating with foreigners is a skill honed by experience, requiring language ability and cultural adaptability, the apparatus should be staffed by the highest-quality personnel, who are encouraged to remain at their work over a long period of time and are relatively free of political patronage and other distractions. The staff should not be large; almost all of its routine work can be farmed out to other departments. But it must be authoritative, with wide-ranging power and responsibility. The head of the apparatus should therefore be close to the President, and be one of the most important members of the Cabinet.

Many of its activities will impinge upon domestic policies. It should therefore have close working relationships with the Office of Management and Budget, which over the years has gained authority for coordinating all domestic regulation and programs. There would then be, in effect, two White House offices with powers to oversee and coordinate executive activities, one focused on domestic matters, and the other on international competition and trade. The two should be designed to work increasingly closely together.

This, then, is our ideal, and the White House Office of the United States Trade Representative (USTR) is the most promising institution to approximate this ideal. First, to a limited degree, it has already done so during the past decade, under the able leadership of William Eberle, Frederick Dent, Robert

Strauss, Reubin Askew, and—since 1981—William E. Brock. Second, the USTR as it is currently organized could theoretically and legally perform almost every function set forth above. It is close to the President and the OMB. It is above all other departments and agencies, and is thus able to coordinate their interests and employ their resources. It is firmly tied to Congress by a unique statute, and at the same time presides over a time-tested array of business and labor advisory committees. Its small staff is regarded as among the most competent in Washington.

The critical issue today is presidential will. For the USTR to do what needs to be done, the President must want it to do so. To this point, presidents have been ambivalent. Both Presidents Carter and Reagan did their utmost to move the office out of the White House. Finding themselves unable to do so because of Congressional resistance, each reassessed his position and determined to keep the USTR where it is. But the office still needs substantial reinforcement if it is even to approach its immense task.

The idea for the current USTR emerged in Congress in the early 1970s as frustration grew with the old procedures for trade negotiation. There were two problems: first of all, the United States, the leading proponent of free trade in the world, was, Congress felt, being "taken" by other countries, which would not play by the "rules of the game." The "cheaters," such as Japan and France, were continually confronting us with sophisticated and subtle procedures and relationships with which we could not compete. Among these were close coordination among government, business, and labor, and a varied collection of nontariff barriers. Second, our negotiators would often go to international meetings and hammer out a deal, only to have it upset when it was submitted for approval to Congress.

In 1973, representatives of ninety-eight nations met in Tokyo and agreed to begin multilateral trade negotiations—"the Tokyo Round"—to reduce tariff and nontariff barriers and to reform the General Agreement on Tariffs and Trade (GATT), the global mechanism for implementing international trade agreements. Leaders in Congress, the executive branch, business, and labor were eager to avoid the fiascoes of the past. A new structure for making trade policy was thus established in the 1974 Trade Act. It consisted of three major elements:

First, Congress changed its role from the detailed drafting of trade bills to a more general oversight, by committing itself to consider trade agreements resulting from the Tokyo Round as an entire package to be voted on without amendment. Congress further agreed to a fixed and expedited timetable for considering trade agreements. In this way, it provided the negotiators with the assurance that their agreements abroad would be considered promptly and on their overall merit, leaving maximum flexibility for international deal-making. Congress also insulated itself from the interest-group pressures that had caused so much trouble in the past, and thus prevented any ensuing trade legislation from being bled to death by a thousand small wounds.

Second, the Special Trade Representative (STR) was greatly strengthened, and given cabinet rank. Congress expected the office to be a single strong focal point within the executive branch for determining trade policy, and for making tradeoffs between the positions held by various departments and agencies. The STR chaired a series of intergovernmental coordinating committees that thrashed out final American positions. Location in the White House, as well as dual responsibility to both Congress and the executive branch, gave the office authority, and also allowed it to bridge the gap between the two branches of government.

The third innovation of the Trade Act of 1974 was the creation of an extensive set of advisory committees, composed of members from the private sector, to consult with and advise the American negotiators. When Congress deliberately insulated itself from the special pleading of interest groups, it also mandated the executive branch to listen to them, and to incorporate their recommendations into American trade policy. In this way, diverse interests could be taken into account before and during the formulation process, rather than after agreements had been reached. Congress maintained its responsibility for oversight by requiring each committee to submit a final report to it.

According to Geza Feketekuty of the USTR Office staff: "The idea was that the negotiators should get as many of these groups as possible on board with what they were doing. At the end of the negotiations, each of the committees was required to report to the Congress on the extent to which the executive branch took their advice into account, and the extent to which they were satisfied with the outcome. If they said they were unhappy, the

Congress wasn't going to agree with what was negotiated."[12] In 1982 there were forty-five private advisory committees with nearly a thousand members, representing a wide variety of interests in agriculture, industry, and labor.

Obviously, this consensus-making structure was new, and required some time to work effectively. Participants from both public and private sectors had to set aside years of adversarial relations to work together to formulate common strategies and tactics.

As the Tokyo Round began to heat up, the consensus-making activities of the USTR increased. When American negotiators needed to know what a specific tariff reduction was worth, or how much of a problem a certain nontariff barrier really was, they turned to the pertinent advisory committee for the answers. An American company that found itself having difficulties getting its products into a foreign market could ask for help through its advisory committee. Congress sent representatives to meetings of the private advisory committees and the intergovernmental coordinating committees. The USTR became a central information exchange—a "switchboard," as it was called—on trade policy, a function which helped to ensure a coherent formulation of American trade positions.

The ability of the USTR to turn its information resources into an effective tool for consensus-building was greatly enhanced by the appointment of Robert Strauss as Special Trade Representative by President Carter in 1977. Unlike former STRs, Strauss had no experience in trade or international affairs; rather, he was a politician, most recently having been chairman of the Democratic Party. His talents were in putting together coalitions and building support for a position. With the full support of the President, he applied these skills to the task of building a broad consensus for the agreements coming out of the Tokyo Round. Tradeoffs had to be made, both large and small: the Italians, for example, complained about restrictions on almonds and eyeglasses. Opposition from the bourbon industry to the removal of a nontariff barrier on whiskey imports was neutralized by concessions gained on tobacco. Steel was less than satisfied with the trade agreements, but was mollified by adjustments in the wording of domestic legislation. Above all, GATT and free trade had to be preserved, and this could be accomplished only by building a broad consensus for multilateral negotiations in the United States through a combination of domestic and international deal-making.

Strauss was able to use the central position of the USTR and strong presidential support to become, in effect, a broker, building consensus between the U.S. and foreign governments, between agencies and departments of the executive branch, between Congress and the executive, and between government and the private sector. He was able to use his cabinet rank, the consensus-building resources of the USTR, its close White House ties, its special relationship to both Congress and the executive, and particularly its institutionalized ties to the private sector, to achieve broad agreement on the Tokyo Round conclusions. A significant measure of his success was the near-unanimous passage by Congress of the domestic legislation implementing the Tokyo Round agreements, a welcome departure from the incoherent results of previous multinational negotiations.

The kind of consensus-building engaged in by the USTR during the Tokyo Round was an unaccustomed activity for the American government. There have been many examples of ad hoc coalitions being formed under strong leadership, often in times of crisis, but the United States has few institutions that encourage continuing cooperation among sectors that are normally adversaries. As a link between Congress and the executive, and particularly with its extensive outreach to agriculture, business, and labor through the private advisory committees, the USTR was able to obtain broad agreement among diverse groups on both trade strategy and tactics.

This ability, it should be noted, was enhanced by the exclusion of the public from the inner workings of the USTR. Private advisory committee meetings were exempted from the "sunshine" provisions of the Federal Advisory Committee Act. Participants on all sides credited this exemption with enabling the committees to get down to the business of bargaining with a minimum of institutional posturing. The committee sessions provided an opportunity for a mutual exchange of views and a forum for hammering out compromises. While representing diverse interests, the participants were able to unite behind what they believed to be the national interest, a position that negotiators could then confidently take to the bargaining table.

Those who have spoken about their participation in the Tokyo Round were quick to point out that they did not get everything they wanted. Without exception, though, they agreed that they were better off being on the inside of a consensual process than on the outside of an adversarial one. Their general conclusion was that the new procedures not only helped the process of policy formulation to function better, but that they also produced good results. For the first time, U.S. representatives were able to promote American interests on an equal footing with their international competitors, and the broad support for the Trade Adjustments Act of 1979 (which implemented the Tokyo Round agreements) suggested a widespread consensus that the agreements were in the national interest.

The reaffirmation by the 1979 act of the changes made in 1974 reflected congressional confidence in the efficacy of this new system, as well as in the results it produced. The expedited procedures for considering trade legislation in Congress were maintained. The office of the USTR was made permanent. The system of private advisory committees was reauthorized, and its mandate expanded from provision of advice on negotiations to implementation of the agreements and ongoing consultation on trade policy. According to the report of the House Ways and Means Committee on the 1979 Trade Act:

> The continuation of this type of mechanism will be of critical importance in ensuring effective implementation of the 1979 agreements, evaluating and refining those agreements, managing problems in key trading sectors, and shaping overall U.S. trade policy objectives and priorities.[13]

Although many countries have close ties between their governments and their private sectors, particularly when considering international issues, such is not the case in the United States. As Phyllis Bonanno, director of the Office of Private Sector Liaison at USTR, put it, "You have a private sector in the United States unlike any other in a developed country in the world. Our private sector and our government do not walk hand in hand the way the Japanese, Germans, and French do."[14] Americans are much

more comfortable with adversarial than with consensual procedures, and because of our fundamental belief that the common
good emerges from the competition of each group pursuing its
own particular interests, we look askance at efforts to bring those
interest groups together to work out and articulate common
goals.

The USTR and its consensus-making activities during the
Tokyo Round did not escape this criticism, and the initial ambivalence expressed by private-sector members of the advisory
committees certainly reflected this view. Over time, though, as
the participants worked together, most of the doubters were converted. They concluded—as noted above—that being on the inside from the beginning was much more effective than attacking
from the outside once positions were established.

To some observers, that was precisely the problem. According
to George Eads, who was on the Council of Economic Advisors
in the White House during the Tokyo Round:

> It wasn't a case of the designated representatives of government
> saying, "These codes are in the national interest. Let's figure out
> some way to get them passed." It was a whole series of bilateral
> deals. It was political brokering in the best American sense of that
> word—log-rolling. The risk is, first, that once the government
> knows the power it has attained, it's tempted to use that power.
> Second, once there is a group identified as the place to which you
> go to lobby, lots of power will be assembled at that place. In some
> ways, it's good to have the lobbying points dispersed and diverse.[15]

In short, suggested Eads, rather than serving as a mechanism for
determining the national interest, a consensual instrument such
as the USTR can become a place for the cynical promotion of the
interests that are represented, at the expense of those that are
not.

Eads's comments cannot be dismissed lightly. They reflect
powerful elements of the American creed. But it seems clear that
the incoherence that he believes protects less powerful interests
is a luxury in today's competitive world. The USTR apparatus,
or something like it, is not a choice but a necessity. The question
we must pose is, How can this vital instrument be safeguarded
from undue influence by private interests, and allowed to focus
on the public interest? One might add further that the "public

interest'' does not exist as some absolute concept, arrived at in a political vacuum. On the contrary: the definition of the public interest must emerge from exactly the kind of pulling and hauling that the USTR apparatus is now set up to manage.

What seems essential is that business, government, and labor understand their roles and responsibilities clearly. Here again the thoughts of Irving Shapiro and Ruben Mettler are particularly relevant. Says Shapiro:

> If we want better government, business had better help develop the alternative policy choices and lay them out so that people who have the political power can make wiser choices.
>
> Policy choices must be made through the political system. The role of the private sector is to help the political system do the job better.[16]

And Mettler:

> There is no question that the United States has to become more competitive. We have neglected the health of our economic system. But there is no remedy which can be put into place outside of the political process. It is all very well for private groups of academics, business people, or whoever to meet and talk and recommend, but when the chips are down it is through the political process that national policy changes are made in the United States.[17]

Eads's comments, and those of Bradford Stroup of Data General, raise legitimate questions about representation on the committees of the USTR. Stroup is concerned about the large, established computer companies that built plants in Europe, Japan, and other countries before many nontariff barriers were erected, and which are naturally not eager to see those barriers removed. "These big companies have a dominant place on the USTR's Electronics and Instrumentation Advisory Committee," he said. "It's hard to get the government to listen to the problems of the smaller, newer companies. I think there ought to be fuller participation by the industry as a whole. To some extent, I suppose, that's our fault. We haven't been pushing as hard as we ought for membership. I think we should work harder at it. But then there's always the question of where we make our effort in Washington. Do we do better concentrating on the Defense Department, for example, or working through the USTR advisory committees?"[18]

In addition to the "end-run" problem, and the big *vs.* the small and old *vs.* new representational issues, there is the question of which segments of an industry are represented. Membership on the Commerce Department's Steel Tripartite Committee of 1978–79 was mostly limited to the large integrated carbon-steel manufacturers, who were in the deepest trouble. Few of the smaller plants—the mini-mills referred to earlier, and the specialty steel companies—were represented. The 1974 Trade Act authorized limited government loans and loan guarantees to companies injured by foreign competition. Help was restricted, however, to those companies that had already suffered losses in sales and production. The result was too little help channeled too late, to the least competitive elements of the industry. It seems an odd point to need emphasis, but it does: winners, as well as losers, must have a say in national strategy.

The interests of American workers present a number of representational problems. There are many industry sectors that have not been organized by labor. Unions are often structured in ways that do not conveniently fit the advisory committee titles, and some industries, such as the semiconductor industry, have virtually no unions at all. The problem has to some extent been avoided by the USTR's practice of placing industry and labor on separate committees. But labor representation will be a continuing difficulty until traditional union organization is extended to unorganized industries, or some form of company union system, as in Japan, can be established. It is significant that on the new Services Policy Advisory Committee (which pertains to banking, insurance, shipping, and other services), industry and labor representatives are for the first time meeting together. Union members include the presidents of the communications and electrical workers' unions, the pilots' union, hotel and restaurant employees, and the seafarers' union.

If labor organization makes tripartite arrangements difficult, so does that of industry. Unlike in Europe or Japan, much of American industry is not well organized. "Banks, for example, are a very heterogeneous lot," said Geza Feketekuty. "It is difficult for the American Bankers Association to represent effectively the full diversity. In fact, service industries generally are not well organized at all politically." It is an incoherence that—like that of labor—will eventually need attention.

The USTR apparatus represents a radical—if pragmatic—departure from several components of traditional American ideology. It would have failed if the foundation for its authority and legitimacy had not been carefully laid. Its consensus-building activities diminish the separation of the Congress from the Executive, and are protected from publicity. The USTR seeks to organize and reduce (if not to restrict) interest-group activity; it recognizes that the marketplace is not free and open, and that therefore government policies and leadership are required to organize a national strategy; it presumes that consensus and cooperation among government, business, and labor are better than conventional adversarialism. As noted earlier, these are conclusions and goals loaded with inflammatory potential: without a clear and precise mandate from Congress, carefully nurtured and preserved, the instrument would almost certainly be deemed illegitimate, and its authority would erode.

Initially, the USTR apparatus was conceived by Congress as an instrument with a narrow purpose—that of conducting trade negotiations with other countries. But in 1974, and again in 1979, Congress extended the USTR's purview to include all of trade policy. Today, we must define what "trade policy" is. As I have suggested, it seems to be inseparable from a host of other government policies affecting United States competitiveness in the world, including fiscal, monetary, employment, and environmental strategies. Congress should state clearly whether it intends the USTR office to think coherently about the impact of all those policies on U.S. fortunes in the world. What role, for example, is the USTR supposed to play with respect to the massive, mounting problems of the steel, auto, and textile industries? How far does its mandate extend? William Brock has admitted that "trying to use the process for the ongoing management of trade and competitive problems is more difficult than when you have major negotiations underway with deadlines to be met." Its authority over nontariff issues could logically impel it into virtually every aspect of these problems, foreign and domestic. Is that what Congress wants?

Since 1976, the steel advisory committee of the USTR has been meeting every three months. It made an important contribution to the subsidies code in the 1979 law.[19] The 1982 industry suits— aimed at preventing foreign governments from subsidizing their steel producers in Europe, Brazil, South Africa, and South Korea —brought steel under the jurisdiction of the Commerce Department, charged with enforcing antidumping and countervailing- duty laws. But as law enforcement turns inevitably into negotiations, the steel issue needs the coordinating capabilities of the USTR. The U.S. cannot have a sensible steel policy without, for example, taking into account the interests of American banks. The big steel producers of the 1990s will certainly include Brazil and Mexico; each plans to double or triple its capacity. Each also owes from $60 billion to $80 billion to foreign banks, mostly American.

The Reagan administration has urged the International Monetary Fund to force debtor countries to tighten their belts and pay their debts. The banks in wealthy nations have applauded this notion. The economics that the administration is urging upon the poor nations run as follows: consume less, save and invest more, and liberate your entrepreneurs. With the additional investment funds that become available, they will make products for export to the U.S. and elsewhere, earning the foreign exchange that will enable the debtors to pay their debts.

We must note, however, that one such product will almost certainly be steel, probably produced and exported inexpensively. Will the banks applaud as vigorously as such behavior continues to erode the steel industries of Europe and America, which also, after all, have debts to pay? And if the United States is to become increasingly dependent on cheap steel from developing countries, would we not prefer more of it to come from Mexico—nearby, and heavily in debt to our banks—than from South Korea? Trade policy is only one part of a total economic policy, which in turn is inseparable from foreign political and military policies, and from domestic policies as well.

Enlargements of the responsibilities of the USTR can be expected to cause confrontations with the older cabinet departments, such as Commerce, Agriculture, Labor, and Treasury, upon whose staffs the office draws. Although there is good reason to locate the apparatus at the highest and most central level, namely the White House, the relationships with other parts of the executive branch will need continuing attention. If business discovers it can gain more by seeking special treatment through a cabinet department, it will make the job of the USTR more difficult, and will ultimately weaken it.

There are other problems in the path of the USTR if and when it moves from the relatively low-profile task of trade negotiation to the high-stakes role of formulating an American strategy for international competition. As the issues with which it deals escalate in importance, the major players may be reluctant to put up with the behind-the-scenes quality of its operation. Even now, some business representatives resent the fact that they cannot get to the real decision-makers through the advisory-committee structure. When the chips are down, they want to see the STR himself or other top policy-makers in government. In addition, there are growing complaints that the White House is using advisory-committee appointments to reward political supporters, which reduces the effectiveness of the committees and diminishes their stature.

Undoubtedly the success of the USTR to date has been partly due to the persons who have headed it: their personal qualities, their access to the President and his inner circle of advisers, and their political influence. But unless the importance of the office is recognized for what it is, its leadership will inevitably deteriorate, and it will be unable to fulfill its expanded mission.

Centers of decision on trade matters will proliferate. In 1983, there were already signs that this was happening, as issues that should have been dealt with through the USTR were being taken up separately by Commerce, Defense, State, Congress, and elsewhere. This is a trend that must be reversed if the USTR is to assume a greater role.[20]

Leaders of government, business, and labor have a clear choice. They can continue acting as they have, or they can help to build a mechanism to formulate U.S. trade policy, and contribute to a national strategy to regain strength in an increasingly competitive world. Today, the voice of business is particularly important, because its influence in Washington is at a relatively high level. Because it has much of the knowledge and competence necessary to make these choices wisely, it has responsibility to make this contribution.

Business can use its influence to help build a national capacity for coherent strategy formulation; it can help to create a procedure through which goals and policies can be set and a consensus behind them developed. In my judgment, business can do this best by strengthening the USTR apparatus, encouraging strong support for it from the President and his staff, enhancing the role of the advisory-committee structure by using it and protecting it from misuse, and by acting on the premise that the prospects of business are linked to the ability of the nation as a whole to prosper.

11

Possibilities for
the Future

The behavior and authority of the government, corporations, and trade unions in the United States are changing as they confront inexorable pressures, global and domestic. As these changes occur, issues of competence arise.

Government, whose authority is rooted in the consent of the governed and the mechanics of interest group pluralism, faces the necessity of defining community need over a relatively long time span. It must—it will—fix goals and priorities, and design policies to carry them out. Somehow, it will concoct a national strategy. The questions are: when, how, and how well? The attendant problems are twofold: developing a consensus to support its new role, and organizing the competence to implement what the consensus endorses.

Implementation will depend upon business, especially large, publicly held corporations. The authority of corporate managers, once rooted exclusively in property rights delegated by shareholders, is moving more toward government—requiring harmony with community need—and toward the managed, who demand a share of control in return for cooperation in promoting the health of the enterprise and the community.

Trade unions, whose authority has traditionally been derived from the collective contract, adversarially bargained in the interests of their membership, now face the necessity of consensus for the good of both their membership and the firm.

The competence of all three institutions depends upon a recognition of their new bases of authority, and on a reorganization to combine their various skills and resources in the most effective manner.

The American disease is an ideological schizophrenia, revealed in ambivalence and inadvertence as our institutions move hesitantly and pragmatically to cope with necessity, and depart from a known and cherished ideology to one that is confused and at times menacing. The symptoms are distrust, division, and delay, exhibited in economic decline, political uncertainty, and social disintegration.

Although the signs of the disease are in many ways physical, the causes are psychological, philosophical, and religious. "In a curious, persistent way, our problem as a nation arises from a surplus of moral energy," Daniel Patrick Moynihan once said. "Our great weakness is the habit of reducing the most complex issues to the most simplistic moralisms. Moralism drives out thought. As a result, we have acquired bad habits of speech and worse patterns of behavior, lurching from crisis to crisis with the attention span of a five-year-old. We have never learned to be sufficiently thoughtful about the tasks of running a complex society." [1]

The moralism to which Moynihan referred derives from the traditional American ideology, Samuel Huntington's "American Creed," which at its core is a religious conviction. Polls revealed in the 1970s that 94% of Americans believed in God, and 71% in life after death—astonishing figures when compared to other nations. In Japan, for example, the comparable figures were 44% and 18%. [2] Concomitant with these beliefs is a concept of contractual relationship with the Almighty, wherein man receives God's blessing according to his works on earth. The rules governing these works, the definition of virtue and right thinking, have approximated the traditional ideology. For example, James Watt, the former Secretary of the Interior, regards it as God's will that man subdue the earth. George Gilder, a high priest of Reaganomics, has written: "Economists who distrust religion will always fail to comprehend the modes of worship by which progress is achieved."[3] And OMB director David Stockman, in his celebrated *Atlantic Monthly* interview, said of the supply-side theory, "The whole thing is premised on faith."[4]

The problem is twofold. Our faith itself is waning: faith in material progress, in the certitude of specialized scientific knowledge, and in the quasi-automatic flow of goodness from self-interested competition. Inevitably, a new faith is waiting to be born. But many institutions are not waiting; they are departing from the old faith before the new one has clearly emerged. As the theologian Hans Küng told students at the Harvard Divinity School: "For one thing is certain: that today, against the background of modern science, the question of God calls afresh for a decision—from unbelievers and believers."[5]

Given our current disarray, it is tempting to prescribe theological remedies for the American disease; and indeed, would-be physicians abound, some of them undoubtedly dangerous in their dogmatic certainty about who and what is moral, and who and what is not. We shall refrain from theological speculation in these pages; suffice it to say that religion in the next decade is likely to be an increasingly prominent, and perhaps scary, part of our national evolution. It will require our serious and careful attention.

Secular remedies, though, must start with politics. Over the years, there have been a number of good arguments made against the prescriptions in this book for changes in the relationships among government, business, and labor. These arguments are offered as reasons why such changes should not occur. In that sense, they are interesting—and perhaps even valid—but they are irrelevant if the changes I describe are real or impending. Indeed, such arguments are distracting, and therefore dangerous, forms of wishful thinking, which only delay the time when serious people will seek to manage our real choices.

The prospect of a strong, coherent government—capable of defining community need, and designing a national strategy with business and labor in order to improve our competitive posture in the world, for example—raises legitimate specters: of fascism, of smothering bureaucracy, and of waste. Some see it as a prescription not for change, but rather for the maintenance of the status quo. But the choice is not whether we can return to the old ways. Rather, it is whether we can intelligently manage the new. Such intelligent management will require the inspection and renovation of deeply held ideological assumptions.

This, it seems, is the paramount task of leadership in whatever calling. Political leaders and their parties should stop trying to hedge their bets, seeking to cover both ideologies inexplicitly, moving opportunistically to the new while failing to see the consequences of doing so. We must reinvigorate the debate between the political parties—a task easily accomplished if both would only focus on the real questions. For example:

Are we to support equality of opportunity, or of results? How will we avoid the elevation of mediocrity? Is there a place for hierarchy? If so, how is access gained to the elite, and how are those at the bottom assured of fairness?

If there are rights of membership, there must also be duties. How are these duties fairly defined and enforced, by government, by business, and by labor?

If pure competition in the marketplace is insufficient to define community need, what combination of governmental and nongovernmental organization will define it? At what level? Through what process? Will we have the nerve and persistence to cut consumption and increase investment in new productive capability? If so, will we do it fairly?

If government's role increases in importance as a definer of community need, how do we recast the government to make it efficient, respected, and authoritative? And how do we relate it to business and other nongovernment groups, whose skills, competence, and viewpoints are essential?

If an adequate grasp of the current reality necessitates a holistic consciousness of systems and their interrelationships, what must we do to make schools and their curricula pertinent, so that students will regard learning as the *sine qua non* for understanding and fulfillment, rather than an irrelevant pursuit of barren specialties? How can schools be related to the communities they serve, so that they are contributors to the life and product of that community, instead of irrelevancies?

These are political questions. As such, they need to be addressed by politicians and their parties, as well as by leaders of business and labor. The answers have little to do with old labels: Republican or Democrat, liberal or conservative. They spring from an understanding of necessity in the face of an altered reality.

If our leaders and their institutions ignore what they must do, they can expect the worst: an increased alienation from them and all that they represent, a surge in violence, and a drift toward anarchy. Already it is possible to see the coalition of revolution in America: the underclass, the chronically unemployed, many members of minority communities, and intellectuals with no place to go. We can hear their complaint, and anticipate their battle cry: "exploitation of the poor by the rich, who control a careless and corrupt government in league with self-centered corporations, which conspire to sustain the pursuit of suicidal military superiority."

This is not a time for timidity or resignation; we must husband our resources and think carefully about how to make the most of them. To this end, let us first consider government, and then the corporation.

The United States, like other western democracies, suffers from an excess of government. There are several categories of evidence. The first is economic: government spending has become greater than the private sector can afford. The second is political: democratic decision-making processes have become overburdened. The channels are clogged with more than they can handle; as a result, only those issues that generate the greatest pressure are confronted, and then in a way that is biased toward those with the most power. The third is philosophical: as our government has undertaken more and more activities and performed them less efficiently, its authority and legitimacy have eroded. Government that moves everywhere gets nowhere, and by overstretching the capacity of democratic government, we have weakened rather than strengthened it. As a consequence, people have moved out of the system. Taxes are harder to collect; voting participation is low; and underground economies flourish.

It is therefore necessary to reduce the quantity of government, and at the same time make it more efficient. In doing this, we confront the fact that there are a number of inevitable community needs which only government can define, such as international competition, the environment, resource allocation, income distribution, and social justice. These needs will not lessen in importance, and they must be dealt with effectively. Here there are two issues: the level of governmental attention—local, state, national, or international—and the relationship between governmental and nongovernmental institutions such as business and labor unions. Both of these elements must be managed correctly if we are to have a government which is at once both smaller and more effective.

Cooperation and partnership between government, business, and labor is more efficient than conflict. Coherence and cooperation must be the instruments we employ to reduce the size and extent of government. They are also the means by which government can enhance its focus and authority. Since cooperation raises new problems of legitimacy and authority, it must be done carefully, making sure that government retains the authority that it would be inappropriate for others to assume, and seeing to it that the forms of cooperation are designed to ensure legitimacy, continuity, and utility over time.

Stated another way, the principal reason we have so large and so expensive a government is that we are reluctant to be explicit about its authority and its role. Put bluntly, we wish it would expire even as we acknowledge its increasing responsibilities.

Henry Schacht said in an interview:

> We'll never get a super planning agency in this country, but we definitely need more planning by government—that is, a greater ability to gather and analyze data, so that the politicians at least understand what they are dealing with and what their choices are. . . . The nation badly needs an industrial policy. We need a tracking mechanism for the GNP [gross national product] so that we know where investment is going, what's happening to our competitive advantage, what are the choices concerning maturing industries like autos, steel, textiles, and so on. I envisage an agency which would be fundamentally concerned with diagnosis, not prescription. We also need a national manpower policy to train and locate jobs for the unemployed steel workers, for example, so that we are not forced to maintain an expensive and inefficient status quo for social and political reasons. We also need a national policy

concerning industrial location. There is no reason why industry should be allowed to put a plant wherever it wants. New plants should go where surplus labor exists.

I view the role of government as being that of a systems manager. It is the only instrument we have for gathering together the competing demands of society and making some rational sense of them. Once it decides the direction we are going to take and the priorities we should observe, it should leave the implementation to business with as much freedom and flexibility as possible.[6]

Fletcher Byrom commented on the refusal of many of his colleagues to face up to the demands of reality:

They think I'm a pessimist when I tell them that the ship is sinking. But that's not a defeatist statement *per se*. It depends on the attitude with which the crew receives the message. A lot of businessmen I know don't believe there is a crisis. That's a problem —escapism, pure and simple.

We need a national strategy, a reliable one that we can count on and build toward. The big problem with government regulation is not so much its quantity as its unpredictability. Uncertainty is bad for business, because you can't make long-run investment decisions.

Of course, we need a national manpower retraining and education policy and the schools need to be related more closely to the employment needs of business. Of course, we need industrial policy in such industries as steel, for example. There ought to be six to ten steel plants in deep-water ports capable of making six to ten million tons of semi-finished steel and carrying it through continuous casting into slabs. Then those slabs should be dispersed around the country to rolling mills which are close to the markets. This would require a joint decision by government, industry, and labor, a national policy—not some elaborate government planning—just a policy.[7]

Charles Brown of AT&T spoke of the need for a policy in his industry:

This business badly needs some coherence in government policy. I don't think there is a country in the world where a matter of such national import as telecommunications is decided in such an irrational and untidy process. If it were not so serious, it would be ludicrous. . . . It seems to me that there must be some way that government can identify those things which are truly of national import, maybe using something like the Federal Reserve Board, which has some independence from politics and the pressures of private interests. Without such a process, and some reliable ground rules about what the national interest is, it is very hard for a company like ours to have the long-term orientation that is so essential.[8]

Why do more business leaders not speak up more forcefully? Why do they not march on their friends in Washington and demand adjustments? There are practical reasons. They are naturally preoccupied with their own tasks; they do not want to waste what influence they have on that which is not explicitly their business; and they wonder whether anyone would listen. One business leader described going to a White House breakfast. "The President popped in and out, and that was it. He seemed to say that either we were his friends and were therefore supposed to do his bidding, or we were not, in which case he was not interested in listening." In short, there is no forum, no continuing apparatus, through which government and business can communicate. Finally, businessmen also are concerned about the competence of government officials to understand and act on advice which they might offer.

There are also ideological reasons. However unrelated to the reality of modern business, the old hymns have enduring appeal. In the words of Irving Shapiro:

> Businessmen generally have been pretty dumb about politics, and they still are. Their attitude toward Washington is schizophrenic. They are very ambivalent about government. But after all government has got to decide the national interest. If it doesn't, no one will. If we're going to get the kind of government we need then we have to have more respect for the public service. We should think in terms of recruiting highly competent, intelligent, dedicated people and paying them enough so that they can live decently. They've got to be committed to the public sector, not the private sector. There are a number of excellent people like that in Washington today and we'd be in big trouble without them.[9]

The reticence of business has prompted Kenneth Andrews of Harvard to write:

> In the interest ultimately of some degree of newly productive consensus, I think we need more interim disagreement and challenge to the assumptions, practices, attitudes, and conventions that we

know are inadequate to a changing world, to a renewal of world competitiveness, and to a cooperative relationship linking government, management, and labor. Rather than silence in the face of absurdity, or resignation to what used to be considered the inevitable, we need more protest in the ranks of management—not against government or other external "enemies"—but against those universal management conventions that should be struck down.[10]

There have been a number of interesting recent proposals regarding an appropriate mechanism to bring business, government, and labor together for the purpose of building a consensus about national priorities, and shaping policies to implement them.

"The government should make the Commerce Department the focal point for industrial policy, broaden its powers and change its name," writes Bruce Scott, whose pioneering work on the concept of national strategy makes him virtually unique in American academia. He, like the Administration, has suggested the merger of the Office of the United States Trade Representative in the White House with Commerce into a new Department of Industry, Trade, and Commerce (ITC). "ITC should have primary responsibility for promotion of U.S. exports and the power to authorize joint ventures to promote research or accelerate the development of new technology, ventures that would be exempt from the antitrust laws." The new department would work closely with business "to establish a more legitimate form of dialogue to identify and evaluate industrial problems."[11] The dialogue should be protected against antitrust liability, and exempt from the "sunshine provisions" of the Federal Advisory Committee Act.

Scott has also recommended legislation to provide a federal charter for companies that would guarantee employment security for all employees with at least ten years' service. This would not supersede state charters, but would be an alternative for those companies who wished "to tailor their schemes of governance" for greater efficiency by providing workers with a greater sense of participation and commitment. The federal charter would carry with it various tax incentives to make it appealing to shareholders as well as employees.[12]

In the closing days of the Carter administration, the AFL-CIO proposed a more elaborate device—a National Reindustrialization Board, "consisting of representatives of the public, labor, and industry, which would recommend the priority and magnitude of reindustrialization to be undertaken in various industrial sectors and geographic regions, in light of the national economic and security interests." [13] The board would supervise a Reindustrialization Financing Corporation (RFC), which would make or guarantee loans to finance reindustrialization in the various regions of the country.

Congressman Stanley Lundine of New York has proposed a National Industrial Development Board, composed of corporate leaders, union heads, government officials, and "major representatives of the public interest." Its purpose would be to "develop a consensual response to key problems of industrial revitalization." It would determine "the industrial development priorities for the United States, furnish policy recommendations on particular problems which are referred to the Board by congressional committees and executive agencies, and provide credible, consensus-backed information on the domestic and global economic situation." The board would be strictly advisory, which its sponsors felt would insulate it from "the corrosive effects of special interest lobbying." [14]

Frank Weil, Assistant Secretary of Commerce for International Trade in the late 1970s, recommends a Federal Industrial Coordination Board, independent of the executive branch and Congress, similar to the Federal Reserve Board. It would have broad responsibilities for developing a "long-term national industrial strategy" for recommendation to the Congress and the President, and "implementing the . . . strategy . . . through stimulation of capital and human resources into appropriate areas." [15]

While each of these proposals has strong merits, my own preference would be for the route suggested in the previous chapter: a program to take advantage of the existing mandate and experience of the USTR office in the White House, and to develop its capacity to serve as a focal point for the design and implementation of a national strategy together with business and labor. I think that to combine the USTR with the Commerce Department would be unwise for several reasons. It would, for example, make it more difficult to recruit and retain the caliber of public servant required. It would deny the office its White House connection, which would reduce its political clout and eliminate its coordinating and mediating authority over all over departments and agencies. (The departments of Agriculture and Labor, for example, would resent a Commerce-originated edict.) Finally, it would diminish the unique relationship between USTR and Congress that is now embedded in the dual reporting system and the operation of the advisory committees.

As the United States moves in the direction of a more coherent, explicit formulation of goals and policies, there will be predictable objections. This is true for both of the two key elements of the proposals I have outlined. First, I envisage a federal authority with responsibility for calculating all of the related effects of different government policies, programs, and regulations, macro and micro, on business and labor. In one sense, this seems only sensible—government should, after all, know what it is doing, and the Office of Management and Budget, as we have seen, has been moving in this direction for more than a decade. Yet this focus of authority is still far from established, and there are many adherents of the old assumptions who feel it is neither practical nor desirable to make government coherent in this way.

Secondly, the federal government, in cooperation with business and labor, must define community-need priorities, and design governmental policies toward industry in such a way as to promote the fulfillment of those priorities. For reasons spelled out in earlier chapters, I believe that we have little choice in this regard: government, business, and labor must assume this responsibility. But there will be winners and losers in this process; and, unless precautions are taken, the winners will tend to be the powerful and the influential, the best organized—in short, the representatives of the status quo. The losers will likely be others: the new, the young, the industries of the future, small business, the unorganized, the consumer. Japanese experience shows that this bias against change can be overcome, but not without clear effort, especially by business. MITI was opposed to Japanese entry into the auto-export market in the early 1960s, for example; the car companies forced their way in, however, and their persistence eventually paid off.

"We've just got to keep everybody's feet to the fire so that

America gets competitive," said Ruben Mettler of TRW. "To do this we need policies to help those who are hurt, but we must avoid the temptation to intervene prematurely or in the wrong way. All of us in business or in labor must feel a new sense of discipline. The way for the labor movement to recover its strength—and I hope it does—is to enhance the competitiveness of the national economy. Those unions which do should get enormous support from the business community." [16]

Can a democratic government ever choose to scuttle elements of a dying industry to turn it around? The answer is a conditional yes: it can, but only if it has good and sufficient procedures for coping with the impact on workers, banks, shareholders, and the affected communities. Several years ago, the Japanese closed eight steel plants without laying anyone off. We could perform similarly if we tried.

Then there is the question of whether and how the U.S. government can force an industry to rationalize, to cut back, and to modernize—as, for example, Fletcher Byrom has advised for the steel industry. History suggests that the government lacks both the will and the power. Steel brought antidumping suits against foreign producers in an attempt to reduce imports, causing no small embarrassment to the larger political and economic interests of the United States. The government proceeded to "buy off" the industry with protective measures—trigger-pricing and quotas—and provided the industry with the economic incentives to modernize for competitiveness. Still, the government had no way of forcing the industry to do so.

Finally, as we consider the procedures for building a consensus about national strategy, it is worth recalling the thoughts of John T. Dunlop, who for more than twenty years has been among the nation's leading consensus-makers, both in government and out:

> Consensus-building is problem solving and pragmatic. It relies heavily on the art of listening, and listening perceptively between the lines of formal positions. It is devoted to the quest for irreducible facts, for the actual and the tendencies. It requires candor and mutual respect. It exhausts charity, patience, and persuasion. . . .
>
> Consensus-building does not depend upon political might or the exercise of governmental or market power. It does not thrive in strident tones or in programs or platforms. It is not congenial to doctrinaire adherence to the left or to the right. [17]

Consensus-building, says Dunlop, requires a continuing forum, a place where all concerned can slowly develop the trust, confidence, and understanding necessary for agreement. It must allow for private discussions where responsible leaders can abandon their institutional cloaks, at least temporarily, and talk frankly. It requires professional staff work and careful leadership to focus attention on well-defined and limited issues. And finally, it cannot be a substitute for the formal decision-making procedures of the private or public sector. "It can only provide a sense of direction, smooth social conflict, and speed formal processes." [18]

It remains to be seen how and how well government, business, and labor will resolve these difficulties as they attempt to cope with the real world of the 1980s. But they will proceed more effectively and efficiently if they realize that they are operating within a context of communitarianism, and not individualism.

Inseparable from the design of new relationships between big business and government and labor is the matter of corporate governance: the procedures by which corporate purposes and direction are set, and management is selected and compensated. In general, of course, consumer desire or community demand in the marketplace determines the goods and services that a corporation provides, and rewards the effectiveness of managers in doing so. But in seeking to satisfy the market profitably, as noted in Chapter 3, managers are governed by four sources of authority: the equity market, shareholders; the debt market, the banks; the managed, all those who work for the company; and the government. In some countries—Japan, for example—the relationships among these four sources are carefully coordinated. In the United States, however, managers receive conflicting signals.

Reliance on shareholders and the institutions that purport to represent them can lead to short-term horizons for the corporation. Signals from the banks, except in catastrophic cases like Lockheed and Chrysler, appear to be muted; instead, trust is placed in the good sense and prudence of management itself. Union insistence on a voice in governance is unpredictable: it may affect anything from plant location to management salaries to investment policies. At root, it seems that managers themselves often decide that what they know how to do or enjoy doing is de facto the corporate purpose. For example, an executive of an oil company told me: "Look, what we know how to do is drill holes in the ground and find oil. If that isn't what we should be doing, then maybe I should quit." In explaining his decision to remain in the steel business and resist the diversification strategies of other steel companies, Republic Steel's chairman E. Bradley Jones said: "That's what we know, and that's what we have to maintain in order to be whatever we're going to be in the future." [19]

At the heart of the matter is the authority of the manager, the right to manage. Behind authority is the question of legitimacy: what is acceptable and justified in the eyes of the communities within which the manager manages? The transition from individualism to communitarianism discussed in this book clearly affects the answers to these questions.

The large corporations of America have, in the name of efficiency, satisfaction of demand, financial necessity, and so on, grown so big as to be fundamentally different from what they were fifty years ago. Once they were, in fact, private property, their owners readily discernible and their managers controlled by the owners. Today they are collectives in limbo, their managers emerging from an obscure, internal, hierarchical process, which springs more from some consensus of the corporate membership than anything else. At the same time, the real world in which the corporation operates has also changed radically. Competitive pressures from nations whose systems are functioning more efficiently than ours compel change. Expanding knowledge about the ecosystem—as well as changes in education, and popular expectations of increased rights of membership—have made many old ways unacceptable.

Large corporations in the United States are not only the backbone of our economic structure; they also supply the life-blood to our social and political institutions. They are in almost every sense "public" institutions; their funds come from the public, they employ the public, their purposes are public, and their effects are public. It therefore follows that their efficiency and their control are also of public concern. The public interest is not met if they are efficient but inadequately controlled; similarly, the public must object if corporations are controlled in ways which make them inefficient. Since the definition of the public interest in the United States is the task of government, large corporations and government are and must be intimately related. Increasingly, the leaders of large corporations recognize this fact.

We have observed that many great corporations of the United States resist both regulation and antitrust action in the name of the national interest (community need)—economies of scale, efficiency, national defense, a positive balance of payments, or whatever. They are thus departing from individualism, and appealing—sometimes on somewhat parochial grounds—to incipient communitarianism. If they are successful, they are of necessity faced with the following question: Who decides the community need? Is it the corporation, the government, or both, in some partnership? If the answer is partnership, who is the senior partner, and what are the terms of the relationship?

We have also observed the transition from contract to consensus that many corporations are undergoing in their management/labor relations. In conceiving of this transition as an ideological phenomenon (as opposed, let us say, to a merely behavioral one), we are obliged to consider the implications comprehensively. Many interests and much bureaucratic power in both unions and management rest on the idea of contract, deriving from it authority and legitimacy—not to mention jobs and money. The procedures for managing in a consensual system are by no means clear. Organizations surely have no less need for authority: the question is, What should the source of that authority be, and how should it be derived and administered? The contract, furthermore, has been a time-tested device for protecting individuals against abuse, and for providing many forms of security. It has, however, tended to divide workers and managers to sustain hierarchies, and to confine the ability of the managed to influence the managers to certain prescribed areas. Nevertheless, if we move away from it, predictable anxieties will arise as the old protections are removed.

Denuding the corporation ideologically, we can say it is supposed to gather resources, design and make goods or services, and distribute them to the communities it serves. In order to do this, it must develop skills, provide motivation, and exert effective organizational control over itself. It should do this as efficiently as possible, maximizing benefits and minimizing costs. Such a description of a corporation is noncontroversial: it fits any community, anywhere; it delineates the competence required to manage successfully.

Now let us introduce ideology. What goods and services does the corporation make? Who decides? What resources does it use? What are the effects of its functions on the communities around it? Internally, what are acceptable and effective means to motivation and control? If there is hierarchy, who gets in, who goes up, and how? Again, who decides? Finally, what is a cost and what is a benefit, and what happens to the surplus of benefits that is assumed to accrue? Again, who decides? Questions like these concern rights and authority, and it is here that ideological analysis is most useful.

Recalling the possible sources of managerial authority—property rights of shareholders, banks, the managed, and the state— boards of directors have been rooted in the first, legally empowered to manage the business of the corporation as representatives of the shareholding owners. Time and events, however, have moved boards away from their traditional roots. Shareholders have neither the desire nor the ability to "own" in any real sense. They are investors, pure and simple, and if they do not obtain an acceptable return on their investment in one firm, they generally put their money into another. Although corporate annual meetings include an "election" in which shareholders "select" directors, this is largely ceremonial in character. Management in fact picks the directors, and directors—understandably—tend to support the will of the management. Suffice it to say that a dubious situation results: directors are responsible for hiring, firing, and fixing the salaries of top executives, especially the chief executive officer, and at the same time they owe their position as directors to these same executives.

The pragmatic evolution of the corporation and its board of directors has thus engendered an obvious ideological aberration. Boards of directors, and consequently corporate management, no longer can claim property rights as a basis for their authority and legitimacy, and any new basis for such authority is not clear. There are only two ways to rectify the situation: we can rehabilitate property rights, or we can move to one of the alternate sources of authority—in particular, the state or the managed.

The wide variety of proposed solutions to the problem can be viewed in terms of these two possibilities.

Kenneth Andrews, a student of boards of directors, writes that "the dignified, well meaning, competent, but largely inactive board of the past, relaxed in its support of the chief executive who brought it together, is being asked to cast off its old skin. It is now expected to show itself as the active, informed, and objective guardian of the shareholders' and the public's interests." [20]

Marvin Chandler, retired chairman of Northern Illinois Gas Company, wrote: "The widespread criticism of many boards as too cozy is warranted, though industry staunchly defends the status quo. If industry doesn't clean up the boardroom, others will. The directors' allegiance *must* be to the others of the business—the shareholders—not to management. To achieve the basic purposes, the majority of the board must be strong, independent, unhesitant in probing, querying, taking issues, saying no, and above all, in constantly appraising the CEO." He deemed an "insider" board "an absurdity." [21]

Christopher D. Stone, professor of law at the University of Southern California, has suggested the appointment of "limited public directors" for two kinds of companies. The first is "the company which has been afoul of the law so repeatedly that further trust in existing corporate control measures seems misplaced," and which therefore needs a kind of an "in-house probation officer." The second is the company in an industry that seriously affects the community need in areas where that need has not been fully defined. He cites chemicals, paper, steel, nuclear energy, and multinationals, which "present special problems relating to our foreign relations and monetary stability." International banks, defense contractors, and aircraft manufacturers also come to mind. In the case of "demonstrated delinquency," appointment of the public director should be made by the courts. With respect to the second category, the appointment would be made by the SEC. In both cases, the public director would be selected in close consultation with management. [22]

In January 1978 the Business Roundtable issued a "Statement on the Role and Composition of Boards of Directors of the Large Publicly Owned Companies," which essentially defended the status quo except for endorsing "the strong tendency of U.S. corporations" to have a majority of "outside" directors on the board.[23] The Roundtable statement is a good illustration of ideological ambivalence and its inherent difficulties. The paper begins by focusing on large, publicly held corporations, rather than those companies with a "small and cohesive group of shareholders" who really do function as owners.[24] It goes on to say what is unexceptionable: "An effective decision-making process requires an hierarchical organization so that there will be clear lines of authority to resolve differences and clear accountability for results." Management must have authority, says the statement, and this it derives together with "legitimacy from the board of directors."[25]

The statement implies that the board derives its authority and legitimacy from the shareholders, but it ignores the problem that most shareholders neither have nor want to have anything to do with the naming of directors. Furthermore, it is quite clear that Roundtable managers do not want them to have any more to do with it: "Proposals to enlarge materially shareowner participation in corporate governance all run into . . . stubborn practical difficulties, and are likely to be of interest only to very small and unrepresentative groups of corporate critics."

Where directors get their authority is thus left obscure, an obscurity that manifests itself in the following sentence: "The directors are stewards—stewards of the owners' interest in the enterprise and stewards also of the owners' legal and ethical obligations to other groups affected by corporate activity."[26] There are two obvious flaws in this logic. First, if the corporation is run by owners (shareholders) and hired hands (management), then it is surely odd that the hired hands should engage those (directors) who are supposed to supervise them on behalf of the owners. Second, how can a director—or anyone else, for that matter—be a steward (that is, a servant or housekeeper) of an obligation? And what are these obligations of the owners? If the Roundtable truly meant that the directors should be investigative watchdogs, ensuring that corporate managers obey the law, then they should have gone a step further and explained how directors can be expected to police reliably those to whom they are obligated for their jobs, fees, and perquisites.

The Roundtable's ambiguity only increases when it describes

the relationship between the board and the CEO—"challenging yet supportive and positive," "arm's length but not adversary," and finally, "The board should stimulate management to perform at the peak of its capacity not by carping, but by setting high standards and providing level-headed encouragement."[27]

None of this comes close to the problem; it only makes a dubious situation more suspect. The fact is that the great, publicly held corporation has moved away from every concept of ownership. Directors are not connected in any real way to shareholders. They are appointees of management; whether they are "outside" or "inside" is of no real significance. And yet, at the same time, they are expected to be accountable to a variety of vague "groups affected by corporate activity." The Roundtable explicitly rejected the idea that these groups or "constituencies" should name directors to represent their interests on the board, as it rejected the notion that workers should be represented on the board.[28] Directors are left increasingly vulnerable to charges and lawsuits without any clear legitimacy.

The remedies that have been proposed by the SEC for dealing with the rights and the responsibilities of boards of directors are no better; they also perpetuate the tired fiction of property. The commission has pressed for more "outsiders" on the board. Former Chairman Harold Williams suggested that the board should be composed entirely of outside members except for the CEO. Prodded by the SEC, the New York Stock Exchange has required all listed companies to maintain an audit committee of the board that is exclusively composed of outside directors. It is unclear, however, how these outsiders should be selected, what exactly they should do, and whether the committee should have a staff to carry out its obscure functions.

The commission ignored several problems: what, for example, makes outsiders appointed by insiders any more legitimate than insiders appointed by insiders? Further, in applying its orders to all companies listed on the Stock Exchange, it failed to take account of the fact that some small companies may well be able to employ property rights as an acceptable legitimizer of management authority, even though they also wish to sell a percentage of their shares publicly. It failed to perceive that, in fact, many companies in America do not need to abandon the old ideology, with which their practice is perfectly consistent.

Furthermore, as Lee Smith has observed in *Fortune*, eliminating inside management from the board of directors is inevitably a sham. The board must and should rely on the top managers of a company for information and expertise, whether or not those managers are board members. Other advantages to having managers on the board seem compelling: "Having insiders on the board also gives the outside directors an opportunity to evaluate the senior managers who will one day be candidates for the chief executive's job." [29]

Victor Brudney, Weld Professor of Law at Harvard, in a careful study of the role and behavior of outside directors, concluded that there was little evidence that they had any particular impact on the problems of corporate management that they were supposed to treat. Looking first at issues of managerial integrity, Brudney found that independent directors rarely adopt the adversarial role which their independence implies. Indeed, they are "apt to view management's demands congenially," and avoid conflict in the boardroom. A study of cases involving self-dealing or misappropriation of corporate assets by management "does not disclose many instances of outside directors' having dissented from the subsequently challenged managerial appropriations." "The essential limitations on independent directors' ability to monitor self-dealing remain—limited access to information, limited incentives and sanctions, and the constraints of the boardroom context against a background of social and economic relationships with members of management." [30]

He found even less evidence that outside directors were particularly effective in monitoring management's efficiency in maximizing shareholder wealth or in behaving responsibly. A study of SEC documents regarding questionable payments to politicians at home and abroad, for example, showed that outside directors "were not often very diligent or alert, and that on many occasions they, and sometimes most inside directors, did not know about the payments and therefore played no role in stopping them." [31]

Brudney concluded that "the independent director is not the institution to legitimate corporate power or to substitute for regulation in the interest of investors or society." [32]

The SEC has also sought to invigorate shareholder democracy, requiring corporations to inform shareholders in greater detail about directors' activities, fees, and corporate ties. It opened the door for a number of shareholder resolutions concerning corporate conduct—including, for example, Lockheed's sales to the U.S.S.R., and numerous other firms' business dealings in South Africa. It has required management to provide information to shareholders about an increasing variety of activities that it says are "significantly related" to company business.

This seems a particularly clear example of how burdensome regulations can spring from confusion about where authority lies. Who should, and who will eventually, decide American policy toward the U.S.S.R. and South Africa? Surely not corporate shareholders, directors, or self-perpetuating managements. When the interests of the whole nation are clearly at stake, such decisions must be made by government in the national interest. Pretending that an annual meeting of shareholders can produce significant or acceptable policy decisions in such cases is patently absurd.

Meanwhile, as corporate leaders and the SEC fail to address the problem, government regulation escalates, as the Congress and the regulators say tacitly: "If the governance of the corporation is inherently illegitimate, we must step in directly to make sure that it does no wrong." But given government's fragmentation, and its inability to match one tradeoff carefully with another, increased regulation tends all too often to be clumsy, inefficient, and expensive.

The best solution to the problems of governance of large corporations has to meet two tests: (1) it should contribute to the greatest efficiency and effectiveness of the corporation, and of government in its relations with the corporation, and (2) it should provide corporate management with a reliable and acceptable basis of authority and legitimacy. One without the other is useless. Old-time socialism, for example, is increasingly discredited even among socialists, because in the name of legitimacy it often destroys efficiency. Perhaps the most striking feature of the Japanese economy is the degree to which its institutions are both efficient and legitimate. The United States in the 1970s, while groping for boundaries within which business can be made legitimate, was throttling business efficiency, thereby causing inflation, unemployment, and a loss of world market share to those who were better able to meet these two tests simultaneously.

How can we apply these requirements to fashion an efficient and effective board of directors? As Myles L. Mace's research has revealed, their members confront enormously important and complicated questions.[33] They must be experienced, intelligent, well-informed, diligent, and courageous. They must have the confidence of the managers whom they supervise. They must be persons of broad vision who can see the long-term interests of their corporation and its place in the larger scheme of things. They should not be excessively preoccupied with the short-run issues of operating management. Their interests must be those of the corporation, but not those of any particular group of persons associated with the corporation. To obtain the services of such estimables, we must certainly pay them well—such paragons of virtue could not come cheaply! More important, though, their authority and legitimacy must be clear. They cannot be under constant suspicion. As honorable people, they must be honored.

How can they obtain this authority and legitimacy? As I have demonstrated, directors of large, publicly held corporations cannot obtain it either from shareholders or from management. Nor, indeed, can they derive it from any collection of transient interest groups or constituencies. Authority and legitimacy can come to directors of large corporations, as Stone suggested, from government, or it can derive from all of the members of the corporation, or, as a practical matter, from both.

Is this a radical conclusion? Perhaps it seems so at first glance. But we must consider the *reality* of modern corporate control instead of the myth. The head of today's great public corporation comes to hold that position through competence and skill. But I believe he has two singular abilities: he is able to obtain the support of those whom he manages, and he knows how to work with government.

The CEO is elevated, as it were, on a cushion of broadly based support within the corporation. "I think there is a lot of bubbling up from below when it comes to the selection of the CEO," Howard Love, chairman of National Steel, said.[34] The successful executive knows how to put together "winning teams"; he knows, in short, that for all of the myths of the hierarchy, with God and property rights hovering somewhere above its apex, his actual right to manage comes from those whom he manages, within a context set by government. Today we see countless ways in which this process is being perfected, both through closer cooperation with government and through the encouragement of increased participation by corporate employees in the decisions that affect their work and lives.

As this happens, it is naturally of increasing importance that all corporate employees care about their company and its long-term interests, rather than their own short-term gains. This means that increasing attention must be paid to employment security, to lifetime employment, to creating a sense of commitment and loyalty on the part of the employee toward the firm of which he or she is a member. (Hence, Scott's proposal for a federal charter for companies desiring to move in this direction.)

The shareholders are becoming investors, pure and simple. The stock market is nothing more or less than a place where corporations go to raise money, as they go to banks, or government, or other sources of money. In this situation it is clear that management has no special relationship to shareholders; indeed, all corporate employees have an identical interest in their firm's ability to raise money. Workers and managers know equally that if they need money from the stock market, they must pay for it, one way or another.

Managers and managed must perfect what they have begun, to build the mechanisms of consensus to take the place of the old structures. What these mechanisms will be is hard to predict. There should be great variety, however, to fit the different needs and different circumstances of different corporations, and of the several groups within corporations.[35] As they develop, they will be reflected in law, and from this process will grow new strains of legitimacy for the new authority.

But there is an element of legitimacy that obviously cannot come from inside the corporation, because it pertains to the various communities which the corporation affects. We must conclude that it is through government that these communities should express their needs and concerns. This brings us back to the second attribute of the contemporary corporate leader.

Although business is burdened by regulation and exasperated by government's inefficiency, most corporate leaders acknowledge its necessity. The chemical industry, we saw, after being bruised and buffeted as a result of the ecological damage caused by its products, ultimately played an active role in designing the

Toxic Substances Control Act, and became engaged in helping government to apply and enforce it. In many areas, the old adversarial relationship of business and government has already been supplanted by a collaborative partnership. Both sides have realized that their own interests depend on cooperation.

We conclude, therefore, that the authority of corporate executives—their right to manage—is increasingly derived from the managed on the one hand and government on the other. If we assume that this reality is here to stay, and this seems a reasonable assumption, then the solution to the problem of corporate governance is clear: we must shape and lend discipline to what in fact is already underway.

The primary task of directors should be to make the corporation as effective as possible over the long run. The definition of "effective" and "long" should emerge from a consensus of the corporate membership, and from the various levels and components of government that the corporation affects. The implementation of the definition that is arrived at requires a close working relationship between directors and managers. Directors should be chosen and their tasks prescribed by three groups: managers, managed, and government. Shareholders of large, nonproprietary corporations should be understood to be investors, and all laws and regulations should be rewritten to relieve corporate management of the burden of regarding them as owners, and to provide the investors with the information they need in order to invest wisely.

This proposal necessitates a sharp distinction between the nonproprietary corporation and the proprietary company—the latter can continue to operate within the old ideology. Here again we are only recognizing and giving order to a reality. The small businesses of America realize that they have little in common with the members of the Business Roundtable. They are fundamentally different, because their legitimacy comes from a different ideology. Both big and small have a place; both need legitimacy and authority; to obtain it, they must look to different quarters.

The implementation of this suggestion for corporate directors needs careful thought. My own preferences correspond with those of Christopher Stone: the Federal Reserve Board, or perhaps the SEC, could compile a list of distinguished citizens who are able and willing to serve as corporate directors. This list would probably include many, if not most, of those who are now outside corporate directors, including the increasing number of "professional" directors who do nothing else but serve on boards.[36] Business-school deans, university presidents, business and professional organizations, and major interest groups throughout the country would be invited to submit candidates for inclusion on the government list. The list would be broken down by industry, with government designating which persons were fitted by knowledge and experience to serve on the boards of companies in particular industries.

Each company board would be chaired by the chief executive officer. It would be his responsibility to prepare annually a slate of directors. One half he could choose freely from outside or inside the company. The other half he would select from the appropriate government list. The slate would be submitted to all corporate employees with ten years or more seniority, affording them an opportunity to consider it and to make proposals for additions to, or subtractions from, either of the two lists, providing the proportions remained unchanged. These same senior employees would elect the final board by a majority vote.

A CEO would thus have a compatible board of directors that would be legitimized both by government and by that portion of the managed with a proven commitment to the company. If management to that point had been performing its job properly, it seems likely that its proposed slate would gain majority acceptance. Management would thus be able to work with a legitimate board, largely of its own choosing.

Under such an arrangement, the board of directors would take on new importance, new legitimacy, and new authority. The directors designated by government would have a special responsibility to consider the relationship between the corporation and the needs of the communities it affected. This could include a range of activities: providing employment in urban areas, safeguarding the environment, or contributing to the nation's balance of trade. Management would benefit by having directors who were intimately informed about the company, and who could help perfect its relationships with government. In this way, government's definition of community need could be made more precise and timely, and the corporation's connection to it more effective. Regulation and intervention by government could be reduced as cooperation developed.

In the words of Control Data's William Norris, "The role of directors should not be that of corporate cops, as many people advocate, but that of industrial statesmen. The director's major activity should be to advocate cooperation between business and government. Equally important, the director should work to foster cooperation within the ranks of big business itself—between big business and small business, and between big business and other sectors of society." [37]

Internationally, government-designated directors representing the several nations or regions in which a multinational corporation might operate could be of assistance to both the corporation and the communities it affected by perfecting the fit between them. Arrangements among multinational corporations that are now either suspect or illegal might be made beneficial to all concerned. I am reminded of a report several years ago of an American and a Japanese oil company, each seeking to buy petroleum in Ecuador. The Ecuadorians said, in effect, we will sell oil to whoever buys bananas, because it is on the banana plantations that we have our social and political difficulties. The American oil company lacked the capacity to handle bananas; the Japanese, because of their more integrated structure, willingly took the fruit. Today, because our directors are fundamentally suspect, cooperation between companies quickly takes on the semblance (or reality) of collusion. This need not be so, if directors could become fully legitimate.

Similarly, directors could play a more effective role in creating mechanisms inside the corporation that would give all employees a sense of commitment and increased motivation. This should result in greater productivity, as awareness increased of the realities that the corporation faced in world financial and product markets.

There are weaknesses in this approach that must certainly be guarded against. (I am sobered, though not daunted, by the fact that no chief executive to date has warmed to it.) The thoughts of Irving Shapiro, as expressed in the following exchange, are shared by many. They are unquestionably sensible, although I do not think they are conclusive.

"I would quickly concede," he said, "that our theoretical model of the shareholder giving authority to management and management being responsible to the shareholders doesn't reflect reality. It's something of a fiction; sort of a phony. But I reject your premise that letting a board provide for its own membership corrupts the process. Good boards can be created. I sit on some very good ones, such as those at Citicorp and IBM, where the members have a strong sense of commitment to both the corporation and the national interest."

I asked: "But even if you had the Twelve Apostles on the board and the process by which they got there was not regarded as legitimate, wouldn't you still have a problem?"

Shapiro: "I recognize the issue you raise. There is no fully satisfactory answer. I don't think that putting a government seal of approval on a list of names really solves the problem. It could make it worse if a number of political hangers-on had to be accommodated. I might accept your idea if I were prepared to accept the proposition that management should be making public policy, but I'm not willing to do that. Ultimately, boards are going to be judged by the quality of the people on them and the public perception of them. There isn't any perfect system for doing it."[38]

There are a number of very fine lines to be drawn here. Certainly as government and business come together there are the dangers of concentration of power, corporate statism, and elitism. These can be minimized, however, if governmental directors represent a broad plurality of interests. Openness can also help; as the government-business partnership develops, its terms should be fully disclosed.

Then there is the matter of privacy of board activities, which is important if we are to keep healthy levels of competition among firms. Can directors who are designated by groups other than management be trusted to observe confidentiality? It seems to me that the answer is yes: employee-designated directors should have as much interest in corporate performance as any others, as should government designees if they have a clear understanding of the new rules and their role.

Shapiro's comments imply an obvious question: why do *anything* which will make our government bigger, and increase the range of its interventions? To this, I respond emphatically that we should not; in fact, I believe that this plan would have exactly the opposite effect. It would help make government smaller by making its intervention more coherent. Similarly, it would enable government to shrink through enhanced effectiveness. I can envision regular meetings of government-designated directors with pertinent Washington agencies to discuss the problems of particular industries, and to work out solutions. The suspicion of special interests serving their selfish aims would be absent from such a process, and the results might well be more satisfactory to both sides than the current arrangements.

Frederick V. Malek, deputy director of the Office of Management and Budget from 1972 to 1976 and later an executive of Marriott Corporation, has written that "the greatest organizational weakness within the government today" is its extreme structural fragmentation, and "the inability to hold any one person or organization responsible for performance."[39] It does not seem overly optimistic to suggest that government-designated directors of major corporations could play an important role in forcing an integration of our splintered government by calling attention, in a convincing way, to the disparate and often contradictory effects of its policies and regulations. They could also serve as an important channel for information from business to government. Malek describes the dismal failure of the old Federal Energy Agency to develop a coherent energy policy, and attributes that failure in part to the inability or unwillingness of the FEA to include representatives of the energy industry in its deliberations.[40] Such failures will surely be repeated unless a politically acceptable way of relating corporate leadership and government on a regular basis is found.

What corporations have most to fear from government is not policies deliberately destructive of business interests, but inadvertent, incoherent, shortsighted, fragmented, and ineffective supervision. A clarification of the business/government relationship is the best and only way to protect both against such harassment and against hobbling.

In conclusion, let me first emphasize that I am not advocating the ideological transition to communitarianism that is described in this book. (The old creed is, I should say, as dear to me as it is to anyone.) Rather, I am observing that the transition is happening. Some institutions, like the corner grocery store, will remain securely rooted in traditional ideas, but our major institutions have been moving, and will continue to move, in the face of change in the real world. The old ideas will never die in America; they will in some way be combined with the new ones. In this combination lies our opportunity and our challenge.

On the other hand, I fervently advocate a recognition of the fact of this transition, and a clear delineation of the choices with which it confronts managers and leaders regarding the roles and relationships of government, big business, and labor.

In some areas, I have been unable to go beyond merely spelling out what these choices seem to be. For example, if public policy and practice move away from both equality of opportunity and equality of result towards the notion of hierarchy, then policymakers must contemplate how to manage the hierarchy so that it is politically acceptable, socially desirable, and economically viable. In such areas, I hope that others will have a clearer view than I, as time and experience sharpen the issues.

In other cases, I have gone further to recommend some specific actions that should be taken to define community need more reliably, to determine rights and duties more effectively, to fix the role of government more efficiently, and to organize institutional relationships more sensibly. To summarize these, here are a few specific steps that might be taken to cure the American disease:

1. Expand and strengthen the Office of the USTR as suggested in Chapter 10, linking it more closely to the Office of Management and Budget. These two White House offices, with their special ties to Congress and an invigorated USTR advisory structure, should be the principal mechanisms for making national strategy—that is, for selecting priorities and coordinating all federal policies and programs so as to fulfill those priorities. They would also be the means of achieving a national consensus behind the strategy.

2. Establish other government, business, and labor mechanisms at different points in the federal government, as proposed in Chapters 5 and 6, for the efficient design and implementation of specific policies in such areas as toxic substances, energy,

electric-power generation, safety, health, affirmative action, and manpower training and utilization.

3. Amend the antitrust laws to prohibit price-fixing, but to allow industry consolidation and cooperation for the fulfillment of the national interest, domestically and in world competition.

4. Consolidate and modernize the steel, automobile, and other troubled industries, according to a definition of the national interest. Provide research and other support to the high-technology industries upon whose success the nation's future depends.

5. Obtain more flexibility of choice for federal spending by reducing defense expenditures, and by restraining cost-of-living escalators attached to non-need-related income-transfer programs, such as Social Security, as in Peter Peterson's suggestion in Chapter 1. Provide special transfers for the "truly needy."

6. Increase federal revenues by a value-added tax that would constrain consumption and allow for a channeling of funds to investment for competitiveness.

7. Provide substantial federal subsidies for business and union training programs to absorb the unemployed, and federal outlays for the renovation of the nation's infrastructure.

8. Redesign corporate governance procedures to assure labor's cooperation for competitiveness, and align corporate activities with national priorities, as suggested in Chapters 3, 9, and 11.

All of these actions are interrelated; they cannot be implemented separately. My interviews for this book indicate that, taken together, these proposals would attract considerable national support. Nevertheless, it is clear that they represent a departure from traditional ideology, and are therefore controversial. To be successful, they will require the recognition of a new ideology, to sustain and legitimize them.

Such a departure would certainly be a radical one. But the transformation of the American economic system in the last fifty years has itself been both radical and revolutionary. It would be strange indeed if the general principles of corporate governance that served the institutional needs of the 1930s served as well today. They do not, and we are suffering the consequences of this mismatch daily, on many fronts.

The course of American history suggests that this country's most remarkable attribute has been its capacity for continuing, radical change, and that among the most forceful agents and architects of that change have been the leaders of great corporations. For the most part, the change has been to their credit. But the time has come to contemplate the full effects of the corporate revolution, and, without malice or blame, to rebuild the foundations underlying what we are achieving.

Notes

CHAPTER 1

1. *Newsweek*, April 20, 1981.
2. *Wall Street Journal*, May 6, 1982.
3. *Business Week*, January 11, 1982.
4. Donald L. Koch, speech before the Florida Economics Club, August 20, 1982, p. 3.
5. *Business Week*, January 11, 1982.
6. Davis Dyer, Mark Fuller, Malcolm Salter, and Alan Webber, *The Auto Industry and the American Economy*, pamphlet, pp. 3–6.
7. William J. Abernathy, Kim B. Clark, and Alan M. Kantrow, "The New Industrial Competition," *Harvard Business Review*, September–October 1981, p. 73.
8. "Managing Our Way to Economic Decline," *Harvard Business Review*, July–August 1980, p. 69.
9. Amitai Etzioni, "Choose We Must," *The Individual and the Future of Organizations* (Georgia State University), Spring 1980, p. 27.
10. "Japan in the Chips," *New York Review of Books*, November 19, 1981.
11. "Can Industry Survive the Welfare State?" *Harvard Business Review*, September–October 1981, pp. 300–305.
12. Interview, May 1982.
13. Jerome B. Cohen, *Japan's Postwar Economy* (Indiana University Press, 1958) p. 196; quoted in Bruce R. Scott, John W. Rosenblum, and Audrey T. Sproat, *Case Studies in Political Economy: Japan, 1854–1977* (Harvard Business School, 1980), p. 82.

14. In the Report of the Committee for the Study of Labor Questions, Japan Federation of Employees' Association (Nikkeiren), March 1981, p. 24.

15. *The United States and Japan*, 3rd edition (Viking, 1964; original edition, Harvard University Press, 1950, pp. 50, 51), quoted in Scott et al., p. 109.

16. I am indebted to Professor Bruce Scott for his development of the concept of national strategy.

17. "Behind Japan's Success," *Harvard Business Review*, January–February 1981, p. 84.

18. Ibid. See also Ezra F. Vogel, *Japan as Number 1* (Harvard University Press, 1979).

19. "Japan's Strategy for the '80s," *Business Week*, December 14, 1981.

20. Figures from Peter G. Peterson, *The U.S. Competitive Position in the 1980s —And Some Things We Might Do About It*, The Center for International Business, March 1981.

21. *Business Week*, December 14, 1981.

22. Daniel Yankelovich, *New Rules* (Random House, 1981), p. 25.

23. Ibid., p. 182.

24. Lester Thurow, "The Moral Equivalent of Defeat," *Foreign Policy*, Spring 1981, p. 121.

25. Interview, January 28, 1982.

26. Thurow, op. cit., p. 115.

27. Bruce D. Henderson, "New Strategies for the New Global Competition," The Boston Consulting Group, pamphlet, 1981, p. 1.

28. C. Fred Bergsten, "The United States and the World Economy," *Annals* of the American Academy of Arts and Sciences, #460, March 1982, p. 12.

29. *Business Week*, March 24, 1980.

30. *Business Week*, September 14, 1981.

31. "The Secret of Japanese Productivity," *Chief Executive*, Spring, 1981.

32. Letters to the Editor, *Harvard Business Review*, November–December 1981, pp. 238–40.

33. Conversation with Professor Yoshi Tsurumi, quoted in Tsurumi, "Productivity—The Japanese Approach," *Pacific Basin Quarterly*, November 6, 1981.

34. *Industry Week*, May 17, 1982.

35. Athos and Pascale, *The Art of Japanese Management* (Simon and Schuster, 1981), p. 201.

36. Ibid., p. 205.

37. *Japan's Cooperation for the Revitalization of American Industry: Summary of the Study*, Nikko Research Center, Tokyo, 1981, pp. 5–17.

38. *America's Competitive Edge: How to Get Our Country Moving Again* (McGraw-Hill, 1982).

39. Ibid., p. 225.

40. Ibid., p. 231.

41. "The Automobile Crisis and Public Policy," an interview with Philip Caldwell, *Harvard Business Review*, January–February 1981, pp. 79, 81, and 82.

42. "Why the U.S. Needs an Industrial Policy," *Harvard Business Review*, January–February 1982, p. 79.

43. See "Towards an Effective Industrial Policy," Robert A. Leone and Stephen P. Bradley, *Harvard Business Review*, November–December 1981.

44. *Wall Street Journal*, July 23, 1981.
45. Ibid.
46. *Wall Street Journal*, September 4, 1981.
47. See Edward Meadows, "Bold Departures in Antitrust," *Fortune*, October 5, 1981.
48. *Wall Street Journal*, July 23, 1981.
49. Interview, New York City, February 4, 1982.
50. *New York Times Magazine*, January 17, 1982.
51. Ibid.
52. William Greider, "The Education of David Stockman," *Atlantic Monthly*, December 1981.
53. *Wall Street Journal*, January 21, 1982.
54. *Economist*, September 18, 1981. All subsequent quotations from Rohatyn in this chapter are from this same source.

CHAPTER 2

1. See George C. Lodge, *The New American Ideology* (Alfred A. Knopf, 1975), pp. 22–23.
2. See George C. Lodge, *Engines of Change: United States Interests and Revolutions in Latin America* (Alfred A. Knopf, 1970), Chapter 4.
3. Strictly speaking, I should say that the Lockean ideology, as I have described it, embraces not only Locke's own writings, but also the development and refinement of his thought by David Hume, Adam Smith, and Charles de Montesquieu. Garry Wills expands on this intellectual tradition in his excellent book *Explaining America* (Doubleday, 1981).
4. Samuel P. Huntington, *American Politics: The Promise of Disharmony* (Harvard University Press, 1981), p. 63.
5. This harsh interpretation of Locke followed and differed from that of many of the Founding Fathers—Thomas Jefferson, for example—for whom individual fulfillment and happiness required a "moral sense" of participation in and obligation to a community, as in the ideal of "the gentleman."
6. Huntington, op. cit., p. 39.
7. This lack of confidence is well documented by public opinion surveys in *The Confidence Gap* by Seymour Martin Lipset and William Schneider (The Free Press, Macmillan, 1983).
8. Informal remarks to JD/MBA students, Fox Club, Cambridge, Mass., April 15, 1982.
9. Jacques Maritain, *Reflections on America* (Scribner's, 1958), p. 118.
10. See Daniel Bell, "The Cultural Contradictions of Capitalism," *Public Interest*, Fall 1970.
11. William Greider, "The Education of David Stockman," *Atlantic Monthly*, December 1981.
12. Quoted in Herman E. Drooss and Charles Gilbert, *American Business History* (Prentice-Hall, 1972), p. 264.
13. See "Hearings Before the Committee on the Judiciary, United States Senate, 92nd Congress, Second Session, on Nomination of Richard G. Kleindienst of Arizona to be Attorney General" (Government Printing Office, 1972).

14. The decision of the Justice Department in 1981 to drop its antitrust suit against AT&T is a contemporary example.
15. Greider, op. cit.
16. Even Herbert Hoover, when he was Secretary of Commerce, was an advocate of planning, as Professor Ellis W. Hawley has pointed out (see "Herbert Hoover, the Commerce Secretariat, and the Vision of an Associative State, 1921–1928," *Journal of American History*, June 1974, pp. 116ff).
17. Those who are interested in a more detailed consideration of the nature and derivation of the concept of ideology, the evolution of communitarianism and individualism in western civilization, the historical development of Lockeanism in America, and the emergence of communitarianism around the turn of the century and its subsequent unfolding, may wish to consult *The New American Ideology*, cited above.
18. Daniel Yankelovich, *New Rules* (Random House, 1981), p. 14.
19. Ibid., pp. xix and xx.
20. Ibid., p. 146.
21. Ibid., p. 147.
22. Ibid., p. 238.

CHAPTER 3

1. "The Crisis of '82," Address to the Yale Political Union, Yale University, September 10, 1981.
2. Samuel P. Huntington, *American Politics: The Promise of Disharmony* (Harvard University Press, 1981), Chapter 2 and elsewhere.
3. Ibid., p. 102.
4. I have been greatly helped in this definition by Dr. Miles F. Shore, Bullard Professor of Psychiatry at Harvard and the director of the Massachusetts Health Center.
5. Thomas C. Schelling and Grant P. Thompson, *Energy Prices and Public Policy*, Committee for Economic Development, July 1982.
6. Remarks, Economic Club of Chicago, April, 1978, quoted in Claude E. Barfield, Jr., "New Federalism: The Debate Is On," *Journal of the Institute for Socioeconomic Studies*, Summer 1982, p. 28.
7. Renato Tagiuri, "Managing Corporate Identity: The Role of Top Management," *Harvard Business School Working Paper 82–86*, p. 26.
8. Alfred D. Chandler, Jr., *The Visible Hand: The Managerial Revolution in American Business* (Harvard University Press, 1977), p. 492.
9. John B. Schnapp, "Who for the Pedestal Now?," *New York Times*, July 11, 1982.
10. Malcolm S. Salter and Wolf A. Weinhold, *Merger Trends and Prospects for the 1980s*, a paper published by the Office of Policy, U.S. Department of Commerce, December 1980.
11. Dennis C. Mueller, "A Theory of Conglomerate Mergers," *Quarterly Journal of Economics*, 1969, pp. 643–59.

12. Carol J. Loomis, "The Madness of Executive Compensation," *Fortune*, July 12, 1982.
13. "Managing Our Way to Economic Decline," *Harvard Business Review*, July–August 1980, pp. 67–79. See also Robert H. Hayes and David A. Garvin, "Managing As If Tomorrow Mattered," *Harvard Business Review*, May–June 1982, pp. 70–79.
14. Lewisburg, Penn., March 22, 1982.
15. *Business Week*, December 14, 1981.
16. U.S. *v.* IBM, plaintiff's exhibit 4794, quoted in Katherine Davis Fishman, *The Computer Establishment* (Harper and Row, 1981), p. 388.
17. Seymour Zucker et al., *The Reindustrialization of America* (McGraw-Hill, 1982), p. 48.
18. James Fallows, "American Industry: What Ails It, How to Save It," *Atlantic Monthly*, September, 1980.
19. Zucker et al., p. 52.
20. "Public-Private Partnership: An Opportunity for Urban Communities," Committee for Economic Development, New York, February, 1981.
21. These data come from an interview with Dr. Richard R. John, Transportation Systems Center, Department of Transportation, Cambridge, Mass.; and from *U.S. Automobile Industry Status Report*, submitted to the United States Senate Committee on Finance, Subcommittee on International Trade, by the U.S. Department of Commerce, December 1, 1981, pp. 1–17.
22. Ibid., p. 13.
23. Ibid., p. 13.
24. Ibid., p. 10.
25. Philip Caldwell, "The Automobile Crisis and Public Policy," interviewed by Kenneth R. Andrews and Malcolm S. Salter, *Harvard Business Review*, January–February, 1981, pp. 80, 81.
26. *Employment and Earnings*, Bureau of Labor Statistics, U.S. Department of Labor, April 1980, p. 24.
27. Bruce Scott, "Can Industry Survive the Welfare State?" *Harvard Business Review*, September–October 1982, p. 302.

CHAPTER 4

1. Marilyn Chase, "U.S. Electronics Firms Considering Joining in Research Ventures to Counter Japanese," *Wall Street Journal*, March 1, 1982.
2. *National Competition Policy: Historians' Perspectives on Antitrust and Government-Business Relationships in the United States*, Federal Trade Commission, Washington, D.C., August 1981, p. 75.
3. James Fallows, "American Industry: What Ails It, How to Save It," *Atlantic Monthly*, September 1980.
4. "Antitrust and the Association Movement, 1920–1940," in *National Competition Policy*, op. cit., p. 109. See also Ellis W. Hawley, "Herbert Hoover, the Commerce Secretariat, and the Vision of an Associative State, 1921–1928," *Journal of American History*, June 1974, pp. 116–40.

5. Hawley, "Herbert Hoover . . . ," p. 108.
6. Ellis W. Hawley, *The New Deal and the Problem of Monopoly* (Princeton University Press, 1966), p. 35.
7. Ibid., p. 45.
8. Ibid., p. 67.
9. Ibid., p. 50.
10. Ibid., p. 104.
11. Ibid., p. 123.
12. Ibid., p. 484, citing Paul T. Homan in *Political Science Quarterly*, June 1936, p. 181.
13. Louis Hartz, *The Liberal Tradition in America* (Harcourt, Brace and World, 1955), p. 260.
14. Samuel P. Huntington, *American Politics: The Promise of Disharmony* (Harvard University Press, 1981), p. 41.
15. Boston *Globe*, March 19, 1982.
16. January 22, 1970.
17. *Business Week*, January 5, 1974.
18. *Economic Report of the President*, transmitted to the Congress, February 1982 (Government Printing Office, 1982), p. 235.
19. Ibid., pp. 196–98.
20. Ibid., p. 207.
21. Ibid., p. 195.
22. Ibid., p. 96.
23. Ibid., pp. 194–95, 202.
24. Ibid., p. 271.
25. Ibid., p. 204.
26. Ibid., p. 203.
27. Ibid., pp. 180, 349.
28. Ibid., p. 180.
29. Ibid., p. 159.
30. Ibid., p. 209.
31. Ibid., p. 111.
32. Ibid., p. 87.
33. Ibid., p. 94.
34. Ibid., p. 95.
35. Ibid., p. 125.
36. Ibid., p. 177.
37. *New York Times*, April 16, 1981.
38. "Artificial Intelligence: The Second Computer Age Begins," *Business Week*, March 8, 1982.
39. *Economic Report*, op. cit., p. 183.
40. Ibid., p. 186.
41. See generally George C. Lodge, *Engines of Change* (Alfred A. Knopf, 1970).
42. *Economic Report*, op. cit., p. 140.
43. Ibid., p. 30.
44. Ibid., p. 37.
45. Ibid., p. 43.
46. Ibid.

47. *New York Times*, February 11, 1982.
48. Interview, May 27, 1982.

CHAPTER 5

1. William Lilley III and James C. Miller III, "The New 'Social Regulation,' " *Public Interest*, Spring 1977, p. 50.
2. J. Ronald Fox, "Breaking the Regulatory Deadlock," *Harvard Business Review*, September–October 1981, p. 98.
3. November 2, 1981, Washington, D.C.
4. Interview, ibid.
5. Interview, January 6, 1982, Wilmington, Del.
6. Interview, July 20, 1981, Washington, D.C.
7. Robert A. Leone and Stephen P. Bradley, "Toward an Effective Industrial Policy," Working Paper, Division of Research, Harvard Business School, June 5, 1981, p. 2.
8. Ibid.
9. Ibid., p. 3.
10. Ibid.
11. Robert B. Reich, "Why the U.S. Needs an Industrial Policy," *Harvard Business Review*, January–February 1982, p. 75.
12. Ibid., p. 76.
13. Ibid.
14. Leone and Bradley, "Toward an Effective Industrial Policy," *Harvard Business Review*, November–December 1981, p. 94.
15. Robert B. Reich, "Regulation by Confrontation or Negotiation?" *Harvard Business Review*, May–June 1981, p. 84.
16. Ibid., p. 91.
17. William Drayton, "Getting Smarter About Regulation," *Harvard Business Review*, July–August 1981, pp. 38–41.
18. Ronald Reagan, "Government and Business in the '80s," *Wall Street Journal*, January 9, 1981.
19. Much of this history is drawn from *Controlling Oil* (ICH 9-378-048), a case written by George C. Lodge from published sources to be used as the basis for classroom discussion; copyright © 1977 by the President and Fellows of Harvard College.
20. Anthony Sampson, *The Seven Sisters* (Viking Press, 1975). See also *Report and Hearings of the Subcommittee on Multinational Corporations of the Senate Committee on Foreign Relations*, 1975.
21. *New York Times*, January 1, 1920.
22. Sampson, op. cit., p. 66.
23. Ibid., p. 73.
24. Ibid., p. 80.
25. Ibid., p. 103.
26. Ibid., p. 92.
27. Ibid., pp. 95–97.
28. Ibid., p. 102.

29. Senate Multinational Subcommittee Hearings, Vol. 4, pp. 12 and 95.
30. Sampson, op. cit., p. 124.
31. Ibid., p. 125.
32. Ibid., p. 208.
33. Ibid., p. 234.
34. Ibid., p. 261.
35. Ibid., pp. 299, 306.
36. *International Herald Tribune*, March 20, 1975.
37. *New York Times*, October 14, 1977.
38. Daniel Yergin, "Awaiting the Next Oil Crisis," *New York Times Magazine*, July 11, 1982.
39. Daniel Yergin, "Pangloss on the Energy Future: Wishful Thinking," *New York Times*, November 9, 1982.
40. Philip A. Wellons, "Economic Nationalism and International Banking: The Implications for U.S. Policy," an unpublished working paper, Harvard Business School, August 31, 1981, p. 44.
41. Myer Rashish, "Banking and Foreign Policy," speech to the Carnegie Roundtable on Banking and Foreign Policy, New York, November 17, 1981.
42. Art Pine, "Uneasy Western Banks Pulling Back on Loans to the Poorer Nations," *Wall Street Journal*, July 1, 1982.
43. Jeff Gerth, "Records Show Citicorp Acted to Skirt Foreign Bank Rules," *New York Times*, September 13, 1982.
44. Ibid.

CHAPTER 6

1. *Economist*, May 22, 1982, p. 25.
2. See Ezra Vogel, "Guided Free Enterprise in Japan," *Harvard Business Review*, May–June 1978, p. 162.
3. William Drayton, "Getting Smarter About Regulation," *Harvard Business Review*, July–August 1981, p. 39.
4. Statement on Corporate Responsibility, October 1981, pp. 3 and 5.
5. *Public-Private Partnership: An Opportunity for Urban Communities*, a statement by the Research and Policy Committee of the Committee for Economic Development, New York, February 1982, p. 76.
6. Peter Navarro, "Our Stake in the Electric Utility's Dilemma," *Harvard Business Review*, May–June 1982, pp. 87–97.
7. Charles F. Luce, "New Directions in the Electric Utility Industry," remarks at Saranac Lake, N.Y., October 22, 1981.
8. Robert A. Leone and John R. Meyer, "Capacity Strategies for the 1980s," *Harvard Business Review*, November–December 1980, p. 133.
9. Ibid., p. 134.
10. Jeffrey L. Hoffman, analyst at Sanford C. Bernstein and Company, quoted in David G. Santy and James R. Normal, "Inside Wall Street," in *Business Week*, March 16, 1981.
11. Luce, op. cit.
12. Ibid.

13. Conference Record, Federal Energy Regulatory Commission (FERC), Docket No. EL 81-7-000.
14. *Electric Power Supply and Demand for the Contiguous United States, 1980–1989*, DOE/RG-0036 (Rev. 1) (U.S. Department of Energy, Economic Regulatory Agency, Division of Water Supply and Reliability, July 1980).
15. Conference Record, op. cit., pp. I.3 and I.4.
16. Interview, December 16, 1981.
17. FERC Report, pp. 9–10.
18. Ibid., pp. 12–13.
19. Ibid., pp. 100–101.
20. Ibid., pp. 24–34.
21. Ibid., pp. 37–38.
22. Ibid., pp. 101, 102.
23. Ibid., p. 55.
24. Ibid., p. 59.
25. Ibid., p. 60.
26. Ibid., pp. 156, 157.
27. Ibid., p. 152.
28. Ibid., p. 120.
29. See, for example, *Wall Street Journal*, May 3, 1982.
30. Excerpts from Graham Allison et al., *Governance of Nuclear Power: The Director's Dilemma*, mimeo, J. F. Kennedy School of Government, Harvard University, Cambridge, Mass., May 1982, p. 3.
31. Robert Stobaugh, "Energy Future and International Trade," *Journal of International Business Studies*, Spring–Summer 1981, p. 24.
32. Interview, December 16, 1981.
33. Swidler interview, January 1982.
34. See also Mason Willrich and Kermit Kubitz, *Regional Power Generation Companies*, mimeo., paper presented at Public Policy and Corporate Management Program, Kennedy School of Government, Harvard University, May 18, 1982.
35. Charles J. Cichetti and Rod Shaughnessy, "Our Nation's Gas and Electric Utilities: Time to Decide," *Public Utilities Fortnightly*, December 3, 1981.
36. "Monsanto's Early Warning System," John W. Hanley interviewed by David E. Ewing and Millicent R. Kindle, *Harvard Business Review*, November–December 1981, p. 115.
37. This section draws on two Harvard Business School cases prepared by Joseph L. Badaracco under the supervision of the author. They are called Allied Chemical Corporation (A) and (B), ICH Numbers 9-379-137 and 9-379-150, respectively, copyright © 1979 by the President and Fellows of Harvard College.
38. Ibid., p. 5.
39. Ibid.
40. *Wall Street Journal*, February 27, 1976.
41. Allied (A), p. 11.
42. Allied (B), p. 3.
43. Ibid., p. 7.

44. Ibid., p. 9.
45. "Praise for an Ex-polluter," *New York Times*, January 28, 1980.
46. Interview, New York, December 16, 1981.
47. "We Need a Credible EPA," *Chemical Week*, October 21, 1981.
48. "An Unlikely Alliance Against New EPA Cuts," *Business Week*, December 1981.
49. Interviews were conducted by Douglas Nelson in the fall of 1982.
50. Boston *Globe*, June 18 and July 6, 1982.
51. Andy Pasztor, "Many States Complain About Having to Assume Environmental Programs from Federal Agencies," *Wall Street Journal*, August 24, 1982.
52. J. Ronald Fox, "Breaking the Regulatory Deadlock," *Harvard Business Review*, September–October 1981, pp. 97–105; Joseph Bower and William Murphy, *The Chemical Industry Institute of Toxicology*, ICH Number 0-382-167, copyright © 1982 by the President and Fellows of Harvard College; Joseph L. Badaracco, "A Study of Adversarial and Cooperative Relations Between Government and Business in Four Countries," Harvard Business School/DBA Thesis, 1981; Thomas McCraw, *The Ablest Agency and How It Grew: A Brief History of the SEC and Third Party Auditors*, a paper for the U.S. Regulatory Council, April 16, 1981.
53. Thomas K. McCraw, "With Consent of the Governed: SEC's Formative Years," *Journal of Policy Analysis and Management*, 1982, pp. 348, 349, 357.
54. Fox, op. cit., pp. 97–105.
55. See Badaracco, "A Study of Adversarial and Cooperative Relations," op. cit.
56. Christopher D. Stone, *Where the Law Ends: The Social Control of Corporate Behavior* (Harper and Row, 1975), pp. 152–183.
57. Richard H. K. Vietor, "NIPCC: The Advisory Council Approach," *Journal of Contemporary Business*, vol. 8., no. 1, Spring 1979, pp. 57–70.
58. Ibid., pp. 58–59.
59. NIPCC, Council Report; quoted in Vietor, p. 60.
60. Ibid., p. 63.
61. Ibid.
62. Ibid., p. 66.
63. Ibid., pp. 66–67.

CHAPTER 7

1. Address, National Alliance of Business, October 5, 1981.
2. George Gilder, *Wealth and Poverty* (Basic Books, 1981).
3. William C. Norris, "A New Role for Corporations," *Report from the Social Needs and Business Opportunities Conference*, Control Data, September 22, 1982, Minneapolis, Minn., p. 10.
4. Felix Rohatyn, "America in the 1980s: Why the Biggest Problems Are the Biggest Opportunities," *Economist*, September 18, 1981.

5. This estimate of the size of the underclass is based on analysis of data collected by the University of Michigan Survey Research Center by Frank Levy, an economist at the Urban Institute, Washington, D.C.
6. Rohatyn, op. cit.
7. Ken Auletta, *The Streets Were Paved with Gold* (Random House, 1975), p. 253.

CHAPTER 8

1. Garrett Hardin, "Tragedy of the Commons," *Science*, December 13, 1968, p. 1245.
2. Charles Frankel, *The Case for Modern Man* (Harper & Bros., 1955), p. 203.
3. U.S. Congress, Senate Committee on Foreign Relations, Subcommittee on Multinational Corporations, *Hearings on Multinational Corporations and United States Foreign Policy*, 94th Congress, 1st Session (U.S. Government Printing Office, 1976, Part 12, pp. 16–17 and 19–24).
4. "Lockheed Says It Paid $22 Million to Get Contracts," *Wall Street Journal*, August 4, 1975.
5. Senate Hearings, op. cit.
6. *New York Times*, May 7, 1972.
7. Josef K. Hoenig to three industry associations, July 5, 1974, mimeo.
8. "Lockheed's Lenders, Who Forced Shakeup, Feud over Its Future," *Wall Street Journal*, April 8, 1976.
9. Foreign Corrupt Practices Act, an amendment to the Securities and Exchange Act of 1934.
10. See Suk H. Kim, "On Repealing the Foreign Corrupt Practices Act: Survey and Assessment," *Columbia Journal of World Business*, Fall 1981, pp. 16–21.
11. *Wall Street Journal*, March 18, 1976.
12. David H. Padden, "Letters to the Editor," *HBS Bulletin*, July–August 1976.

CHAPTER 9

1. Dale D. Buss, "UAW Chief in an Awkward Spot," *Wall Street Journal*, August 12, 1982.
2. *New York Times*, November 8, 1982.
3. *Wall Street Journal*, November 8, 1979.
4. Boston *Globe*, May 3, 1982.
5. Interview, Pittsburgh, December 11, 1981.
6. Adolph A. Berle and Gardiner C. Means, *The Modern Corporation and Private Property* (Macmillan, 1932).
7. Josephine Young Case and Everett Needham Case, *Owen D. Young and American Enterprise, a Biography* (David R. Godine, 1982), p. 374.
8. NAM press release 77-17, December 1, 1977, mimeo, Washington, D.C.

9. "The Automobile Crisis and Public Policy," Philip Caldwell interviewed by Kenneth R. Andrews and Malcolm S. Salter, *Harvard Business Review*, January–February 1981, pp. 77, 81.
10. Encyclical *On Human Work*, Washington, D.C., U.S. Catholic Conference, September 14, 1982.
11. Gail Lauren Sokoloff, "The Creation of an Employee Owned Firm: A Case Study of Hyatt Clark Industries," Harvard College honors thesis, April 19, 1982, p. 1. The buyout estimate was made by Hay Associates, a Philadelphia-based management consulting firm. *New York Times*, February 23, 1983.
12. Sokoloff, op. cit., p. 1.
13. Ibid., p. 44.
14. Ibid., p. 39.
15. Ibid., p. 43.
16. Ibid., p. 48.
17. Ibid., p. 52.
18. Ibid., p. 53.
19. Ibid., p. 54.
20. Ibid., p. 80.
21. Ibid., p. 60.
22. Ibid., p. 61.
23. Ibid.
24. Ibid., p. 63.
25. Ibid., p. 64.
26. Ibid., p. 70.
27. Ibid., p. 95.
28. Ibid., p. 99.
29. Ibid., p. 101.
30. Ibid., pp. 103–4.
31. Ibid., p. 137.
32. *Wall Street Journal*, July 27, 1982.
33. Michael Maccoby, *The Leader: A New Face for American Management* (Simon and Schuster, 1981), p. 76; see also G. C. Lodge and Karen Henderson, *Bolivar*, Harvard Business School Case Services, President and Fellows of Harvard College, 1977.
34. Bert Spector and Paul Lawrence, *General Motors and the United Automobile Workers*, Harvard Business School Case Services, President and Fellows of Harvard College, 1981, p. 2.
35. Ibid., p. 3.
36. Ibid., p. 5.
37. Bluestone interview, Detroit, September 8, 1981.
38. Ibid.
39. Spector and Lawrence, op cit., p. 9.
40. *Harbus News*, April 20, 1981.
41. Bluestone interview, op. cit.
42. Spector and Lawrence, op. cit., p. 16.
43. Martin Douglas, "GM vs. Its Workers," *New York Times*, February 15, 1982.
44. Bluestone interview, March 17, 1982.
45. Watts interview, Washington, D.C., November 23, 1981.

46. University of Massachusetts, speech, January 1982, mimeo, p. 2.
47. Richard E. Walton and Leonard A. Schlesinger, "Do Supervisors Thrive in Participative Work Systems?" *Organizational Dynamics*, Winter 1979, p. 26.
48. Richard E. Walton, "The Topeka Work System: Optimistic Visions, Pessimistic Hypotheses, and Reality," Harvard Business School Working Paper, 1981, p. 22.
49. *Business Week*, May 11, 1981.
50. MacNeil-Lehrer Report, February 15, 1982, transcript, pp. 2 and 4.
51. See, for example, Bayless Manning, "Thinking Straight About Corporate Law Reform," in *Corporations at the Crossroads: Governance and Reform*, edited by Deborah A. DeMott, (McGraw-Hill, 1980), pp. 26–27.
52. John Hoerr, "Smudging the Line Between Boss and Worker," *Business Week*, March 1, 1982.
53. Charles Hecksher, "Unions Play Key Role in Quality of Work Life," *Workplace Democracy*, Winter 1982, p. 18.
54. William J. Abernathy and Kim B. Clark, *Notes on a Trip to Japan: Concepts and Interpretations*, Harvard Business School Working Paper 82-58, p. 8.
55. Press release, March 4, 1981.
56. Thomas J. Schneider, "Quality of Working Life and the Law," speech given at the Kennedy School of Government, Harvard University, November 19, 1981.
57. Ibid.
58. July 7, 1982.

CHAPTER 10

1. Interview with R. F. Mettler, July 14, 1982.
2. Interview, January 6, 1982, Wilmington, Del.
3. Interviews with Charles Brown, May 27, 1982; Fletcher Byrom, December 11, 1982; Howard Love, March 3, 1982; William Norris, September 23, 1981; Henry Schacht, December 16, 1981; and speech at Northwestern University by Frank T. Cary, October 15, 1981.
4. Ira C. Magaziner and Robert B. Reich, *Minding America's Business* (Harcourt Brace Jovanovich, 1981), p. 32; and C. Fred Bergsten, "International Economic Relations," *Transatlantic Perspectives*, February 1982, p. 2.
5. Bruce R. Scott, "Can Industry Survive the Welfare State?" *Harvard Business Review*, September–October 1982, pp. 72, 73.
6. "An Economic Strategy for the '80s," *The Business Roundtable*, Washington, D.C., March 1981, p. 6.
7. Interview, Washington, D.C., February 5, 1982.
8. Statement issued by Reagan/Bush Campaign Committee, Tuesday, September 16, 1980.
9. Interview, Pittsburgh.
10. Edmund Ayoub, chief economist, United Steelworkers, *Steel in the Seventies*, Table 3, mimeo, January 2, 1981.
11. *Economic Report of the President*, February 1982, p. 94.
12. Interview, March 19, 1982, Washington, D.C.

13. Report of the Committee on Ways and Means, U.S. House of Representatives, to accompany H.R. 4537, House Report No. 96-317, July 3, 1979 (U.S. Government Printing Office, Washington, D.C.), p. 187.
14. Interview, January 28, 1982, Washington, D.C.
15. Interview, February 19, 1982, College Park, Md.
16. Interview, January 6, 1982.
17. Interview, July 19, 1982, in Cleveland, Ohio.
18. Interview, April 1982, Boston, Mass.
19. Industry Sector Advisory Committee, No. 11, Report, June 28, 1979, USTR.
20. John Starrels, *Wall Street Journal*, July 9, 1982.

CHAPTER 11

1. Farewell address at the White House, December 1970.
2. Surveys in 1974–75 by Gallup International Research Institute for non-U.S. countries and in 1978 by the American Institute of Public Opinion (Gallup), Princeton Religious Research Center, and the Gallup Organization, Inc., for the United States; cited in Samuel P. Huntington, *American Politics: The Promise of Disharmony* (Harvard University Press, 1981), p. 156.
3. Gilder, *Wealth and Poverty* (Basic Books, 1981), p. 155.
4. William Greider, "The Education of David Stockman," *The Atlantic Monthly*, December 1981, p. 29.
5. Lecture, November 12, 1980.
6. Interview, December 16, 1981, New York.
7. Interview, Pittsburgh, December 11, 1981.
8. Interview, May 27, 1982, New York City.
9. Interview, January 6, 1982, Wilmington, Del.
10. "Letter from the Editor," *Harvard Business Review*, May–June 1982.
11. "Can Industry Survive the Welfare State?" *Harvard Business Review*, September–October 1982, p. 83.
12. Ibid.
13. Statement by the AFL-CIO Executive Council on Reindustrialization, Chicago, August 21, 1980, p. 1.
14. Preamble to proposed legislation, typescript, p. 6.
15. Frank Weil, "Congressional Findings, Purposes, Structure and Powers of Federal Industrial Coordination Board," working paper, pp. 3–6.
16. Interview, July 14, 1982.
17. Lecture, Wharton School Centennial, March 23, 1981. For an excellent discussion of consensus-building mechanisms, see Ray Marshall (former Secretary of Labor), "Government, Markets, and Consensus-Building Mechanisms," *National Productivity Review*, Autumn 1982, p. 445.
18. Lecture, Wharton School Centennial.
19. "Republic Sticking to Steel Despite Growing Dangers," *Business Week*, August 9, 1982.
20. "Board of Directors," *Harvard Business Review* reprint No. 21024, Preface.
21. Marvin Chandler, "It's Time to Clean Up the Boardroom," *Harvard Business Review*, September–October 1975, pp. 5–7.

22. Christopher D. Stone, "Public Directors Merit a Try," *Harvard Business Review*, March–April 1976, pp. 21, 22.
23. "Outside" means appointed by management but not on the company payroll. The Roundtable statement suggested that outsiders be recommended to management by a nominating committee composed of a majority of outside directors.
24. Roundtable statement, p. i.
25. Ibid., p. 6.
26. Ibid., p. 7–8.
27. Ibid., pp. 22–23.
28. Ibid., p. 18.
29. Lee Smith, "The Boardroom Is Becoming a Different Scene," *Fortune*, May 9, 1978.
30. Victor Brudney, "The Independent Director—Heavenly City or Potemkin Village?" *Harvard Law Review*, January 1982, p. 610.
31. Ibid.
32. Ibid.
33. Myles L. Mace, "What Today's Directors Worry About," *Harvard Business Review*, July–August 1978, pp. 30–53.
34. Interview, Pittsburgh, March 3, 1982.
35. See Richard E. Walton, "The Topeka Story," *Wharton Magazine*, Spring 1978; and Karen Henderson and George C. Lodge, *Bolivar*, ICH Number 9-377-123, copyright © 1976 by the President and Fellows of Harvard College.
36. See Stone, op. cit.
37. William C. Norris, "How to Expand R & D Cooperation," *Business Week*, April 11, 1983, p. 21.
38. Shapiro interview.
39. Frederick V. Malek, *Washington's Hidden Tragedy* (Free Press, 1978), p. 218.
40. Ibid., p. 12.

Index

317

Wolff, Alan, 98
women in labor force, 58
work, as a right/duty, 49–50
  see also workfare
worker-owned businesses, 222–7
workers' participation in management,
  20, 52, 214–21 *passim,* 231–5, 291

ESOP, 222
  at GM, 225–31
  see also governance of corporations
workfare, 49–50, 57, 99, 172

Young, Owen, D., 216

A Note About The Author

George C. Lodge was born in Boston in 1927, and after two years in the Navy was graduated from Harvard College in 1950. He was a reporter on the Boston *Herald* for four years, and from 1954 to 1961 served with the U.S. Department of Labor, first as director of information and later as assistant secretary for international affairs. In 1962 he was the Republican candidate for the U.S. Senate from Massachusetts, and then joined the faculty of the Harvard Business School, where he is now professor of business administration. In addition to the present work, he is the author of *Spearheads of Democracy: Labor in Developing Countries*; *Engines of Change: United States Interests and Revolution in Latin America*; and *The New American Ideology*. Mr. Lodge is married and the father of six children.

A NOTE ON THE TYPE

The text of this book was set via computer-driven cathode ray tube in Video Times Roman, an adaptation of a face called Times Roman, designed by Stanley Morison for *The Times* (London), and first introduced by that newspaper in 1932. Among typographers and designers of the twentieth century, Stanley Morison had a strong forming influence, as typographical adviser to the English Monotype Corporation, as a director of two distinguished English publishing houses, and as a writer of sensibility, erudition, and keen practical sense.

Composed by Dix Type Inc., Syracuse, New York
Printed and bound by Fairfield Graphics,
Fairfield, Pennsylvania